The 50 States

WIDE EYED EDITIONS

Welcome explorers, investigators, and lovers of knowledge . . .

TO THE 50 STATES!

Are you ready to embark on a remarkable adventure, with more than 50 infographic maps as your guide?

Unlike other maps that show you each state's rivers and roads, the maps in this book have been made to do something different: to show you each state's story. They are a bit like a photograph that has been taken over hundreds of years! Packed with essential and curious information, they capture some of the achievements of each state, and introduce you to inspiring people from times past right up till today.

All mapmakers make choices about what to include in their drawings. With the choices we have made, our hope is that you will spot something that interests you and perhaps investigate it further, examining other maps, reading books, and asking the people in your life what they know about a particular person, place, or event.

So pack your bags and say later 'gator . . .
the great States await!

EXPLORING THIS BOOK

WELCOME BOX
With so much to investigate, it's good to have a plan! For each state, you may want to start by reading the short introduction.

INSPIRING PEOPLE
Meet six inspiring people who have a connection with the state.

STATE ICONS
Let your eye wander over the icons that celebrate a state's people, places, and history—history that we continue to make every day!

KEY FACTS
These twelve key facts provide a quick snapshot of each state, including the three largest cities.

MOMENTS TO REMEMBER
Discover some of the significant dates in the state's history.

REGION SPOTLIGHT
These bubbles, featuring a collection of key icons, allow you to discover more about one particular place.

Each state's map contains information about which states it neighbors, its **BODIES OF WATER** and **BORDERS**, as well as where it is situated in the country. Did you know that while Hawaii shares its borders with no one, both Missouri and Tennessee border eight other states? We've also included many **STATE PARKS**, **BATTLEFIELDS**, **NATIONAL FORESTS**, and **RESERVATIONS**, and hope they will inspire you to respect and explore the great outdoors. Just remember: these maps have been designed to tell a story: they aren't drawn to scale. At the back of this book, you'll find a guide to the **STATE FLAGS** and a gallery of the **PRESIDENTS** of the U.S. to date, as well as a handy index and some ideas for further reading.

GET TO KNOW THESE SYMBOLS ON EVERY MAP

STATE CAPITAL

LARGEST CITIES

PLACE OF INTEREST

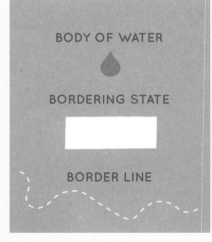

BODY OF WATER

BORDERING STATE

BORDER LINE

INSPIRING PEOPLE

STATE CAPITOL BUILDING

MUSCLE SHOALS
Music greats like the Rolling Stones, Paul Simon, and the Black Keys have recorded in this musical town.

JESSE OWENS
This four-time Olympic gold medalist was born in Oakville.

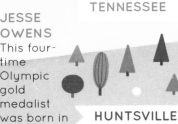

TENNESSEE

RUSSELL CAVE NATIONAL MONUMENT
This large cave was used as a shelter by prehistoric people up to 10,000 years ago!

THE COON DOG CEMETERY
lies in what was a popular coon-hunting camp in Cherokee.

LITTLE RIVER CANYON NATIONAL PRESERVE
is home to the endangered green pitcher plant—a carnivorous plant that eats insects!

DISMALS CANYON
A red-filtered flashlight can help you spot rare glowworms on the canyon walls.

HUNTSVILLE

UNCLAIMED BAGGAGE CENTER
This Scottsboro secondhand store sells skis, iPads, guitars, and other oddball things, all left behind at airports.

HELEN KELLER
1880-1968
This political activist and author was the first deaf and blind person to earn a college degree.

CARL LEWIS
b.1961
This track and field athlete who won 10 Olympic medals and 10 World Championships was born in Birmingham.

NATURAL BRIDGE
At 148 feet long, this 200-million-year-old stone arch is the longest natural bridge east of the Rockies.

ALABAMA CONSTITUTION VILLAGE
Churn butter and join in other 1819-style activities in this open-air museum in Huntsville.

THE BERMAN MUSEUM
in Anniston has curiosities from around the world, including a flute that fires bullets!

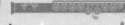

ROSA PARKS
1913-2005
The "first lady of civil rights" led the Montgomery Bus Boycott—a turning point in the fight for racial equality.

RICKWOOD FIELD
Willie Mays and other baseball heroes played here, at the country's oldest minor league ball park.

BIRMINGHAM

CHEAHA MOUNTAIN
Alabama's highest point is named for the Creek Indian word "Chaha," meaning "high place."

CORETTA SCOTT KING
1927-2006
Born in Marion, this civil rights leader helped establish Martin Luther King, Jr. Day as a national holiday.

FALLING STAR
is a Sylacauga statue commemorating a meteorite that crashed into Ann Hodges' house and grazed her while she slept on the couch!

AUBURN UNIVERSITY
A rescued eagle kicks off every Auburn football game with a majestic flight around the stadium.

BIG AL
is the mascot of the University of Alabama Crimson Tide football team, from Tuscaloosa.

MONTGOMERY

THE TUSKEGEE AIRMEN
were a group of African American pilots who overcame prejudice to become one of the most highly respected fighter groups of WWII.

GEORGIA

VOTING IS PEOPLE POWER

USS ALABAMA BATTLESHIP MEMORIAL PARK
In 1964 schoolchildren collected nickels and dimes to raise $100,000 to preserve this warship.

JOHNSTONE'S JUNONIA
The state shell is named for Kathleen Johnstone, a shell lover from Mobile.

5 RIVERS DELTA RESOURCE CENTER
Gator sightings abound here, where the Mobile, Spanish, Tensaw, Apalachee, and Blakeley Rivers all flow into Mobile Bay.

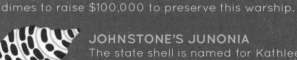

SELMA TO MONTGOMERY NATIONAL HISTORIC TRAIL
In 1965 25,000 people marched these 54 miles to protest for voters' rights.

ALABAMA STATE CAPITOL
The "floating" spiral staircase in this national historic landmark was designed using bridge-building techniques by engineer Horace King.

DEXTER AVENUE KING MEMORIAL BAPTIST CHURCH
The 1955 Bus Boycott was planned here, where Dr. Martin Luther King was once pastor.

THE BELLINGRATH GARDENS
These beautiful gardens in Theodore are home to thousands of flowers.

THE CONECUH NATIONAL FOREST
in Andalusia is home to the gopher tortoise, whose burrows give shelter to hundreds of different animal species.

THE HANK WILLIAMS MUSEUM
celebrates one of country music's first megastars.

MOBILE

OCTAVIA SPENCER
b.1970
This Montgomery-born Oscar winner from the movie *The Help* is also a children's book writer.

DAUPHIN ISLAND
Here, some 300 species of birds rest after migrating from Central and South America each spring.

BOTTLENOSE DOLPHINS
can be seen off Orange Beach. They can hold their breaths for up to 12 minutes and reach speeds of 22 mph!

HARPER LEE
b.1926
The Pulitzer Prize-winning author of *To Kill a Mockingbird* was born in Monroeville.

GULF OF MEXICO

MISSISSIPPI

WELCOME TO THE HEART OF DIXIE

With the letter "A" appearing four times in its name, the 22nd state has plenty of grade A things about it: there's the authentic soul food (fried chicken, pork chops, collard greens, and cheese grits), the astronomic football rivalry (do you root Crimson Tide or Auburn Tigers?), and the alluring antebellum architecture (stately columns and beautiful balconies). Not to mention the achievers, athletes, artists, and authors who all hail from the Heart of Dixie!

Rosa Parks and Martin Luther King, Jr., two of our nation's most heroic role models, planned important moments in the civil rights movement from the state's capital, Montgomery. Their leadership inspired the Montgomery Bus Boycott and the Selma to Montgomery march, paving the way for racial equality.

Alabama has an abundance of country music stars, and is also one of the nation's top producers of poultry, peanuts . . . and rocket ships! So buckle up and blast off for a tour of this grade A state.

KEY FACTS

CAPITAL
Montgomery

LARGEST CITIES
Birmingham
Montgomery
Mobile

BIRD
Yellowhammer

NAMED FOR
Possibly the Choctaw words *alba* and *amo*, meaning "plant gatherers"

STATEHOOD DATE
December 14, 1819

STATEHOOD ORDER
22

FLOWER
Camellia

POSTAL CODE
AL

REGION
Deep South

MAIN TIME ZONE
Central

TREE
Southern longleaf pine

"WE DARE MAINTAIN OUR RIGHTS"

FLORIDA

Some 13,000 years ago a fearless collection of travelers crossed the now-vanished Bering Land Bridge, leaving behind the life they knew in Asia and entering unknown territory.

They came not as we might now—in thick socks, thermal underwear, and down parkas—but in clothes made from animal hides they had skinned and tanned themselves. Incredible!

Today, Alaskans are just as incredible and take part in all sorts of inspiring events that call to mind the heroics of their ancestors. One such event is the Iditarod Trail Sled Dog Race. This tough endurance challenge involves teams of dogs and "mushers" traveling astonishing distances through blizzards and across lands so remote they might go days without seeing another living being—apart from the mighty caribou!

CHUKCHI SEA

JACK LONDON
1876–1916
Californian writer whose adventures in the Yukon gold rush inspired *The Call of the Wild* and *White Fang*.

RUSSIA

GRAY WOLVES
have about 200 million scent cells, which is 195 million more than humans!

LEONHARD SEPPALA
1877–1967
Norwegian-born Seppala's ability to breed, train, and mush sled dogs made him an unbeatable dogsled racer.

IDITAROD SLED RACE
Teams of 16 dogs and a "musher" race almost 1,000 miles from Anchorage to Nome.

BERING SEA

MUSK OXEN
were among the first animals to cross the Bering Land Bridge from Asia.

KATMAI NATIONAL PARK
is home to many salmon-fishing bears.

KEY FACTS

CAPITAL
Juneau

LARGEST CITIES
Anchorage
Fairbanks
Juneau

BIRD
Willow ptarmigan

NAMED FOR
The Aleut word *alyeska*, meaning "great land"

STATEHOOD DATE
January 3, 1959

STATEHOOD ORDER
49

FLOWER
Forget-me-not

POSTAL CODE
AK

REGION
Pacific

MAIN TIME ZONE
Alaska

TREE
Sitka spruce

THE ALEUTIAN ISLANDS
are a chain of 14 large volcanic islands and 55 smaller ones.

KODIAK BEARS
are the world's largest, standing 10 feet tall or more on their hind legs.

ALUTIIQ MASKS
The Native American Alutiiq word for their ceremonial masks means "like a face, but not really."

"NORTH TO THE FUTURE"

THE IÑUPIAT HERITAGE CENTER
See snow goggles from AD 1200 here!

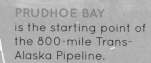

PRUDHOE BAY
is the starting point of the 800-mile Trans-Alaska Pipeline.

BEAUFORT SEA

THE NORTHERN LIGHTS
are best seen during the early hours of the morning between August 21 and April 21.

THE ARCTIC NATIONAL WILDLIFE REFUGE
is home to all three species of North American bear: polar, black, and grizzly.

JUVENILE BALD EAGLE
The majority of America's bald eagles nest in Alaska, such as this juvenile here.

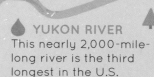

FAIRBANKS

BLITZEN BLVD

ELIZABETH PERATROVICH
1911–1958
A member of the Tlingit tribe, Peratrovich campaigned for equal rights for Native Alaskans.

NORTH POLE
This small town has Christmas-themed street names, such as Santa Claus Lane and Snowman Lane.

YUKON RIVER
This nearly 2,000-mile-long river is the third longest in the U.S.

CANADA

ALASKA STATE CAPITOL
The capital city can only be reached by air or sea— there is no road access.

ANCHORAGE

LAKE ILIAMNA
Alaska's largest lake is said to have a "monster," which some believe to be a sleeper shark.

SNOWIEST SPOT
A record-breaking 81 feet of snow once fell in just one year at Thompson Pass.

JUNEAU

TLINGIT NATION CANOE
Native peoples believe each canoe has its own spirit.

SITKA NATIONAL PARK
In a Tlingit story-telling totem pole, an eagle represents peace and friendship.

THE TONGASS NATIONAL FOREST
is the largest in the U.S. and about the size of West Virginia!

HAROLD GILLAM
1902–1943
An early bush pilot, midwesterner Gillam flew daring rescue operations over the Alaskan wilderness.

DANVILLE
2,835 MILES

SIGN POST FOREST
Here, the homesick make signs showing the miles to their hometowns.

GULF OF ALASKA

HOMER'S HALIBUT
In the city of Homer, some winning catches top 350 pounds!

HUNGRY!
The Baleen whales found near Barren Island can eat up to 9,000 pounds of fish and krill every day!

KENAI FJORDS
At least 38 glaciers flow out of these mountains.

WHALE WATERS
Humpback whales travel 3,100 miles during their annual migration to Mexico.

ADA BLACKJACK
1898–1983
The only survivor of an Arctic expedition, this young Inuit learned to hunt and shoot during her two-year ordeal.

CHANGUNAK ANTISARLOOK ANDREWUK: "SINROCK MARY"
1870–1948
The Iñupiat "Queen of Reindeer" turned a small herd of reindeer into the largest in the state, becoming one of Alaska's richest women.

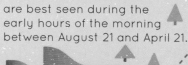

ESTEVANICO
c.1500-1539
This escaped African slave was one of the first non-natives to explore modern-day Arizona.

IRA HAYES
1923-1955
Born in Sacaton, this Pima Native American marine helped raise the U.S. flag at Iwo Jima during WWII.

JAMES TURRELL
b.1943
This artist is best known for the Roden Crater—a volcano cone that he is turning into a naked-eye observatory.

UTAH

MONUMENT VALLEY
Over time, wind and water have worn away layers of soft and hard stone to make these striking rock formations.

CODE TALKERS
The Navajo Nation was home to many of the Navajo Code Talkers who assisted the U.S. military in WWII.

EMMA STONE
b.1988
The co-star of *The Help*, *The Amazing Spider-Man*, and *Zombieland* grew up in Scottsdale.

SANDRA DAY O'CONNOR
b.1930
The first female Supreme Court Justice lives in Phoenix.

NEVADA

THE GRAND CANYON
Some five million hikers, river runners, and splendor seekers visit this 277-mile-long, 1-mile-deep canyon each year.

HOPI CULTURAL CENTER
The Hopi people are known for their kachina dolls, which represent spirits.

CANYON DE CHELLY NATIONAL MONUMENT
This park preserves the historic cliff dwellings of the ancient Pueblo people.

HAVASU FALLS
The Havasupai people have lived near these breathtaking waterfalls for some 800 years.

SAN FRANCISCO PEAKS
Come winter, this volcanic mountain range is covered with snow.

THE PAINTED DESERT
got its name from its multicolored rocks. It's home to burrowing owls, who love to eat dung beetles.

STEVEN SPIELBERG
b.1946
The Academy Award–winning director of *E.T.* and *Jurassic Park* was a boy scout in Phoenix.

LOWELL OBSERVATORY
Pluto—once known as the ninth planet but now downgraded to a dwarf planet—was discovered here in 1930.

RODEN CRATER
Artist James Turrell has spent more than 30 years making an observatory out of this extinct volcano.

JEROME
This ghost town was once home to 15,000 people, mostly miners. Today there are around 450 inhabitants, many of them artists.

METEOR CRATER
NASA astronauts trained in this 50,000-year-old crater to prepare for missions to the moon.

PETRIFIED FOREST
The 225-million-year-old trees here have turned to quartz over time, leaving crystallized logs!

CALIFORNIA

LONDON BRIDGE
In 1968 the founder of Lake Havasu City transported the 1831 London Bridge to Arizona, all the way from England!

ENERGY VORTEXES
The town of Sedona is said to have several spiritual locations with healing energy . . . perfect for yoga!

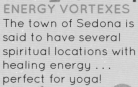

PHOENIX

DON'T CALL ME PIG!
Javelinas or peccaries are common in this state. They look like pigs but are a different species, with straight tusks.

MESA

THE BOLA TIE
is the official state neckwear of Arizona, the first of only three states to have such a thing.

ARIZONA STATE CAPITOL
A wax figure of Arizona's first governor, George W. P. Hunt, sits in the governor's office.

SAGUARO NATIONAL PARK
A saguaro cactus can live for between 100 and 200 years and grow 40 feet tall.

NEW MEXICO

HEARD MUSEUM
Doug Hyde's *Intertribal Greeting* sculpture, showing women from various tribes, welcomes visitors to this Native American art museum.

BIOSPHERE 2
In 1991 eight people were sealed off inside this 3.14-acre glass research center for two years.

TALIESIN WEST
The architect Frank Lloyd Wright built this house, near Scottsdale, using local volcanic rock and cement mixed with desert sand.

DIAMONDBACK BRIDGE
Among many pieces of public art in Tucson is this bridge, shaped like a rattlesnake.

TUCSON

THE KARTCHNER CAVERNS
is one of the world's top ten caves for its range of different mineral deposits. Its stalactites are still growing . . . about 1 inch every 750 years!

GULF OF CALIFORNIA

MEXICO

ARIZONA-SONORA DESERT MUSEUM
This zoo is home to many desert critters, including the Gila monster, whose venom is used to kill prey . . . and treat diabetes!

COPPER QUEEN MINE
Journey 1,500 feet underground and 100 years back in time on a tour of Bisbee's copper mine.

8

WELCOME TO THE GRAND CANYON STATE

The last of the 48 adjoining states to enter the union is full of jaw-dropping sights.

There's the Grand Canyon, of course, from which the state gets its nickname: a dramatic, 277-mile-long gorge carved by the Colorado River. Native Americans have lived in this area for centuries, and today, a visit to the Havasupai Indian Reservation is a must for anyone wishing to marvel at the spectacular blue-green waterfalls along the south side of the Colorado River.

Just as spectacular are the towering sandstone rocks of Monument Valley, the sunset glow of Cathedral Rock, and even the red blooms of the spiny ocotillo plant that brighten the Sonoran Desert every spring.

You'll also find beauty in the creative arts of Arizona's cities, both large and small, such as Tucson and Bisbee. And don't miss the chance to taste state specialties, like jams and salads made from saguaro and prickly pear cacti, or anything roasted over a mesquite fire!

KEY FACTS

CAPITAL
Phoenix

LARGEST CITIES
Phoenix
Tucson
Mesa

BIRD
Cactus wren

NAMED FOR
Possibly the Native American Pima word "arizonac" meaning "little spring"

STATEHOOD DATE
February 14, 1912

STATEHOOD ORDER
48

FLOWER
Saguaro cactus blossom

POSTAL CODE
AZ

REGION
Southwest

MAIN TIME ZONE
Mountain

TREE
Palo verde

"GOD ENRICHES"

MOMENTS TO REMEMBER

AD 500: The Hohokam people begin building a canal system in the Sonoran Desert.

AD 700–1130: The ancient Pueblo people, ancestors of the Hopi and Zuni tribes, live in small towns and farm crops such as corn and squash.

NOVEMBER 1926: A new east-west highway, Route 66, is established from Illinois to California. The section through the Black Mountains in Arizona is so treacherous that some travelers hire locals to drive their cars for them.

MAY 29, 1935: The Hoover Dam is completed, creating Lake Mead, the largest reservoir in the U.S.

AUGUST 14, 1982: The first Navajo Code Talkers Day is observed, celebrating the Native American people who helped send military messages during WWII in codes based on native languages.

FEBRUARY 1990: The Heard Museum in Phoenix hosts its first World Championship Hoop Dance Contest, where Native American dancers use dozens of hoops to tell stories.

JUNE 28, 1994: Arizona experiences its hottest day on record, with temperatures of 128°F in Lake Havasu.

JANUARY 27, 2014: Arizona illustrator Molly Idle wins a Caldecott Honor for her picture book *Flora and the Flamingo*.

SEPTEMBER 28, 2014: Blind adventurers Lonnie Bedwell and Erik Weihenmayer complete a 21-day, 277-mile kayak trip through the Grand Canyon.

MARCH 27, 2015: Identical twin astronauts Mark Kelly (who lives in Tucson) and his brother, Scott, begin a NASA study examining the effects of long-term space travel on the body.

ARIZONA

LOUISE THADEN
In 1936 this pioneering aviator from Bentonville set a world record flight time from New York to Los Angeles.

THORNCROWN CHAPEL
This chapel in Eureka Springs, designed by E. Fay Jones, has 425 windows and over 6,000 square feet of glass!

CRYSTAL BRIDGES MUSEUM OF AMERICAN ART
This Bentonville gallery has a huge collection, including a sculpture of Pinocchio by artist Jim Dine.

AL GREEN
b.1946
This Rock and Roll Hall of Famer sang gospel as a boy in Forrest City.

E. FAY JONES
1921–2004
Born in Pine Buff, this architect built with materials native to the Ozark Mountains.

JOHNNY CASH
1932–2003
This country music icon turned actor and author grew up in Dyess.

BETTE GREENE
b.1934
The novel *Summer of My German Soldier* is based on this award-winning author's childhood in Parkin.

MELBA PATTILLO BEALS
b.1941
This journalist was one of the "Little Rock Nine" and wrote the book *Warriors Don't Cry* about her experiences.

MISSOURI

RUSH GHOST TOWN
This deserted zinc-mining center was once the second-largest town in Arkansas.

BENTONVILLE

FAYETTEVILLE

BUFFALO NATIONAL RIVER
Canoeing is a favorite pastime along the 135 miles of the nation's first national river.

THE OZARK FOLK CENTER
celebrates American folk music and traditional crafts, such as quilting.

JOHNNY CASH
grew up singing songs with his family and working on a cotton farm in Dyess.

THE HAMPSON ARCHEOLOGICAL MUSEUM
in Wilson displays artifacts from a 600-year-old village.

POPEYE STATUE
The city of Alma claims to be the "Spinach Capital of the World" and has a giant bronze Popeye statue.

FLAMIN' TASTY
Local chefs have created delicacies from an unusual food stuff: cacti! Here you can eat it candied, juiced, and they even use it to flavor a unique barbecue sauce.

THE DELTA CULTURAL CENTER
in Helena explores the people and music of the Arkansas Delta area.

FORT SMITH

LAKE OUACHITA
is one of the cleanest lakes in the country, and is home to rare freshwater jellyfish. Don't worry . . . they don't sting!

TOAD SUCK
An annual toad race helps celebrate this town's bizarre name.

LITTLE ROCK

OKLAHOMA

THE LITTLE ROCK NINE
In 1957 nine bright and brave African American teenagers were chosen to integrate Central High School.

HEIFER INTERNATIONAL HEADQUARTERS
In this eco building, which uses only half the energy of a conventional office, they reuse rainwater to flush toilets.

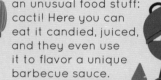

ST. MARY'S CHURCH
Architect Charles Eames designed this church in Helena. The lights represent the world as half in darkness, half in light.

OUACHITA MOUNTAINS
Some of the best-quality quartz crystals in the world are mined here.

BUCKSTAFF BATHHOUSE
Visitors to the city of Hot Springs can soak away their aches in the warm mineral waters here.

ARKANSAS STATE CAPITOL
The six bronze front doors were purchased from Tiffany's of New York for $10,000!

ARKANSAS INLAND MARITIME MUSEUM
Tour the USS *Razorback*, a WWII submarine that rescued downed pilots.

CRATER OF DIAMONDS STATE PARK
Dig for gems at the only diamond site in the world open to the public.

THE ARKANSAS MUSEUM OF NATURAL RESOURCES
The town of Smackover was a top oil producer in the 1920s.

TOLTEC MOUNDS ARCHEOLOGICAL STATE PARK
This ancient site lies southeast of Little Rock. Archaeologists think that a hoop and stick game called chunkey may have been played here 1,000 years ago.

MISSISSIPPI

SCOTTIE MAURICE PIPPEN
b.1965
This Olympic medal-winner and NBA All-Star forward was born in Hamburg.

PECAN
The state nut is not actually a true nut, but a type of fruit!

PINK TOMATO
Warren hosts an annual festival celebrating the state fruit, which is also the state vegetable!

THE LAKEPORT PLANTATION
in Lake Village was once a cotton plantation farmed by slaves, and is now a museum.

WELCOME TO THE NATURAL STATE

Arkansas is truly a diamond of a state. And speaking of diamonds, these precious stones were first discovered here in 1906 at what is now the Crater of Diamonds State Park. Today visitors to the park can dig for their own glittering jewels under the "finders-keepers" policy!

As well as its sparkling gems, Arkansas has many more natural wonders, including its world-famous hot springs (which bubble out of the ground at 143 degrees Fahrenheit) and the breathtaking Ozark–St Francis National Forest. With its beautiful scenery, clear lakes, and magnificent rivers, the "Natural State" is aptly named.

But just as momentous as its landscape is the key role the state has played in American history. In 1957 nine African American students made headlines as the first black pupils to attend Little Rock's all-white Central High School. Today the school is a National Historic Site where visitors can learn about this history-making act of bravery.

TENNESSEE

MOMENTS TO REMEMBER

AD 650: The Plum Bayou people begin building 18 mounds, now known as the Toltec Mounds, which serve as a religious and social meeting place.

JANUARY 10, 1921: Oil is discovered near El Dorado, leading to the Arkansas oil boom.

JULY 14, 1944: The charity now known as Heifer International, based in Little Rock, sends its first shipment of farm animals to Puerto Rico to help reduce hunger and poverty.

1946: Arkansas senator J. William Fulbright creates the Fulbright Program, an international exchange program for talented students. So far more than 300,000 people have taken part!

SEPTEMBER 25, 1957: The "Little Rock Nine" enter Little Rock Central High School escorted by the U.S. Army. These teenagers had volunteered to be the first black students to attend the all-white school, in the face of violent opposition.

JANUARY 25, 1975: Bette Green wins a Newbery Honor for her novel *Philip Hall Likes Me, I Reckon Maybe*, set in rural Arkansas.

JANUARY 20, 1993: Former governor of Arkansas Bill Clinton, who was raised in Hot Springs, begins his first term as U.S. president.

FEBRUARY 24, 1999: Johnny Cash, the singer of "Ring of Fire," born in Kingsland, receives a Grammy Lifetime Achievement Award.

MARCH 29, 2007: Milton Crenchaw, the first African American licensed pilot from Arkansas, and a leading WWII pilot trainer, is awarded a Congressional Gold Medal.

KEY FACTS

CAPITAL
Little Rock

LARGEST CITIES
Little Rock
Fort Smith
Fayetteville

BIRD
Mockingbird

NAMED FOR
The Ogahpah people, who an Illinois tribe described as *Akansa*, or "downstream people"

STATEHOOD DATE
June 15, 1836

STATEHOOD ORDER
25

FLOWER
Apple blossom

POSTAL CODE
AR

REGION
South

MAIN TIME ZONE
Central

TREE
Pine

"THE PEOPLE RULE"

ARKANSAS

OREGON

LASSEN VOLCANIC NATIONAL PARK
boasts all four types of volcanoes . . . and some boiling mud pools!

NATIONAL YO-YO MUSEUM
Find one of the world's biggest yo-yos here: it's called Big-Yo, it's over 4 feet wide, and it can only be played with a crane!

GRIZZLY BEARS
These nocturnal omnivores weigh up to 800 pounds and can run at up to 35 miles per hour.

MOUNT LASSEN
is the aboriginal home of Ishi, who in the early 1900s, taught anthropologists skills of the Yahi people.

BLUE JEANS
The world's first pair of blue jeans were created in California by Levi Strauss and Jacob Davis.

PINK GOLD
In the 1880s, the people of a Chinese fishing camp on San Pablo Bay caught 3 million pounds of shrimp a year.

CALIFORNIA STATE CAPITOL
When the capitol building was finished in 1874, it had cost $2.45 million—that's about $46 million in today's money!

NEVADA

GOLDEN GATE BRIDGE
A team of 50 ironworkers and painters maintain San Francisco's most famous bridge.

SACRAMENTO

BODIE: GHOST TOWN
This once-thriving gold-rush town is now all but abandoned.

SAN FRANCISCO

ALCATRAZ

ENTER THE DRAGON
The Bay area was home to legendary martial arts master Bruce Lee.

This small island was the site of a famous prison whose inmates included gangster Al Capone.

BUFFALO SOLDIERS
were African American soldiers serving after the Civil War. They brought law and order to parks such as Yosemite.

SAN JOSE

SILICON VALLEY
is home to top tech companies such as Apple.

THE JOHN MUIR TRAIL
is named after the wilderness lover who helped create the national park system.

ESPERANZA RISING
Pam Muñoz Ryan's award-winning novel takes place in the San Joaquin Valley in the 1920s.

PACIFIC OCEAN

LOG TUNNEL
Sequoia National Park has the tallest redwood in the world . . . as well as a fallen tree you can drive through!

134°F IN DEATH VALLEY
This is the hottest, driest, and lowest place in the U.S.

ROUTE 66
The famous highway ends on the Santa Monica Pier.

JOSHUA TREE NATIONAL PARK
The park's tallest tree is 40 feet tall and hundreds of years old.

DISNEYLAND
was built on 160 acres of orange groves.

LOS ANGELES

HOLLYWOOD
The letters of the iconic Hollywood sign stand 45 feet tall.

SALLY RIDE
The first U.S. woman in space grew up playing tennis in Los Angeles.

FAITHFUL SWALLOWS
Every March these birds return to roost in Mission San Juan—Capistrano's oldest building.

SAN DIEGO

LA BREA TAR PITS
Fossils of many prehistoric animals have been found here, including saber-toothed cats.

BONES BRIGADE
Fakie, goofy-foot, crooked grind . . . All hail the legendary south Californian skateboarding team.

WEST COAST SWING
is California's energetic state dance.

MEXICO

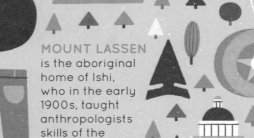

iFORNIA

JOHN MUIR
1838–1914
Naturalist and conservationist, Muir influenced the creation of many national parks.

SHIRLEY TEMPLE BLACK
1928–2014
This singing, tap-dancing child film-star from Santa Monica grew up to become a diplomat.

WELCOME TO THE GOLDEN STATE

California has greeted many explorers, vacationers, and adventurers over the years, including the forty-niners, who came seeking their fortunes in 1849 after the discovery of gold at Sutter's Mill on the banks of the South Fork American River.

Today, this sun-kissed state is a destination for those eager to experience famous attractions such as Hollywood, Disneyland, Yosemite National Park, Angel Island, and the Golden Gate Bridge . . . along with the City of Eternal Sunshine (Coachella), the City of the Silent (Colma), the Avocado Capital of the World (Fallbrook), Dogtown (Santa Monica), the City by the Bay (San Francisco), and the City of Angels (Los Angeles), to name but a few. With over one million acres of state parks, including Yosemite, the Pinnacles, and the Humboldt Redwoods, there is something for everyone in sunny CA!

MOMENTS TO REMEMBER

SEPTEMBER 28, 1542: Portuguese explorer Juan Rodríguez Cabrillo explores what is now San Diego Bay.

JANUARY 24, 1848: Gold is discovered! In the California gold rush, some 300,000 people travel from around the globe to mine for riches.

MAY 10, 1869: The First Transcontinental Railroad is completed, with much of the track built by Chinese immigrants.

APRIL 18, 1906: A powerful earthquake rips through San Francisco, and navy Lieutenant Frederick Newton Freeman leaps into action, guiding tugboats to help save the burning city.

1910–1940: Angel Island in San Francisco Bay sees approximately 300,000 Asian immigrants enter the U.S.

JULY 17, 1955: Disneyland opens, somewhat hastily: in some areas of the park, the paint is still wet!

MAY 16, 1966: The popular band the Beach Boys release their album *Pet Sounds*, featuring unusual instruments such as bike bells and dog whistles.

AUGUST 22, 1966: Farm worker and civil rights activist Cesar Chavez co-founds the United Farm Workers Organizing Committee, which continues to champion farm workers' rights today.

MARCH 8, 1978: Sonoma County is the first place to celebrate Women's History Week. In 1987, Congress declares March to be National Women's History Month.

JANUARY 3, 2007: Californian representative Nancy Pelosi becomes the first female speaker of the U.S. House of Representatives.

KADIR NELSON
b.1974
The award-winning author and illustrator of *Hearts and Soul* and *Henry's Freedom Box* lives in San Diego.

ARIZONA

CESAR CHAVEZ
1927–1993
A childhood farm worker, Chavez later strived to bring better conditions and pay to farm laborers.

LUTHER BURBANK
1849–1926
Born in Massachusetts but living in Santa Rosa, this botanist created 800 new strains of plants.

DOROTHEA LANGE
1895–1965
This photojournalist took pictures of migrant farmworkers during the Depression of the 1930s.

KEY FACTS

CAPITAL
Sacramento

LARGEST CITIES
Los Angeles
San Diego
San Jose

BIRD
California valley quail

NAMED FOR
The fictional warrior Queen Calafia, ruler of a mythical island in a Spanish tale

STATEHOOD DATE
September 9, 1850

STATEHOOD ORDER
31

FLOWER
California poppy

POSTAL CODE
CA

REGION
Pacific

MAIN TIME ZONE
Pacific

TREE
California redwood

"EUREKA" (I HAVE FOUND IT)

COLO

THE BLACK AMERICAN WEST MUSEUM
showcases the achievements of pioneers, explorers, doctors, and other Old West heroes.

COLORADO STATE CAPITOL
The dome of the capitol building contains a mini-capitol made from soup cans!

ARGO GOLD MINE
Pan for your fortune in the mine that milled $100 million worth of gold.

TITANIC SURVIVOR
At the "Unsinkable" Molly Brown's House Museum, you can learn Edwardian etiquette with a Mind Your Manners Tea.

HORSETOOTH MOUNTAIN
One legend has it that a giant was slain here; these days, enjoy camping and water-skiing.

TWO-HEADED MOO
Guess which animal oddity you will find at the Overland Trail Museum?

PRONGHORNS
are the fastest land mammals in the Western Hemisphere.

DINOSAUR MONUMENT
Gape at a 150-foot-long quarry wall embedded with more than 1,500 fossilized dinosaur bones.

GLENWOOD HOT SPRINGS
Swim and soak in a pool as long as a football field.

AURORA

DENVER

CADET CHAPEL
The 17 spires of this U.S. Air Force Academy chapel create an iconic place of worship.

BIG BAND
Glenn Miller started his first band with high school classmates in Fort Morgan.

MIKE, THE HEADLESS CHICKEN FESTIVAL
Every May in Fruita they celebrate a real rooster that lived for 18 months . . . *after* he lost his head!

LOVELAND PASS
Breathtaking views— and nail-biting ascents— await at this 11,990-foot-high landmark.

GARDEN OF THE GODS
Astounding rock formations grace the sites of these former Native American camps.

UTE INDIAN MUSEUM
Visit beautiful Ute tepees, some of which took 14 buffalo hides to make!

MAROON BELLS-SNOWMASS WILDERNESS
Nature lovers flock to the six peaks of this official wilderness area.

ASPEN SHRINES
Curious collections of keepsakes are hidden on the ski slopes of Aspen. They honor Elvis, Snoopy, and other heroes.

ROYAL GORGE BRIDGE
Speed through the air on a zip line 1,200 feet above the Arkansas River!

COLORADO SPRINGS

OWL WOMAN
The Cheyenne Mis-stan-sta helped manage relations between Native Americans and settlers.

KIT CARSON
was made famous through deeds of selfless heroism.

RAILWAY CROSSING

SANDBOARDING
Pros surf the Great Sand Dunes early to avoid burns from the 150°F sand!

MESA VERDE NATIONAL PARK
The ancient Pueblo people built some 600 dwellings into the cliff faces here.

DURANGO & SILVERTON
This 1881 rail line is a must-see for steam engine enthusiasts.

UFO WATCHTOWER
Flying-saucer experts say the San Luis Valley is prime UFO-spotting territory.

R·R·MARKET

R&R MARKET
Dario Gallegos opened this San Luis store in 1857 . . . and his family still runs it!

COMANCHE NATIONAL GRASSLAND
These 435,000 acres of grassland and canyons make for spectacular sunsets.

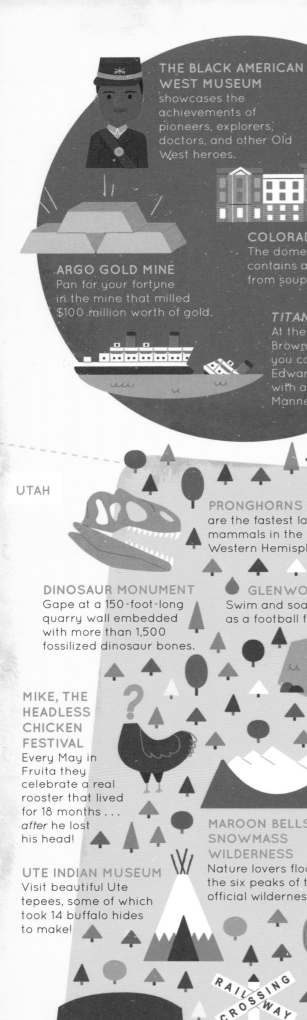

RADO

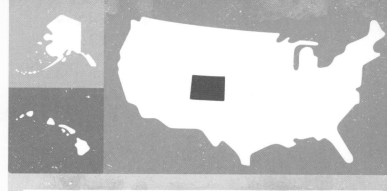

WELCOME TO THE CENTENNIAL STATE

I n 1895, Katharine Lee Bates wrote the lyrics to the song "America the Beautiful" after a breathtaking visit to one of Colorado's highest points, Pikes Peak. Her phrases "purple mountain majesties" and "amber waves of grain" perfectly describe the beauty of this state.

The flat, grassy prairies—where buffalo once roamed—stop mid-state at the base of the majestic Rocky Mountains. These mountains are home to elk, moose, and bighorn sheep. They sit on deposits of silver and gold that beckoned prospectors west in the 1800s.

Today visitors from all over the world flock to Colorado, attracted by the variety of things to see and do. From world-class skiing and mountain vistas to deserts, plains, and river-carved canyons, natural beauty and adventurous pursuits abound in Colorado.

RUTH HANDLER
1916–2002
This Denver native co-founded the toy company Mattel and created the Barbie doll.

FLORENCE SABIN
1871–1953
A Central City native, the "First Lady of American Science" was a groundbreaking medical researcher.

TEMPLE GRANDIN
b.1947
State professor Grandin's insights into animal behavior changed the livestock industry.

ISABELLA BIRD
1831–1904
An English explorer, Bird wrote about her horseback adventures in the Rockies.

CHIN LIN SOU
1836–1894
Originally coming from China to work on the railroad, Chin settled in Denver and became a successful businessman.

GLENN MILLER
1904–1944
This popular swing era trombonist and bandleader went to college at UC Boulder.

OKLAHOMA

KANSAS

MOMENTS TO REMEMBER

1100s: The ancient Pueblo people begin construction of cliff dwellings beneath overhanging cliffs in Mesa Verde.

1842: Mountain man James P. Beckwourth, a former slave, founds the city of Pueblo.

JANUARY 7, 1880: Ute leaders Chief Ouray and his wife, Chipeta, negotiate a reservation resettlement treaty in Washington DC.

MARCH 18, 1898: Activist and bike-riding reporter Minnie J. Reynolds founds the Denver Woman's Press Club (DWPC).

1902: Dr. Justina Ford starts practicing medicine in Denver and is the only female doctor there for the next three decades. She delivered an estimated 7,000 babies in her 50-year career.

NOVEMBER 1910: The Argo Tunnel, the largest mining project in the world, is completed. The tunnel flooded and was shut down in 1943.

1935: Louis Ballast, owner of the Humpty Dumpty Barrel Drive-In, tries a slice of American cheese on his burger and patents the name "cheeseburger."

MAY 7, 1945: Mary Chase wins a Pulitzer Prize for *Harvey*, a play about a man with an imaginary companion: a six-foot-three-and-a-half-inch rabbit!

1975: Retired U.S. Air Force Colonel Hugh Nevins opens a ski school for the blind; Colorado now has several.

MARCH 2008: Skiier Lindsey Vonn wins the overall World Cup title for the first time.

KEY FACTS

CAPITAL
Denver

LARGEST CITIES
Denver
Colorado Springs
Aurora

BIRD
Lark bunting

NAMED FOR
The Spanish for "colored red"

STATEHOOD DATE
August 1, 1876

STATEHOOD ORDER
38

FLOWER
Rocky Mountain columbine

POSTAL CODE
CO

REGION
Rocky Mountain

MAIN TIME ZONE
Mountain

TREE
Colorado blue spruce

"NOTHING WITHOUT PROVIDENCE"

15

Connecticut

HARRIET BEECHER STOWE spent much of her life in Connecticut. She is famous for writing *Uncle Tom's Cabin*, which helped turn people against slavery.

JOHN BROWN The birthplace of this fiery abolitionist is a site on CT's Freedom Trail.

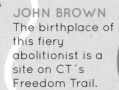

CITY OF TORRINGTON, CONNECTICUT
INC. 1923

OLD NEW-GATE PRISON was once a copper mine, then a prison, and is now a museum.

CONNECTICUT STATE CAPITOL The Gothic-style capitol building was completed in 1878.

HARTFORD

NATHAN HALE STATE FOREST honors one of Connecticut's Revolutionary War heroes.

THE APPALACHIAN TRAIL The U.S.'s longest continuous hiking trail passes through 14 states.

TONY AND SONS' SEAFOOD has been producing some of CT's best shellfish for more than 25 years.

FARMINGTON

was a key town on the Underground Railroad, where escaped slaves were helped to reach freedom. Some used the North Star to navigate.

THE HELICOPTER was invented in CT in 1939 by Igor Sikorsky.

TICK-TOCK The clockmaker Eli Terry invented one of the first mass-produced shelf clocks.

DINOSAUR STATE PARK Visitors can make a cast of a real dinosaur print!

CANDLEWOOD LAKE Here, curious divers can investigate underwater buildings and abandoned farm machinery.

CONNECTICUT RIVER Bald eagles flock here for easy fishing and nesting.

HOOPSKIRT HOOPLA! Made in Derby in the 1850s, these skirts were nearly 6 feet wide!

NEW HAVEN

CHEAP SWEET New Haven produced the first trademarked "lolly pops" in 1931. They sold for a penny!

DANBURY RAILWAY MUSEUM has some historic engines and cabooses (crew's wagons).

GILLETTE CASTLE Discover hidden rooms and secret mirrors in this 24-room mansion.

KNOW-IT-ALL More than 500 brains are on display at Yale University's Cushing Library!

GLASS HOUSE Designed by Philip Johnson, the view from this house is simple: trees and nature!

BRIDGEPORT

LONG ISLAND SOUND

THE BARNUM FESTIVAL celebrates the imaginative circus showman and Bridgeport native P. T. Barnum.

BARBARA McCLINTOCK 1902–1992 Born in Hartford, McClintock's work on plant genetics won her a Nobel Prize in 1983.

PRUDENCE CRANDALL 1803–1890 Crandall fought racial intolerance in her efforts to provide an education for African American girls.

MARIAN ANDERSON 1902–1993 The first African American soloist with the Metropolitan Opera, Anderson moved to a Danbury farm in her retirement.

NOAH WEBSTER
1758–1843
Born in West Hartford, Webster wrote the first American dictionary and grammar textbook.

EUGENE O'NEILL
1888–1953
While in the hospital in Connecticut, O'Neill discovered a passion for writing and went on to win the Nobel Prize.

JAMES W.C. PENNINGTON
1807–1870
An escaped slave, Pennington was the first African American to attend Yale. He wrote the first history of African Americans.

RHODE ISLAND

THE PRAYING MANTIS
is Connecticut's official state insect and an unmatched pint-sized predator.

EDUCATION FOR ALL
The Prudence Crandall Museum honors one of Connecticut's heroes, who opened one of the first schools for African American girls.

NEW LONDON COUNTY

WELCOME TO THE CONSTITUTION STATE

As one of the original 13 colonies it's no surprise that "The Constitution State" has many firsts to its name. For instance, you can read these words thanks to Connecticut native Noah Webster, who published the first American dictionary in the early 1800s—just after the nation's first newspaper started here in 1764. In addition to housing the first law school, public art museum, and pay phone, the fifth state also produced the nation's first tacks and first plows—how about that?

These feats and others are the efforts of the enterprising people who grew up here. Although it's the third-smallest state by area, it's among the most densely populated, which could explain why so many influential people have called Connecticut home. From Revolutionary War hero Nathan Hale to inventor Charles Goodyear, or the best-selling author of *The Hunger Games* trilogy, Suzanne Collins, Connecticut has a knack for producing notable people.

MOMENTS TO REMEMBER

OCTOBER 29, 1764: The *Hartford Courant*, America's oldest continuously operating newspaper, publishes its first edition.

APRIL 1777: 16-year-old Sybil Ludington rides 40 miles at night to warn her father's soldiers of the British advancement, and becomes a hero of the Revolutionary War.

MARCH 14, 1794: Eli Whitney invents the world's first cotton gin: a machine that separates cotton fibers from their seeds.

1806: Noah Webster publishes the first American dictionary, with 37,000 entries including the newly coined American words *squash* and *skunk*.

NOVEMBER 25, 1841: After a long legal battle, Sengbe Pieh and other survivors of the *Amistad* slave revolt return home to Africa.

JUNE 5, 1851: The first installment of Harriet Beecher Stowe's *Uncle Tom's Cabin* appears in the antislavery newspaper *The National Era*.

1858: Ezra Warner invents the world's first can opener—nearly 50 years after the first cans!

1877: The first American bicycles—one of CT's many manufacturing achievements—are produced in Hartford.

1973: Battling bulldozers, Elizabeth George stands in the way of developers trying to dig up the Pequot Indian Reservation.

JANUARY 27, 2003: The author Patricia Reilly Giff, resident of Trumbull, is awarded a Newbery Honor for her book *Pictures of Hollis Woods*.

THE LAST WOODEN WHALESHIP
The *Charles W. Morgan* is docked at Mystic Seaport.

MASHANTUCKET PEQUOT MUSEUM
The world's largest Native American museum brings history to life.

ATLANTIC OCEAN

MONTE CRISTO COTTAGE
Childhood summer home of Nobel laureate Eugene O'Neill.

FOXWOODS
The largest casino in the U.S. employs some 10,000 people.

KEY FACTS

CAPITAL
Hartford

LARGEST CITIES
Bridgeport
New Haven
Hartford

BIRD
American robin

NAMED FOR
The Mohegan word *quinnehtukqut*, meaning "Beside the long tidal river"

STATEHOOD DATE
January 9, 1788

STATEHOOD ORDER
5

FLOWER
Mountain laurel

POSTAL CODE
CT

REGION
New England

MAIN TIME ZONE
Eastern

TREE
Charter (white) oak

"HE WHO TRANSPLANTED STILL SUSTAINS"

17

PENNSYLVANIA

DELAWARE'S ONLY CAVE
The privately owned Wolf Cave in Beaver Valley is the only natural cave in the state!

WILMINGTON

NEWARK

SHELL SHOCK
The Delaware Museum of Natural History, near Winterthur, has North America's second-largest shell collection, behind only the Smithsonian.

FIRST FLAG
The first U.S. flag ever to fly was during the Battle of Cooch's Bridge, September 3, 1777, during Delaware's only Revolutionary War skirmish.

ICE CHAMPS
Olympic figure skaters Johnny Weir and Tara Lipinski trained at the University of Delaware Ice Arena in Newark.

DELAWARE MEMORIAL BRIDGE
is a set of twin bridges joining Delaware to New Jersey. At 3,650 feet, it's the world's longest twin suspension bridge!

PEA PATCH ISLAND
Locals say this island was named when a ship carrying peas ran aground and lost its cargo, which sprouted new pea plants!

NEW JERSEY

JOHN DICKINSON
1732–1808
Called the "Penman of the Revolution," this Founding Father's writings encouraged American independence.

LIGHTS, CAMERA, ACTION!
The movie *Dead Poets Society* was filmed at St. Andrew's School in Middletown.

THE SMYRNA OPERA HOUSE
once served as a town hall, police and fire station, library, movie theater, and jail (complete with barred windows, which are still there today)!

BOMBAY HOOK NATIONAL WILDLIFE REFUGE
More than a million snow geese pass through this salt marsh each year on their way to their northern breeding grounds.

JOSEPH BIDEN, JR.
b.1942
Raised in Wilmington, this six-time senator became the 47th vice president of the United States in 2009.

DOVER

VERY CRABBY
Delaware Bay is home to the largest population of horseshoe crabs in the world.

SUIT UP!
The engineering company ILC Dover has been making astronauts' space suits for 50 years.

CONCRETE WATCHTOWERS
up to 75 feet tall were built along the coastline during WWII as protection against Nazi U-boat attacks.

V(I)P PLANE
Take a tour of an Air Force Two plane, which transported several vice presidents, at the Air Mobility Command Museum in Dover.

DELAWARE LEGISLATIVE HALL
is one of the few state capitols built in the red-brick Georgian style.

THE JOHNSON VICTROLA MUSEUM
celebrates the inventor Eldridge Reeves Johnson, who developed the gramophone (an early record player).

OH, DEERE!
The Messick Agricultural Museum in Harrington displays one of the first mass-produced John Deere tractors.

MILTON
Named for the English poet John Milton, this friendly place has a Town-Wide Yard Sale each fall.

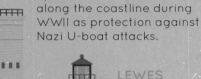

LEWES
Named after an English town, Lewes (pronounced *lou-iss*, not *lose*) is known as "the first town in the first state," as it was settled in 1631 by the Dutch.

THE WORLD CHAMPIONSHIP PUNKIN CHUNKIN
is a contest where people hurl pumpkins from catapults. It began in Bridgeville, with the winner flying 126 feet. Thirty years later, the range is nearly 5,000 feet!

THE CHICKEN OR THE EGG?
Sussex County raises more broiler chickens than any other county in the United States.

NANTICOKE INDIAN TRIBE
DELAWARE

NANTICOKE POWWOW
Every September descendants of the Nanticoke tribe hold a powwow celebrating their heritage.

MARYLAND

ANNIE JUMP CANNON
1863–1941
This astronomer devised a way to remember the classifications of stars (OBAFGKM): Oh, Be A Fine Girl—Kiss Me!

HENRY HEIMLICH
b.1920
This surgeon and medical inventor, born in Wilmington, developed a maneuver to save choking victims.

TAKING SIDES
The Mason-Dixon Line dividing Delaware from Maryland runs through two towns—Delmar and Marydel—whose names come from combining the names of the two states.

PUTTING DOWN ROOTS
The Great Cypress Swamp is the northernmost cypress swamp in the country, with trees that are hundreds of years old.

INTO THE FRYING PAN. . .
A 10-foot-wide, 650-pound frying pan was created in Selbyville for the first annual Delmarva Chicken Festival in order to fry 800 chicken quarters.

wave

WELCOME TO THE FIRST STATE

The nation's second-smallest state is proof that good things come in small packages. Despite its small size (just 96 miles long and, at most, 35 miles wide), the "Small Wonder" state is big in terms of historical importance. As its nickname suggests, it was the very first state to approve the U.S. constitution in 1787.

Delaware was home to people long before that, of course. The Lenni Lenape tribe, whose name means "original people," lived along the Delaware River for thousands of years, hunting, fishing, and farming.

Today, Delaware's 28-mile-long sandy shoreline attracts oodles of beachcombers, enjoying kites and cones on beaches like Rehoboth. Nature lovers will enjoy exploring the wetlands of the mysterious cypress swamps, while young scientists may be inspired by visiting the DuPont Experimental Station and walking in the footsteps of the inventors of nylon and GORE-TEX!

MOMENTS TO REMEMBER

8,000 BC: The Lenni Lenape tribe establish a farming society in the Delaware Bay area.

1610: English sea captain Samuel Argall sails into the bay and names it "Delaware" after the governor of Virginia, Lord De La Warr.

1638: Peter Minuit and the New Sweden Company found the town of New Christina, which is renamed after the Earl of Wilmington 100 years later.

JULY 1, 1776: Continental Congress delegate Caesar Rodney rides all night, through a thunderstorm, from Dover to Philadelphia. He arrives just in time to cast the deciding vote for Delaware in declaring independence from Britain, and has since been known as the "Hero of Delaware."

DECEMBER 7, 1787: Delaware becomes the first state to ratify the U.S. Constitution.

1880: Rehoboth Beach holds what is claimed to be the first bathing beauty contest. One of the three judges is inventor Thomas Edison!

1900: The "Father of American Illustration," Howard Pyle, opens his art studio in Wilmington. Students include N. C. Wyeth and Jessie Willcox Smith.

JUNE 20, 1904: A train driver fails to see a schooner passing through the open drawbridge in Laurel, resulting in a rare collision of train and boat.

FEBRUARY 28, 1935: The DuPont Research Lab, headed by Dr. Wallace Carothers, first produces nylon as an alternative to silk. Three years earlier, they patented neoprene, the first synthetic rubber.

NOVEMBER 6, 2008: Delaware senator Joe Biden is elected the 47th vice president of the United States.

REHOBOTH BEACH
Vacationers have been flocking to this seaside town since the 1870s.

ATLANTIC OCEAN

THE FENWICK ISLAND LIGHTHOUSE was painted in 1880 for a total cost of $5!

EMILY BISSELL
1861–1948
By introducing Christmas seals to the nation, this social worker put her stamp on history!

THOMAS GARRETT
1789–1871
Garrett helped 2,700 runaway slaves travel through Delaware on the Underground Railroad.

KEY FACTS

CAPITAL
Dover

LARGEST CITIES
Wilmington
Dover
Newark

BIRD
Delaware blue hen

NAMED FOR
The Delaware River, which was named after Lord De La Warr, governor of the colony of Virginia

STATEHOOD DATE
December 7, 1787

STATEHOOD ORDER
1

FLOWER
Peach blossom

POSTAL CODE
DE

REGION
Mid-Atlantic

MAIN TIME ZONE
Eastern

TREE
American holly

"LIBERTY AND INDEPENDENCE"

OSCEOLA
c.1804–1838
A fiery leader of Florida's Seminole people, Osceola fought to preserve his tribe's lands.

CITRUS
80% of the U.S.'s oranges and grapefruits are grown in the Sunshine State.

ALABAMA

CIRCUS CLASS
Florida State University is one of only two colleges that offer circus lessons!

GEORGIA

AUGUSTA SAVAGE
Born in Green Cove Springs, this sculptor created *The Harp* for the 1939 World's Fair.

PALM TREES
Florida's state tree, the cabbage palm, has many edible parts.

FLORIDA STATE CAPITOL
A high-rise state capitol was built behind the old one in the 1970s. It took over 3 million man hours!

SEED SPITTING
Every year the town of Chiefland holds a Watermelon Festival: the seed-spitting contest is a favorite!

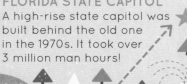

TALLAHASSEE

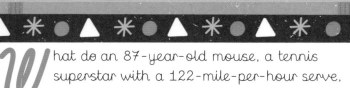

WELCOME TO THE SUNSHINE STATE

MAGNET LAB
Tallahassee's Mag Lab is a state-of-the-art magnet research center.

THE SUWANNEE RIVER
has plentiful catfish, aka mudcat or chucklehead, for anglers to enjoy.

THE YEARLING RESTAURANT
at Cross Creek offers traditional swampland eats such as cooter, frog legs, and alligator!

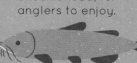

What do an 87-year-old mouse, a tennis superstar with a 122-mile-per-hour serve, and a tailless dolphin all have in common? That's right: Mickey Mouse, Serena Williams, and Winter the dolphin all call the 27th state home. And what about oranges, golf courses, and tourists? You've got it—the Sunshine State has the most in the nation!

The 16th-century explorer Ponce de León named the state for the Spanish celebration *Pascua Florida*, or feast of flowers. This balmy part of the world certainly lives up to its beautiful name, with such natural attractions as the cypress swamps of Everglades National Park, the seashells of Sanibel Island, and the 1,197 miles of glorious coastline teeming with dolphins, manatees, and coral.

Key West locals say that Florida's most beautiful sight is the sun—they host a nightly arts festival and gather to watch the sun sink into the Gulf of Mexico.

GEORGE SMOOT
b.1945
Born in Yukon, astrophysicist Smoot won a Nobel Prize for his work in cosmic microwave background radiation.

GULF OF MEXICO

DALI MUSEUM
Dripping clocks and other surreal artwork from Salvador Dali await you in St. Petersburg.

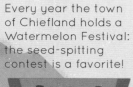

TAMPA

RINGLING MUSEUM
Squeeze into a clown's car at circus king John Ringling's former estate in Sarasota.

ZORA NEALE HURSTON
1891–1960
An author and folklorist, Hurston loved the state so much she once wrote, "I've got the map of Florida on my tongue."

SHAQUILLE O'NEAL
b.1972
Shaq's career as a basketball superstar began with the Orlando Magic, where he broke several backboards.

FLORIDA

20

JACKSONVILLE

ST. AUGUSTINE LIGHTHOUSE
Investigate shipwrecks and hunt for ghosts at this historic lighthouse.

THE GREAT AMERICAN RACE
NASCAR racing began in Daytona. Drivers wear helmets and five-point harnesses, and carry fire extinguishers!

CAPE CANAVERAL
Climb aboard a NASA spacecraft at the Kennedy Space Center!

OCALA National Forest
OCALA NATIONAL FOREST has some 600 lakes as well as rivers and crystal-clear springs.

ORLANDO

THE ZORA NEALE HURSTON LIBRARY
in Fort Pierce is the first stop on this award-winning author's heritage trail.

THE AH-TAH-THI-KI MUSEUM
offers a unique glimpse into the Seminole Green Corn Ceremony.

CHAMPION CIRCUMFERENCE
The famous banyan tree at the Edison & Ford Winter Estates is big enough to fill a football field!

THE BIG CYPRESS NATIONAL PRESERVE
is home to the endangered Florida panther . . . and its predator: the alligator.

KEY WEST

THE ERNEST HEMINGWAY HOME AND MUSEUM
The author's former grounds are now overrun with cats!

KEY WEST FISHING
Ernest Hemingway would often fish around Key West from his boat *Pilar*.

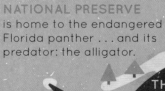

SIDNEY POITIER
b.1927
The first African American to win an Oscar for Best Actor is a lifelong advocate for racial equality. He was born in Miami.

CARL HIAASEN
b.1953
Much of this author's work, whether mystery thrillers or newspaper articles, has centered around Florida.

MINI PRESIDENTS
Find a miniature Reagan, Obama, and all the others at the Presidents Hall of Fame in Clermont.

WALT DISNEY WORLD
Here the very *Brave* can practice archery like Princess Merida.

SINGING TOWER
The 60 bells of the 205-foot-high Bok Tower ring twice daily.

PALM BEACH
is the setting for Judy Blundell's award-winning novel *What I Saw and How I Lied*.

ATLANTIC OCEAN

LITTLE HAVANA
is the place to get Cuban food, such as guava-and-cheese pastries.

GATOR WRESTLING
The Miccosukee people are famed for their reptile wrangling!

EVERGLADES NATIONAL PARK

MIAMI

FLORIDA KEYS

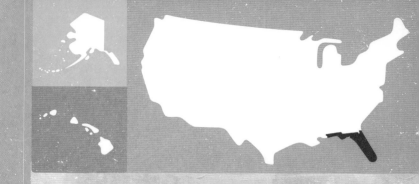

MOMENTS TO REMEMBER

12,000 YEARS AGO: The first humans come to Florida. The ancient Paleo people hunt mastodons, mammoths, and other big game across the Florida peninsula.

APRIL 2, 1513: Spanish explorer Ponce de León arrives in the land he calls *La Florida*, meaning "Land of Flowers."

MAY 1, 1939: Marjorie Kinnan Rawlings wins the Pulitzer Prize for *The Yearling*, the story of a boy and an orphaned fawn set in Ocala National Forest.

1944: During WWII airman Benjamin Green develops an early form of sunscreen that later becomes the popular, cocoa-scented Coppertone.

FEBRUARY 22, 1959: Future NASCAR Hall of Fame driver Lee Petty wins the first Daytona 500 Race . . . average speeds are 135 miles per hour.

JANUARY 14, 1973: After playing a perfect season—winning every game—the Miami Dolphins win the Super Bowl.

MARCH 12, 1978: Little Havana holds its very first Calle Ocho Festival, honoring Miami's Hispanic community with tamales, dances, and mariachi music.

APRIL 12, 1981: The first space shuttle launches from the Kennedy Space Center in Cape Canaveral.

JANUARY 27, 2003: Carl Hiaasen is awarded a Newbery Honor for his novel *Hoot*.

MAY 2014: Engineering student Albert Manero founds Limbitless Solutions, which uses 3-D printers to make prosthetic arms for kids . . . for free!

KEY FACTS

CAPITAL
Tallahassee

LARGEST CITIES
Jacksonville
Miami
Tampa

BIRD
Mockingbird

NAMED FOR
The Spanish phrase *Pascua Florida*, meaning "feast of flowers."

STATEHOOD DATE
March 3, 1845

STATEHOOD ORDER
27

FLOWER
Orange blossom

POSTAL CODE
FL

REGION
Deep South

MAIN TIME ZONE
Eastern

TREE
Cabbage palm

"IN GOD WE TRUST"

TENNESSEE

NORTH CAROLINA

NEW ECHOTA
was capital of the Cherokee Nation and is the start of the Trail of Tears historic trail.

SEAL OF THE CHEROKEE NATION · SEPT. 6, 1839

ETOWAH INDIAN MOUNDS
These huge, flat-topped pyramids were built by ancient people.

GOLD FEVER
first hit the nation when gold was discovered in 1828 in Dahlonega—by accident!

FLANNERY O'CONNOR
1924–1964
One of the best short-story writers of the 20th century, O'Connor often wrote about the Deep South.

JULIETTE "DAISY" GORDON LOW
1860–1927
Inspired by the English founder of the Boy Scouts, Low started the Girl Scouts in Savannah.

CHICKEN CAPITAL
A 1961 Gainesville law forbids eating chicken with a fork!

THE TY COBB MUSEUM
in Royston celebrates one of the greatest baseball players of all time.

JAMES OGLETHORPE
1696–1785
Social reformer Oglethorpe was a British general who founded the colony of Georgia.

CHAMPION CAMPUS
Berry College sprawls over 27,000 acres of woodland and meadows.

ATHENS ROCKS
Bands like R.E.M. and the B-52s helped put the city of Athens on the music map.

AUGUSTA

GEORGIA STATE CAPITOL
The capitol has a statue of "Miss Freedom" on its dome. Her torch lights up at night.

MOUNTAIN MONUMENT
At Stone Mountain, a huge carving of three Civil War leaders is more than half a football field wide!

FORE!
Augusta's highly ranked golf course hosts the Masters tournament.

LITTLE RICHARD
b.1932
This flamboyant performer, born in Macon, composed the chartbusters "Tutti Frutti" and "Lucille."

ATLANTA

BATTLE OF ATLANTA
This pivotal Union victory in 1864 helped elect Abraham Lincoln to a second term.

TRICKSTER TALES
like those of Brer Rabbit are celebrated at the Uncle Remus Museum.

SAVANNAH

The oldest, and perhaps prettiest city in GA is said to be its most haunted, too!

WARM SPRINGS
Native Americans, Franklin D. Roosevelt, and many others have healed in the waters here.

CRAFTY ESCAPE
Ellen Craft disguised herself as a male Southern slaveholder to escape slavery.

COLUMBUS

ALABAMA

GLOWWORMS
The sandy soils of southern GA hide a slimy secret: two-foot-long earthworms that ooze a glowing gunk!

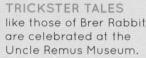

VIDALIA ONIONS
President Jimmy Carter sent out bags of these state vegetables as White House gifts.

JUST PEACHY
Georgia produces more than 40 varieties of peaches.

LIBERTY SHIPS
were cargo ships built in super-quick time during WWII to deliver much-needed supplies to the troops.

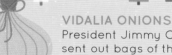

JUST NUTTY
One of GA's biggest crops is celebrated with a 10-foot-tall peanut in Ashburn.

PASAQUAN
is a folk-art haven built by Eddie Owens Martin, who claimed he was instructed to do so in a vision.

THE LUNCH BOX MUSEUM
proudly displays some 3,500 metal lunch boxes, some worth $2,500!

FORT BENNING
is one of the largest army bases in the world, housing over 120,000 people.

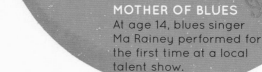

MOTHER OF BLUES
At age 14, blues singer Ma Rainey performed for the first time at a local talent show.

MARTIN LUTHER KING, JR.
1929–1968
Raised in Atlanta, this iconic leader of the African American civil rights movement won the Nobel Peace Prize.

TOMOCHICHI
c.1644–1739
Chief of the Yamacraw Indians, Tomochichi built a positive relationship with Georgia's English settlers, leading to years of peace and abundance.

OKEFENOKEE SWAMP
is home to lots of alligators, some weighing up to 700 pounds!

FLORIDA

WELCOME TO THE PEACH STATE

Even if you've never been south of the Mason-Dixon Line, you've probably heard a song about Georgia. Musicians raised here, including Gladys Knight, CeeLo Green, and, of course, Ray Charles, have sung about this "Empire State of the South," celebrating the beauty and ingenuity of Georgia's lands and people.

"The road leads back to you," sings Ray Charles in the song "Georgia on My Mind," and if you follow that road, you'll find the nation's fourth state rich in hospitality, charm, history, and cultural delights.

Nature lovers are drawn to the stunning scenery of the Blue Ridge Mountains, which mark the southern end of the Appalachian Trail. The nightlife and bustling industry of Atlanta beckon the city-loving traveler, while history fans stroll through Savannah with pleasure. Regardless of your reason for visiting, there's no doubt you'll find much to enjoy in the "Peach State"—including peaches!

KEY FACTS

CAPITAL
Atlanta

LARGEST CITIES
Atlanta
Columbus
Augusta

BIRD
Brown thrasher

NAMED FOR
England's King George II

STATEHOOD DATE
January 2, 1788

STATEHOOD ORDER
4

FLOWER
Cherokee rose

POSTAL CODE
GA

REGION
Deep South

MAIN TIME ZONE
Eastern

TREE
Live oak

"WISDOM, JUSTICE, AND MODERATION"

MOMENTS TO REMEMBER

1000 BC: Native Americans build mysterious earthworks for burials and ceremonies.

DECEMBER 22, 1864: During the Civil War, Union Army General William T. Sherman seizes control of Savannah and presents it to President Lincoln as a Christmas gift!

MAY 8, 1886: The first Coca-Cola is served at Jacobs' Pharmacy in Atlanta. It costs a nickel then . . . and for the next 70 years!

1933: Agriculturalist Naomi Chapman Woodroof begins studying peanuts—research that helps transform them into an essential food product.

MAY 1937: Margaret Mitchell's novel *Gone with the Wind* wins the Pulitzer Prize. She began writing it when she was cooped up with a broken ankle.

1944: Martin Luther King, Jr., enrolls at Morehouse College—age 15—and begins to study theology.

APRIL 13, 1961: Ray Charles wins a Grammy for his cover of "Georgia on My Mind," now the state song.

JANUARY 20, 1977: Former peanut farmer Jimmy Carter is inaugurated and walks down Pennsylvania Avenue to the White House: a presidential first!

JANUARY 23, 1986: Macon-born Little Richard, made famous by his hit song "Tutti Frutti," is one of the first artists honored in the Rock and Roll Hall of Fame.

JULY 19, 1996: Some 10,000 athletes and 2 million tourists arrive for the Summer Olympic Games in Atlanta.

ATLANTIC OCEAN

CAPITAL
Honolulu

LARGEST CITIES
Honolulu
Pearl City
Hilo

BIRD
Nene

NAMED FOR
Possibly the Polynesians' name for their homeland

STATEHOOD DATE
August 21, 1959

STATEHOOD ORDER
50

FLOWER
Yellow hibiscus

POSTAL CODE
HI

REGION
Pacific

MAIN TIME ZONE
Hawaii-Aleutian

TREE
Candlenut

"THE LIFE OF THE LAND IS PERPETUATED IN RIGHTEOUSNESS"

★ WELCOME TO THE ALOHA STATE

The moment you enter Hawaii, you will be surrounded by the Aloha Spirit, a friendly attitude embraced by those in the 50th state. The Hawaiian word "aloha" means something like "joyfully sharing life" and is used in greetings, farewells, and expressions of love. If you live in the Spirit of Aloha, you will be alert, kind, honest, humble, and respectful of the land and other people.

This beautiful, tropical-island state has a long history of different settlers bringing new influences. For instance, Polynesian settlers brought taro, ginger, and coconut, a Spanish adviser introduced coffee and pineapple, and, once the sugar industry took off, workers from China, Japan, the Philippines, Portugal, and other nations journeyed to these islands, bringing a host of different languages and cultures.

Locals and visitors alike celebrate the foods, customs, and language that are a result of this delightful mix of backgrounds.

GARDEN ISLE
Jurassic Park is one of more than 70 movies filmed in Kauai's tropical rain forests.

SPOUTING HORN
Though legend says this coastal fountain is caused by a monstrous lizard, we know it's just waves being forced through a lava tube.

DRIP, DROP
Mount Waialeale gets 460 inches of rain a year, making it the rainiest spot in the U.S.!

MENEHUNE FISHPOND
In Hawaiian mythology, the Menehune were tiny people who built this huge pond in just one night.

THE FORBIDDEN ISLAND
Only those personally invited can visit the privately owned Ni'ihau.

KAUAI

NIIHAU

BETHANY HAMILTON
b.1990
At age 13, Hamilton lost her left arm in a shark attack. She went on to become a winning pro surfer.

DUKE KAHANAMOKU
1890–1968
A five-time Olympic swimming medalist, Honolulu-born Kahanamoku is known as the "Father of Modern Surfing."

PHILIP KUNIA "GABBY" PAHINUI
1921–1980
A master slack key and steel guitarist, Pahinui earned his nickname when he wore gabardine pants to his gigs.

LILI'UOKALANI
1838–1917
The last queen of Hawaii reigned during a turbulent time and was forced to give up her throne to avoid violence.

PATSY MINK
1927–2002
Maui-born Mink was the first Asian American woman elected to Congress.

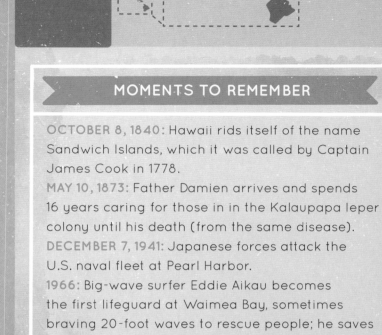

HAWAII STATE CAPITOL
The open-air design of the capitol building celebrates the elements, allowing sun, wind, and rain to enter.

FIRE DANCE
competitions are held each year at the Polynesian Cultural Center.

AMAZING MAZE
The Dole pineapple plantation is home to an almost 2-mile-long maze: the largest in the world!

THE USS *ARIZONA* MEMORIAL
honors those who lost their lives at Pearl Harbor during WWII.

IOLANI PALACE
is the 1882 home of King Kalākaua.

FLOWER POWER
Made with flowers, leaves, and shells, Hawaii's traditional garlands—called lei—show respect, congratulations, welcome, or appreciation.

KAMEHAMEHA I
c.1758–1819
"Kamehameha the Great" unified the islands of Hawaii as king after he conquered each in turn.

OAHU

KAILUA

HONOLULU

MOLOKAI

PEARL CITY

LANAI

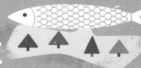

MOLOKAI FISHPONDS
13th-century fishers built dozens of these ingenious rock-walled enclosures.

LĀHAINĀ BANYAN TREE
This 60-foot-high fig tree has 16 trunks!

LĀHAINĀ HARBOR
Heavily hunted in the mid-1800s, humpback whales now frolic in these shallow waters.

MAUI

KAHOOLAWE

GARDEN OF THE GODS
The unusual rock towers of Keahiakawelo look as if they're straight out of a Martian landscape.

SHIPWRECK BEACH
Many vessels have sunk in Kaiolohia Bay, including the *London*, which was carrying a cargo of gold!

CRESCENT-SHAPED CRATER
Molokini, a partially submerged volcanic crater, is a snorkeling wonderland.

CAPTAIN COOK
The British explorer Captain James Cook was killed in 1779 in Kealakekua Bay.

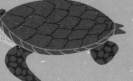

GREEN SEA TURTLES
were once endangered in Hawaiian waters, but their numbers are slowly increasing again.

PLACE OF REFUGE
Criminals who had broken sacred laws sought mercy at Puʻuhonua o Hōnaunau, which is now a historical park.

STARGAZING
The dormant, 13,796-foot high Mauna Kea volcano hosts 13 telescopes run by astronomers from 11 countries.

HAWAII

LA . . . THAT WAY!
It's a long way to the mainland! There are about 2,500 miles between Hawaii and Los Angeles.

HILO

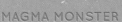

MAGMA MONSTER
Kīlauea, whose crater walls measure up to 400 feet, is the world's most active volcano.

COLORFUL SANDS
Volcanoes, not crayons, created the black and green sands of Hawaii Island.

MOMENTS TO REMEMBER

OCTOBER 8, 1840: Hawaii rids itself of the name Sandwich Islands, which it was called by Captain James Cook in 1778.

MAY 10, 1873: Father Damien arrives and spends 16 years caring for those in in the Kalaupapa leper colony until his death (from the same disease).

DECEMBER 7, 1941: Japanese forces attack the U.S. naval fleet at Pearl Harbor.

1966: Big-wave surfer Eddie Aikau becomes the first lifeguard at Waimea Bay, sometimes braving 20-foot waves to rescue people; he saves hundreds during his career.

NOVEMBER 7, 1978: Hawaiian is recognized as an official language of the state, after its use was banned when Hawaii became a U.S. territory.

JANUARY 3, 1983: The volcano Kilauea begins a long-lasting eruption, which continues over 30 years, destroying more than 200 buildings.

JANUARY 24, 1985: Ellison Shoji Onizuka, an astronaut born in Kealakekua, orbits the earth 48 times as a NASA mission specialist.

NOVEMBER 1, 1993: Ukulele star Israel Kamakawiwo'ole releases *Facing Future*, which becomes Hawaii's first platinum album.

JUNE 26, 2005: At age 15, shark-attack survivor and amputee Bethany Hamilton shreds the waves and wins her first national surf title.

JANUARY 20, 2009: Honolulu-born Barack Obama becomes the first president from Hawaii and the nation's first black president.

WASHINGTON

SILVERWOOD
The biggest theme park in the Pacific Northwest features a crazy coaster that twists through four underground tunnels!

JOSEPH ALBERTSON
1906–1993
Albertson founded his chain of grocery stores in Boise, and was a generous contributor to Idaho's colleges.

CECIL D. ANDRUS
b.1931
Andrus was governor of Idaho for 14 years. This passionate environmentalist also served as U.S. Secretary of the Interior.

GREGORY "PAPPY" BOYINGTON
1912–1988
This Coeur d'Alene-born WWII fighter pilot won the Medal of Honor and the Navy Cross.

EZRA POUND
1885–1972
Born in Hailey, Pound was a key figure in the modernist poetry movement.

SACAJAWEA
c.1788–1812
Guide and interpreter for Lewis and Clark on their exploration of the West, Sacajawea was born near the Salmon River.

SILVER VALLEY
This region is one of the world's richest mining areas, with silver, copper, tungsten, and garnets.

APPALOOSA
The Nez Perce people have a special connection to this elegant horse breed.

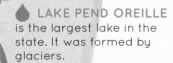

LAKE PEND OREILLE
is the largest lake in the state. It was formed by glaciers.

IDAHO PANHANDLE

CATALDO MISSION
See the state's oldest standing building, which was built without nails!

VERNON BAKER
from St. Marie was the only living African American WWII veteran to be awarded a Medal of Honor by President Clinton in 1997.

THE STAR GARNET
is a rare gem that can only be found in India and the Idaho Panhandle National Forests.

WALLACE
In 2004 a mayor proclaimed the town of Wallace the center of the universe . . . and since it can't be proven otherwise, it *must* be true!

CADDIE WOODLAWN
The award-winning author of this book, Carol Ryrie Brink, was born in Moscow, Idaho.

OREGON

BARBARA MORGAN
In 2007, this elementary-school teacher completed a NASA mission.

THE NEZ PERCE NATIONAL FOREST
covers more than 2 million acres of land and includes rugged canyons and fragrant cedars.

LANA TURNER
1921–1995
Born in Wallace, this movie star was discovered by a Hollywood scout in a malt shop while playing hooky from high school.

MONTANA

THE CRATERS OF THE MOON NATIONAL PRESERVE
spreads over 1,100 square miles. It has ancient lava flows so big they can be seen from space!

IDAHO STATE CAPITOL
The Idaho state capitol is the only state capitol heated by hot springs.

SUN VALLEY
Strap on your skis for a slalom!

THE LUCKY PEAK NURSERY
Every year, this nursery grows millions of trees to replace damaged forest.

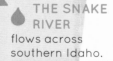

ARCO
In 1955 Arco became the first town in the world to be powered by atomic energy.

BOISE

MERIDIAN

NAMPA

WORLD CENTER FOR BIRDS OF PREY
Discover the secret life of raptors here.

SHOSHONE ICE CAVES
Even when temperatures top 100°F outside, you'll need a warm coat to visit!

THE SNAKE RIVER
flows across southern Idaho.

HAGERMAN FOSSIL BEDS
Here, scientists uncover around 3,000 fossils a year, including bones of saber-toothed cats and mastodons.

BLACKFOOT

SHOSHONE FALLS
These 212-foot-tall, 1,000-foot-wide waterfalls are known as the "Niagara of the West."

CITY OF ROCKS
Clip on your carabiner in this national reserve.

NEVADA

UTAH

WELCOME TO THE GEM STATE

Idaho is twice as large as all six New England states combined, and is one of the country's least densely populated states. Since forests cover 40 percent of Idaho, this makes sense!

The Gem State is rich in soaring mountains, plunging canyons, and 3,100 miles of rivers—more than any other state. And, as its state nickname promises, Idaho is home to 72 types of precious and semi-precious stones, including the garnet, opal, and topaz. Excavations have also unearthed beautiful materials of another kind: the obsidian arrowheads of tribes such as the Nez Perce, Shoshone, and Paiute. These finds are some of the oldest indigenous artefacts in the country.

As well as being a treasure trove of wilderness and wildlife, Idaho is home to some 25,000 farms. Well known as the potato capital of the world, Idaho is also one of the U.S.'s top producers of dairy products and wheat.

MOMENTS TO REMEMBER

c.500 BC: Indigenous tribes begin drying salmon on wooden racks . . . early jerky!

NOVEMBER 1804: Shoshone woman Sacajawea joins Lewis and Clark's famous expedition across the western U.S. as an interpreter and guide.

FEBRUARY 20, 1860: Elias Davidson Pierce strikes gold in the Clearwater River. A gold rush ensues.

APRIL 16, 1896: Teacher Abigail Scott Duniway helps secure Idaho women the vote. The state becomes the fourth to grant this right.

AUGUST 20, 1910: Forest ranger Ed Pulaski leads a crew of 40 to safety during a huge forest fire called the Big Blowup. He later invents the Pulaski: a firefighting tool still used today.

1921: For a science project, 14-year-old inventor Philo T. Farnsworth develops an image receiver: a key component of the world's first electronic televisions.

1923: At age 14, future potato-baron J.R. Simplot starts his first company; he goes on to be Idaho's richest citizen and one of its biggest philanthropists.

DECEMBER 20, 1951: The Idaho National Laboratory successfully produces electricity from nuclear energy for the first time.

1966: Grocery-store owning philanthropists Joe and Kathryn Albertson form a foundation that has since given more than $240 million to Idaho's communities and education system.

IDAHO POTATO MUSEUM
See the world's biggest potato chip here!

SHOSHONE-BANNOCK POW-WOW
Join revelers for a day of dancing and a feast of buffalo.

J.R. SIMPLOT
Known as the "French Fry King," Simplot introduced the world to frozen fries in 1953.

KEY FACTS

CAPITAL
Boise

LARGEST CITIES
Boise
Nampa
Meridian

BIRD
Mountain bluebird

NAMED FOR
An invented word said to derive from the Shoshone language meaning "gem of the mountains"

STATEHOOD DATE
July 3, 1890

STATEHOOD ORDER
43

FLOWER
Syringa

POSTAL CODE
ID

REGION
Rocky Mountain

MAIN TIME ZONE
Mountain

TREE
Western white pine

"LET IT BE PERPETUAL"

JANE ADDAMS
1860–1935
Born in Cedarville, the "Mother of Social Work" was the first woman to win the Nobel Peace Prize.

RICHARD J. DALEY
1902–1976
This working-class Irish American was Chicago's mayor for 21 years.

MILES DAVIS
1926–1991
Anyone who knows Davis's work as a jazz musician and trumpet player considers him the very embodiment of *cool*.

ROBIN WILLIAMS
1951–2014
Chicago-born Williams was a genius comedian and film actor. The Oscar and Emmy winner was also one of the founders of Comic Relief.

WELCOME TO THE PRAIRIE STATE

Though of average size as far as land area goes, there is nothing else that's ordinary about the country's fifth-most populous state. Just think of all the influential people that have hailed from Illinois, from Abraham Lincoln and Ronald Reagan to Hillary Clinton and Michelle Obama.

And then there's the nation's third-largest city, Chicago, whose cultural institutions include the Wrigley Field stadium, the Art Institute (the second-largest art museum in the U.S.), and Millennium Park, with its well-loved silver sculpture, "Cloud Gate" (or the "Bean" to locals). Decades before these attractions emerged, visitors journeyed to the Windy City for the 1893 World's Fair, where they experienced the first ferris wheel and first movie theater. Legend has it that they might also have tasted an early version of the popcorn treat Cracker Jack!

The Prairie State has a wild side, too. In the Wildlife Prairie State Park, bison, bears, and cougars still roam.

ALBERT SPALDING
The future baseball maker from Byron started off as a pitcher—earning $40 a week!

ALL ABOARD
The massive Railway Museum in Union has tons of train treats for junior conductors.

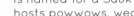

BLACK HAWK STATE PARK
is named for a Sauk tribal warrior and hosts powwows, weddings, and hikes.

ROCKFORD

PUMPKIN PARTY
Every fall the city of Sycamore celebrates its Pumpkin Festival.

PLOW POWER
John Deere's equipment innovations improved farming in the 1800s; the company started in Grand Detour.

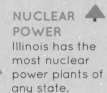

NUCLEAR POWER
Illinois has the most nuclear power plants of any state.

CHICAGO

ROBERT ALLERTON PARK
This 1,500-acre park has many unusual features like the Chinese Maze Garden and House of the Golden Buddhas.

IOWA

VISIT THE SUN!
It is 46 feet in diameter and found at the Riverfront Museum in Peoria.

AURORA

STARVED ROCK
Come winter, the waterfalls in this state park freeze into spectacular icefalls!

LINCOLN LUCK
Rubbing the nose of the Great Emancipator's statue in Springfield is supposed to bring you luck.

SPRINGFIELD

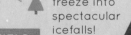

THE MUSEUM OF SHIP MODELS
includes a 27-foot model of the *Queen Mary*—made using a million toothpicks!

ROCKOME GARDENS
As well as an Amish museum and a Raggedy Ann museum, this park has rock sculptures and a tic-tac-toe-playing chicken!

ILLINOIS STATE CAPITOL
The 12-foot-high doors of the capitol's House and Senate chambers weigh 300 pounds each!

MISSISSIPPI RIVER

FORGOTTEN CITY
The remains of a sophisticated prehistoric native civilization are lovingly preserved at Cahokia Mounds.

KASKASKIA DRAGON
For a buck you can see the 25-foot-tall metal dragon in Vandalia breathe fire!

PIZZA WARS
Locals champion the deep dish, though thin crust rules in other states.

THE CAVE-IN-ROCK
was a hideaway for outlaws, perhaps even the notorious Jesse James; it's now part of a state park.

MISSOURI

SUPER CITY
The founder of the Super Museum in Metropolis started his Superman collection when he was 10 years old!

KENTUCKY

FERMILAB
Bison keep the lawn tidy outside this important physics lab.

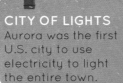

CITY OF LIGHTS
Aurora was the first U.S. city to use electricity to light the entire town.

DANCE ROOTS
Anthropologist, activist, and dancer Katherine Dunham celebrated African and Caribbean dance.

LINCOLN PARK ZOO
is the nation's oldest public zoo—and it's free!

WRIGLEY FIELD
HOME OF CHICAGO CUBS

WRIGLEY FIELD
Cubs loyalists cherish the ivy-covered stadium that gum built.

FRANK LLOYD LEGO®
Future architects can build LEGO® models at Frank Lloyd Wright's famous Robie House.

CARL SANDBURG
1878–1967
Starting out as a journalist for the *Chicago Daily News*, Sandburg later received two Pulitzer Prizes for poetry and another for a biography of Lincoln.

FRANK LLOYD WRIGHT
1867–1959
One of the greatest American architects, Wright was influenced by the buildings and landscapes around Chicago.

INDIANA

MOMENTS TO REMEMBER

3 MILLION YEARS AGO: The Illinoian glacier covers much of North America.

SEPTEMBER 16, 1836: After buying his own freedom, former slave Free Frank McWorter founds the town of New Philadelphia.

FEBRUARY 1, 1865: Illinois becomes the first state to ratify the 13th Amendment to abolish slavery.

NOVEMBER 28, 1865: The U.S.'s first motor race is held between Chicago and Evanston, in snowy conditions: the winning driver's average speed was just 7.3 mph!

OCTOBER 8, 1871: A barn fire sweeps through Chicago, destroying some 18,000 buildings and leaving 100,000 people homeless.

MAY 1, 1893: The World's Fair opens, featuring many inventions including the first Ferris wheel.

DECEMBER 10, 1931: Jane Addams, founder of the social work profession in America, becomes the first U.S. woman to win the Nobel Peace Prize.

OCTOBER 26, 1947: Hillary Rodham Clinton—future First Lady, senator, presidential nominee, and Secretary of State—is born.

MARCH 17, 1961: The Chicago Plumbers Union dye the river green on St. Patrick's Day . . . and every St. Patrick's Day since!

JUNE 17, 2001: Richard Peck wins the Newbery Medal for his novel *A Year Down Yonder*.

KEY FACTS

CAPITAL
Springfield

LARGEST CITIES
Chicago
Aurora
Rockford

BIRD
Northern cardinal

NAMED FOR
The French version of the Algonquin word for "warrior"

STATEHOOD DATE
December 3, 1818

STATEHOOD ORDER
21

FLOWER
Violet

POSTAL CODE
IL

REGION
Great Lakes

MAIN TIME ZONE
Central

TREE
White oak

"STATE SOVEREIGNTY, NATIONAL UNION"

MICHAEL JACKSON
1958–2009
The "King of Pop" who recorded *Thriller*—the best-selling album of all time—was born in Gary.

DAVID LETTERMAN
b.1947
The Indianapolis-bred *Late Show* funnyman funds a scholarship at Ball State University, where he studied.

NORMAN BRIDWELL
1928–2014
The creator of the *Clifford the Big Red Dog* books was born in Kokomo.

A CHRISTMAS STORY
This hilarious movie (with its famous leg lamp) is based on Jean Shepherd's experiences of growing up in Hammond.

INDIANA DUNES NATIONAL LAKESHORE
has sand dunes that rise to almost 200 feet . . . race you to the top!

STUDEBAKER NATIONAL MUSEUM
This South Bend car company started out making horse-drawn buggies!

MICHIGAN

JOHN GREEN
b.1977
The award-winning author of *The Fault in Our Stars* was born in Indianapolis.

LARRY BIRD
b.1956
An Indiana State University basketball legend, Bird returned as head coach, then president of the Pacers.

MADAM C. J. WALKER
1867–1919
The U.S.'s first female self-made millionaire invented and produced hair treatments in 1910 Indianapolis.

POKAGON STATE PARK
has a refrigerated toboggan run where speeds can top 40 mph!

FORT WAYNE

SECHLER'S PICKLES
Whether you like them hot, sweet, or spicy, this St. Joe mainstay has the pickles for you.

POPCORN KING
Before making it big in Valparaiso, Orville Redenbacher first sold popcorn from the back of his car.

A GIRL OF THE LIMBERLOST
The author Gene Stratton-Porter is celebrated in Rome City, where she studied the wildlife of the Limberlost Swamp.

FRANCE PARK
This old Logansport quarry, popular with scuba divers, is home to an underwater school bus and several 7-foot-long paddlefish!

PURDUE UNIVERSITY
The college mascot is a railroad engine called the Boilermaker Special, which represents Purdue's engineering heritage.

ROTARY JAIL MUSEUM
Prison guards in Crawfordsville could rotate wedge-shaped cells around a hub, allowing one cell at a time to be opened.

JAMES DEAN
The star of *Rebel Without a Cause* grew up in Fairmount, which hosts an annual festival.

THE WORLD'S LARGEST BALL OF PAINT
has some 23,000 layers of paint and is still growing in Alexandria!

INDIANAPOLIS

INDIANA 33 STATE

PERIODIC TABLE DISPLAY
Greencastle's DePauw University presents the chemical elements in a beautiful wall-sized exhibit.

SMITH MEMORIAL LABYRINTH
This Hawthorn Park labyrinth is a place of quiet reflection.

THE TULIP TRESTLE
At 2,295 feet long, with a height of 157 feet, this bridge over Richland Creek is one of the longest railroad trestles in the country.

Fe

THE BIG BRAIN
This 7-foot-tall model at Indiana University is the largest anatomically correct model brain in the world!

EMPIRE QUARRY
The Empire State Building was made from limestone from this quarry.

INDIANA BASKETBALL HALL OF FAME
This is New Castle's shrine to basketball greats like Larry Bird and the Milan high school team who inspired the movie *Hoosiers*.

OHIO

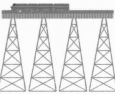

ILLINOIS

THE WEST BADEN SPRINGS HOTEL
was built in 1902 so visitors could benefit from the healing properties of the nearby mineral springs.

THE LINCOLN LIVING HISTORICAL FARM
lets visitors experience life as Abraham Lincoln might have during the 14 boyhood years he spent in what is now Lincoln City.

ANGEL MOUNDS HISTORIC SITE
is one of the best-preserved prehistoric Native American sites in the U.S. The ancient settlement dates from AD 1000.

EVANSVILLE

BLUESPRING CAVERNS PARK
Bedford's 21-mile-long underground cavern is home to albino crickets, spiders, crayfish, and other creepy critters.

SANTA CLAUS, INDIANA
A group of volunteer elves respond to some 13,000 letters sent to this small town each Christmas!

SANTA CLAUS

INDIANAPOLIS STATE CAPITOL
The state house was rebuilt in 1888 after the House Chamber's ceiling collapsed!

INDY 500
For more than 100 years cars have raced 200 laps around the 2.5-mile Speedway track. These days, speeds top 200 mph.

THE INDIANAPOLIS ART CENTER
has classes, camps, and exhibits like *Twisted House*, a sculpture by Indiana artist John McNaughton.

THE MAJOR TAYLOR VELODROME
is named for Marshall Taylor who, in 1899, won the cycling world championship, becoming only the second black athlete to become a world champion in any sport.

KENTUCKY

So what on earth is a Hoosier? People from Indiana have been called Hoosiers since the 1830s, but nobody can be certain why. Wherever the nickname came from, the people of Indiana have embraced the name with pride! After all, there is much to be proud of here at "the crossroads of America!"

For instance, the beautiful limestone of Bedford has been an essential part of key monuments such as the Empire State Building, the Pentagon, and the National Cathedral.

Too, Indiana is famous the world over as the host state for the Indy 500: a 500-mile-long motor race held at the Indianapolis Speedway every May. Often called the "greatest spectacle in racing," the Indy 500 was first held in 1911. But it's not all high-octane motor sports. Chilled-out Indiana has many more relaxing destinations such as its sun-kissed cornfields, lush forests and hills, and golden lakeside sand dunes.

KEY FACTS

CAPITAL
Indianapolis

LARGEST CITIES
Indianapolis
Fort Wayne
Evansville

BIRD
Northern cardinal

NAMED FOR
a word meaning
"Land of the Indians"

STATEHOOD DATE
December 11, 1816

STATEHOOD ORDER
19

FLOWER
Peony

POSTAL CODE
IN

REGION
Great Lakes

MAIN TIME ZONE
Eastern

TREE
Tulip
poplar

"THE CROSSROADS OF AMERICA"

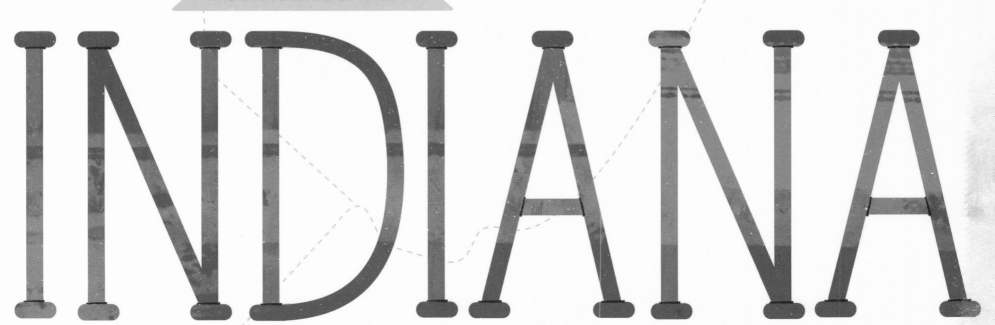

INDIANA

MOMENTS TO REMEMBER

1826–1847: From their home in what is now Fountain City, Levi and Catharine Coffin help more than 2,000 runaway slaves escape to freedom.

MAY 4, 1871: The first major-league baseball game is played in Fort Wayne.

NOVEMBER 15, 1885: Indiana poet James Whitcomb Riley publishes "Little Orphant Annie," warning children to beware of goblins!

MAY 15, 1902: The Indianapolis Soldiers and Sailors Monument is dedicated. Since then, this towering pillar has become an icon of Indiana.

FEBRUARY 10, 1910: The entrepreneur Madam C. J. Walker moves to Indianapolis, where she opens a hair salon and beauty school. She will later be seen as America's first female self-made millionaire.

JANUARY 31, 1970: The Jackson Five's first single, "I Want You Back," tops the charts. Michael Jackson and his four brothers were all born in the city of Gary.

JUNE 1987: The human rights activist Cleve Jones, born in West Lafayette, founds the AIDS Memorial Quilt: the largest piece of folk art in the world.

MAY 24, 1992: Lyn St. James is the second woman to compete in the Indianapolis 500 race, and the first woman to win the Rookie of the Year Award.

2008: The Fort Wayne Wizards, a minor league baseball club, change their name to the Fort Wayne TinCaps in honor of local legend Johnny Appleseed, who wore a tin pot on his head.

JANUARY 18, 2010: Phillip Hoose wins a Newbery Honor for *Claudette Colvin: Twice Toward Justice*.

HAYDEN PRAIRIE
The rare tallgrass of "Iowa's Rain Forest" bursts with different species of plants and birds.

HOBO MUSEUM
At this museum of traveling workers in Britt, you can find out how hobos left notes for each other on trails. A kitten sketch meant a kind lady lived nearby.

EFFIGY MOUNDS
Visit Harpers Ferry to see these Native American mounds. Some are shaped like bears, birds, lynx, and other animals.

WEST LAKE OKOBOJI
A popular spot for fishing, motor boating, and water skiing, this is Iowa's deepest lake.

MOREL HUNTING
North Iowa is prime hunting territory for edible morel mushrooms.

FORT ATKINSON
Many forts of the 1700s and 1800s played a part in the fur trade, with Native Americans trading beaver fur for tools.

THE LARGEST POPCORN BALL
in the world can be found in Sac City! It measures 8 feet across and weighs more than 5,000 pounds.

GREAT GROTTO
The walls of the Grotto of the Redemption in West Bend are made of stones, fossils, and gems.

STUMPTOWN KID
Cedar Rapids natives Carol Gorman and Ron J. Findley's novel is about race, baseball, and loyalty in the 1950s.

CEDAR RAPIDS

HIGH TRESTLE TRAIL BRIDGE
This 13-story bridge was once a rail track but is now a bike trail.

THE GENTLE DOCTOR
At Iowa State University you can see this famous sculpture of a vet by the artist Christian Petersen.

DEVONIAN FOSSIL GORGE
Near Iowa City you can explore a fossilized ocean floor from before the time of the dinos!

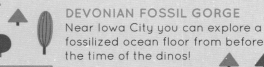

THE DeSOTO NATIONAL WILDLIFE REFUGE
on the banks of the Missouri is home to raccoons, coyotes, great blue herons, egrets, and many more species.

DES MOINES

CAPTAIN KIRK'S BIRTHPLACE?
Every year Trekkies gather in Riverside for a pre-birthday party!

IMES COVERED BRIDGE
Madison County is famous for its covered wooden bridges, and Imes Bridge is the oldest one left.

1901

TODD HOUSE
This house in Tabor belonged to the minister John Todd and was a stop on the Underground Railroad.

DIRTY SNOWBALL
Born in Red Oak, astronomer Fred Whipple discovered that comets are made up of dirt and ice.

THE KNOXVILLE RACEWAY
is known as the "Sprint Car Capital of the World."

AMERICAN GOTHIC HOUSE
This house in Eldon featured in Grant Wood's famous painting. Outside, you can pose for your own masterpiece!

CORN
Iowa is the U.S.'s largest producer of corn and grows some 2.3 billion bushels a year.

JOHN WAYNE
1907–1979
An iconic Western movie star, Wayne was born in Winterset.

THE IOWA STATE FAIR
annually showcases a 600-pound butter cow—and once had a butter Harry Potter!

IOWA STATE CAPITOL
The state house has a 19,000-pound round glass floor under the gold-plated dome.

BALLOON FESTIVAL
Dozens of hot-air balloons take to the air at the National Balloon Classic festival in Indianola.

JOHN WAYNE BIRTHPLACE MUSEUM
The 6'4" movie star needed custom-built station-wagons to ride comfortably. See one of them at this museum in Winterset.

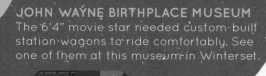

ELIJAH WOOD
b.1981
Born in Cedar Rapids, Wood was a child actor, then starred in *The Lord of the Rings*.

32

GRANT WOOD
1891–1942
Born in Anamosa, Wood created a new American art style with his world-famous painting *American Gothic*.

NATIONAL MISSISSIPPI RIVER MUSEUM
Stay overnight in the crew's quarters of a river dredge boat in Dubuque!

VANDER VEER BOTANICAL PARK
In winter, the lagoon here hosts the Silver Skates children's speed race.

DAVENPORT

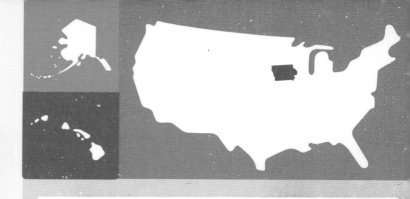

WELCOME TO THE HAWKEYE STATE

There's no shortage of things to see and do in the 29th state. Iowa has great universities, cosmopolitan cities, and plenty of agricultural activity—after all, it is 92 percent farmland!

Every August for more than 150 years, hundreds of thousands of visitors have flocked to the state fair. It is one of the biggest in the country, with livestock competitions, ribbon-winning food specialties, and even a 600-pound cow sculpted from butter.

Iowa has a diverse history. The annual Meskwaki Powwow honors Iowa's Native American heritage through song, dance, and crafts. The Hawkeye State's nickname is a tribute to Chief Black Hawk, leader of the Sauk Indians. Other groups have also played a part in Iowa's history, including Dutch, German, Scandinavian, Czech, and Slovak settlers. Each group celebrates its traditions with festivals and eats—not surprising for a state that produces a tenth of America's food!

ILLINOIS

ESTHER PAULINE FRIEDMAN & PAULINE ESTHER FRIEDMAN
1918–2002 • 1918–2013
These twin advice columnists, Ann Landers (Esther) and Dear Abby (Pauline), grew up in Sioux City.

ART "SUPERMAN" PENNINGTON
b.1923
After a successful career in the Negro League, this baseball star moved to Cedar Rapids.

GEORGE WASHINGTON CARVER
c.1860–1943
Born into slavery, Carver became a botanist and inventor who made many important discoveries. He was the first black faculty member at Iowa State University.

MOMENTS TO REMEMBER

AD 500: Native Americans begin sculpting a collection of shaped mounds of earth now known as the Marching Bears.

MAY 31, 1840: The government founds Fort Atkinson to protect the Winnebago Indians after they are forced from their Wisconsin homeland.

JULY 6, 1881: 17-year-old Kate Shelley risks her life to save a passenger train in Boone during a treacherous storm. She crosses a perilous, damaged bridge to sound the alarm.

MARCH 4, 1929: Herbert Hoover, born in West Branch, is sworn in as the 31st president.

1936: Wilbur Schramm begins the Iowa Writers' Workshop at the University of Iowa. To date, 17 graduates have won Pulitzer Prizes.

AUGUST 26, 1973: The first RAGBRAI (Register's Annual Great Bicycle Ride Across Iowa) begins, with riders cycling from west to east across the entire state. Today, it is the oldest, largest, and longest recreational bike touring event in the world.

MAY 26, 1994: Cedar Falls native Marc Andreessen, co-author of Mosaic (the first widely used Web browser), becomes one of only six people inducted in the World Wide Web Hall of Fame.

FEBRUARY 1, 1999: Mount Vernon resident Jacqueline Briggs Martin wins the Caldecott Medal for her picture book *Snowflake Bentley*.

MARCH 22, 2228: James T. Kirk, captain of the starship *Enterprise*, will be born in Riverside. Fans celebrate at the annual Trek Fest!

KEY FACTS

CAPITAL
Des Moines

LARGEST CITIES
Des Moines
Cedar Rapids
Davenport

BIRD
Eastern goldfinch

FLOWER
Wild rose

NAMED FOR
The Ioway tribe, who camped near the Iowa River.

STATEHOOD DATE
December 28, 1846

STATEHOOD ORDER
29

POSTAL CODE
IA

REGION
Midwest

MAIN TIME ZONE
Central Standard

TREE
Oak

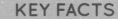

"OUR LIBERTIES WE PRIZE AND OUR RIGHTS WE WILL MAINTAIN"

WELCOME TO THE SUNFLOWER STATE

Made famous in the 1939 movie *The Wizard of Oz*, Kansas is a piece of classic America. Right in the center of the country, this state is a destination for history lovers who will be spoiled for choice with its museums and historic sites, from Civil War battlefields to the boyhood home of President Eisenhower.

In terms of farming, the ranchers and cowboys of Kansas produce some of the highest numbers of beef cattle in the country. And the sunflower state is also big on wheat and—you guessed it—sunflowers! The usually sunny 34th state is known for its occasionally extreme weather. The thunderstorms here sometimes spawn tornadoes—Kansas has around 100 twisters a year. Dodge City is officially the windiest city in the U.S., and hailstones weighing more than 1½ pounds once fell on Coffeyville!

From its wide prairies to its sparkling lakes and rolling rivers, visitors here are sure to agree, there's no place like Kansas!

COLORADO

KEY FACTS

CAPITAL
Topeka

LARGEST CITIES
Wichita
Overland Park
Kansas City

BIRD
Western
meadowlark

NAMED FOR
The Kansas River, which
was named after the
Kansa tribe

STATEHOOD DATE
January 29, 1861

STATEHOOD ORDER
34

FLOWER
Wild
sunflower

POSTAL CODE
KS

REGION
Midwest

MAIN TIME ZONE
Central

TREE
Cottonwood

"TO THE STARS THROUGH DIFFICULTIES"

NEBRASKA

MONUMENT ROCKS
Oodles of fossils have been found in these ancient chalk beds.

STERNBERG MUSEUM OF NATURAL HISTORY
See an exhibit of a Gove County fossil showing how a 14-foot Xiphactinus ate a 6-foot Gillicus shortly before dying.

THE BIG EASEL
The town of Goodland boasts an 80-foot easel with a giant sunflower painting.

FORT LARNED
A company of African American "Buffalo Soldiers" served here in the 1860s.

READY AND FORWARD

DODGE CITY RODEO
Bull riders must stay atop a bucking bull for eight seconds, holding on with just one hand!

INTERNATIONAL PANCAKE DAY
Every Shrove Tuesday, people in Liberal race through town, flipping flapjacks as they run.

TORNADO ALLEY
About 100 of the U.S.'s average 1,000 tornadoes a year happen in Kansas.

AMELIA EARHART
1897–disappeared 1937
This pioneering pilot disappeared over the Pacific Ocean in an attempt to fly around the world.

JANELLE MONAE
b.1985
The six-time Grammy nominated psychedelic soul and R&B singer-songwriter was born in Kansas City.

KANSAS

LEBANON
is the geographic center of the main block of U.S. states; add in Alaska and Hawaii and the center moves to South Dakota.

OZ MUSEUM
This Wamego attraction celebrates L. Frank Baum's books and *The Wizard of Oz* movie.

KANSAS STATE CAPITOL
The 1923 elevator in the state house can't be operated without an attendant.

AMELIA EARHART BIRTHPLACE MUSEUM
One reason Earhart chose her first plane was that it was light enough for her to move without help!

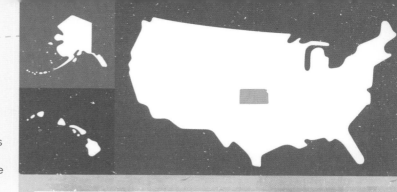

TWINE TOWN
It takes eight or so people to hug this enormous ball of twine in Cawker City.

ROCK CITY
Climb and pose and marvel among some 200 huge sandstone spheres.

KANSAS CITY

TOPEKA

OVERLAND PARK

GARDEN OF EDEN
S. P. Dinsmoor spent 22 years creating some 150 concrete sculptures of huge insects, angels, trees, and more.

TALLGRASS PRAIRIE
This national preserve in the Flint Hills protects one of the last pieces of tallgrass prairie in the country.

BROWN V. BOARD OF ED. HISTORIC SITE
This museum tells the story of the teachers, secretaries, welders, students, and ministers who helped end segregation in schools.

MISSOURI

WICHITA

LITTLE SWEDEN
A herd of 31 fiberglass Dala horses roam the streets of Lindsborg—can you spot them all?

BIG BRUTUS
It takes 900 gallons of Omaha Orange to paint this 16-story-high electric shovel, now found at the mining museum in West Mineral.

OKLAHOMA

QUIVIRA NATIONAL WILDLIFE REFUGE
The endangered least tern is one of the 500,000 migratory birds that visit these protected marshes.

THE COSMOSPHERE AND SPACE CENTER
in Hutchinson is home to many space artifacts that couldn't fit into the Smithsonian!

UNDERGROUND SALT MUSEUM
Venture 650 feet beneath the ground to tour this 980-acre salt mine in Hutchinson.

BOTANICA
Discover 9 acres of gardens, a tremendous tree house and a musical maze in this museum.

OLD COWTOWN MUSEUM
Visit a jail, a saloon, and a buffalo trading post at this open-air living museum.

KEEPER OF THE PLAINS
Blackbear Bosin donated this 44-foot steel sculpture as a tribute to the Native American tribes who continue to gather at this sacred site.

THE MID-AMERICA ALL-INDIAN CENTER
proudly displays flags of some of the 549 recognized Native American tribes.

KANSAS SPORTS HALL OF FAME
Here you can find out about sporting greats such as James Naismith, the inventor of basketball.

BLACKBEAR BOSIN
1921–1980
A statue by this Comanche-Kiowa artist stands where the Wichita tribe once lived.

ERIN BROCKOVICH
b.1960
The story of this Lawrence-born legal clerk's work as an environmental activist was made into a movie.

LYNETTE WOODARD
b.1959
This gold-medal-winning Olympic basketball player was born in Wichita.

LOIS RUBY
b.1977
Ruby's time in Wichita inspired her historical books *Steal Away Home* and *Soon Be Free*.

ALLEN ALLENSWORTH
1842-1914
Louisville-born Allensworth escaped slavery, became an army nurse, was a U.S. military chaplain, and founded a California town.

MUHAMMAD ALI
b.1942
This Olympic gold-winning boxer, raised in Louisville, won the World Heavyweight Championship three times.

INDIANA

LOUISVILLE SLUGGER MUSEUM & FACTORY
A pro baseball player will order some 120 bats a season! Find out more bat facts here.

THE KENTUCKY DERBY
is held at Churchill Downs. Jockeys must have excellent balance and strength: many can do nonstop sit-ups for 4 minutes!

DERBY PIE
Kern's Kitchen fiercely protects the recipe of this chocolate and nut pie, invented in Prospect.

125 Slugger

USS *SACHEM*
Kayakers can visit the ghostly ruins of this naval ship anchored on the Ohio River in Petersburg.

VENT HAVEN MUSEUM
In Fort Mitchell you'll find some 800 ventriloquists' dummies—the world's largest collection!

THE VIETNAM WAR MEMORIAL
in Frankfort honors Kentuckians who died in Vietnam; a shadow passes over each name on the anniversary of their death.

KENTUCKY STATE CAPITOL
A 34-foot clock made of 10,000 flowers sits behind the capitol in Frankfort.

FRANKFORT

LEXINGTON

LOUISVILLE

U.S. BULLION DEPOSITORY
No single person knows the complete combination to access the Fort Knox vault, home to much of the U.S.'s gold reserve.

JOHN JAMES AUDUBON STATE PARK
This park is named in honor of a bird lover who discovered and studied many birds while living in Henderson.

ILLINOIS

THE STEPHEN FOSTER STORY
is a musical performed in Bardstown about "the father of American music" who wrote "My Old Kentucky Home."

ROSIE THE RIVETER
This icon of a hard-working WWII woman was partly based on aircraft factory worker Rose Will Monroe, born in Pulaski County.

"BLUE MOON OF KENTUCKY"
Bluegrass music is a type of folk music born in Kentucky. The "Father of Bluegrass," Bill Monroe, wrote the state bluegrass song.

BERNHEIM ARBORETUM
has an art program where artists contribute to the landscape. Artist Myung Gyun You made the sculpture *Photosynthesis* in 2014.

DUNCAN HINES
Born in Bowling Green, the "Cake Mix King" started off as a restaurant reviewer.

ABRAHAM LINCOLN BIRTHPLACE
The 16th president was born in a humble cabin in Hodgenville.

MISSOURI

BOWLING GREEN

TRAIL OF TEARS

MAMMOTH CAVE NATIONAL PARK
is home to 400 miles of passages and caverns, making it the world's longest natural cave system.

HOUSEBOAT VACATIONS
are popular in the lakes around Jamestown and Monticello.

BLACKBERRY POWER
Also known as brambleberries or thimbleberries, the state fruit is high in Vitamin C.

THE TRAIL OF TEARS COMMEMORATIVE PARK
in Hopkinsville holds an annual powwow with dance and food, honoring the rich Native American heritage.

TENNESSEE

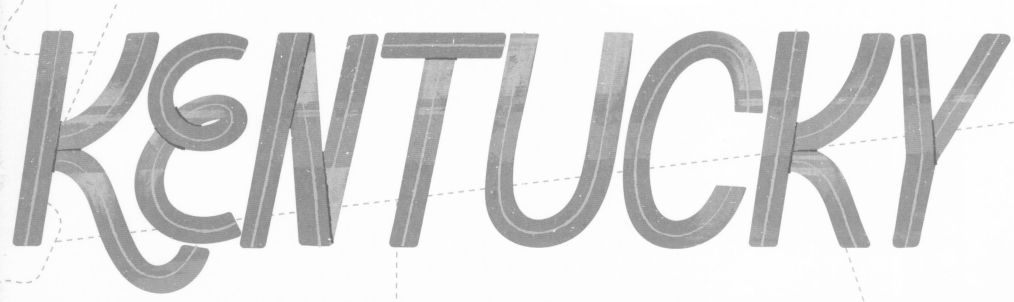

KENTUCKY

VAMPIRES DON'T WEAR POLKA DOTS
Marcia Jones and Debbie Dadey wrote the first Bailey School stories in the cafeteria of the school where they taught.

SEABISCUIT
This champion thoroughbred, who became a symbol of hope during the Great Depression, was bred at Claiborne Farm, near Paris, KY.

OHIO

JENNIFER LAWRENCE
b.1990
The star of *The Hunger Games* was born in Louisville.

DIANE SAWYER
b.1945
Born in Glasgow, this news anchor blazed a path for women journalists.

WEST VIRGINIA

VIRGINIA

REPTILE ZOO
Some snake venom is used in cancer research—see it extracted at the zoo in Slade!

RED BIRD RIVER
This fork in the Kentucky River, near Manchester, is named after a Cherokee chief who helped the white settlers in the area.

CUMBERLAND FALLS
The largest waterfall in Kentucky is famous for its "moonbow"—a rainbow made by the light of the moon.

BIG SOUTH FORK SCENIC RAILWAY
A historic train in Stearns takes passengers to Blue Heron, an abandoned coal mine.

WELCOME TO THE BLUEGRASS STATE

Kentucky is a real melting pot, mixing the warmth and friendliness of the South with the industry of the North, and the old traditions of the East with the pioneering spirit of the West.

In springtime, Kentucky's pastures bloom with blue buds, giving the state its nickname. But it's not all about bluegrass—the landscape of Kentucky is just as varied as its culture. The 15th state has more miles of running water than any state except Alaska, so with its plentiful rivers and lakes, nearly 900,000 acres of national forests, and 52 state parks, Kentucky is a destination for outdoor adventurers keen to enjoy hiking, fishing, rafting, camping, and caving.

The elegant farms and fields of central Kentucky are known as "horse country," as this is where some of the top racehorses in the world are bred. Every May the state hosts the famous Kentucky Derby, and the country holds its breath for "The Greatest Two Minutes in Sports"!

MOMENTS TO REMEMBER

APRIL 12, 1861: The Civil War begins and, as a border state, Kentucky sends troops to both the North and South, sometimes pitting brother against brother.

JULY 10, 1925: 24-year-old Paducah-native John Scopes is taken to court for teaching the theory of evolution to high school students; the Scopes Trial is the first trial ever broadcast on national radio.

JANUARY 1937: The first gold is moved into the vault at Fort Knox; it now holds 147.3 million ounces valued at $42.22 per ounce.

MARCH 2, 1940: The champion racehorse Seabiscuit, born in Kentucky, wins the Santa Anita Handicap; it is his last race before retirement.

JANUARY 2, 1943: The Kentucky Wildcats basketball team start their record-breaking 129-game home-court winning streak—it lasts for 12 years!

JUNE 1, 1981: The first Corvette to be built in Kentucky rolls off the assembly line at the new General Motors plant in Bowling Green.

SEPTEMBER 12, 1987: Hopkinsville holds its first Trail of Tears Powwow to commemorate the 150th anniversary of the forced removal of Native American people from their homelands.

JUNE 14, 2003: Some 60 descendants of the Hatfield and McCoy families gather to sign a truce, officially ending a famous feud that began in the 1800s along the Big Sandy River.

JANUARY 11, 2011: George Ella Lyon, an author born in Harlan, wins the Schneider Award for *The Pirate of Kindergarten*—the story of a girl who wears an eye patch to school to help her see better.

KEY FACTS

GEORGE CLOONEY
b.1961
This Lexington-born actor, voice of *Fantastic Mr. Fox*, is also a United Nations Messenger of Peace.

LORETTA LYNN
b.1932
This country music star, who sang "Coal Miner's Daughter," was raised in Butcher Hollow.

CAPITAL
Frankfort

LARGEST CITIES
Louisville
Lexington
Bowling Green

BIRD
Northern cardinal

NAMED FOR
Possibly the Iroquoian word "ken-tah-ten," meaning "land of tomorrow"

STATEHOOD DATE
June 1, 1792

STATEHOOD ORDER
15

FLOWER
Goldenrod

POSTAL CODE
KY

REGION
South

MAIN TIME ZONE
Eastern

TREE
Tulip poplar

"UNITED WE STAND, DIVIDED WE FALL"

SHREVEPORT
is the birthplace of Evelyn Ashford, a four-time Olympic gold medalist.

THE BONNIE & CLYDE FESTIVAL
is held in Gibsland every year.

AMERICAN ROSE CENTER
Smell the 20,000 rosebushes at the nation's largest rose gardens.

DRISKILL MOUNTAIN
You can't climb any higher in this state than Driskill's 535 feet.

NATCHITOCHES
Louisiana's oldest town was the setting of the movie *Steel Magnolias*.

THE OUACHITA RIVER
is lined for most of its length with woodland.

WELCOME TO THE PELICAN STATE

TOLEDO BEND RESERVOIR

THE ALEXANDRIA ZOOLOGICAL PARK
is home to about 500 animals, including cougars.

During Thomas Jefferson's presidency, the United States made the Louisiana Purchase, doubling the size of the country by buying from France a massive chunk of land that now covers parts of 15 states. Today, the size of Louisiana is considerably smaller! But that historic purchase is not all that Louisiana is famous for.

The people of Louisiana have long inspired us with their talent and strength, from the state's early days to the aftermath of Hurricane Katrina. What's more, Louisiana is overflowing with festivals and good food. Travelers from all over the world swear by the cuisine: spicy Creole crawfish and blue crab are just some of the state's culinary delights. And, if there's one place that knows how to celebrate, it's New Orleans, where the annual Mardi Gras festival features more than 75 floats and 60 marching bands!

LIBERTY CENTER

THE AUDUBON PILGRIMAGE FESTIVAL
in St. Francisville celebrates spring.

LIBERTY THEATER
This theater once hosted big names such as musician Tex Ritter.

THE EVANGELINE OAK
is one of the most photographed trees in the world, and an inspiration for Longfellow's poem, *Evangeline*.

LOUISIANA STATE CAPITOL
At 450 feet tall, Louisiana's art-deco style capitol building is the tallest capitol in the U.S.

BATON ROUGE

LAKE CHARLES
is the birthplace of Michael DeBakey, who was a world-class heart surgeon.

THE *FESTIVALS ACADIENS ET CRÉOLES*
celebrates the craft, music, and food of Cajun culture.

CHARENTON
The Chitimacha people are expert basket-weavers, making red, black, and yellow baskets from local river cane.

TEXAS

SWAMP TOURS
Meet an alligator snapping turtle on a tour of one of Louisiana's many swamps.

AVERY ISLAND
Spice lovers can join a Tabasco® factory tour.

MR. CHARLIE
is the only place in the world where you can walk around an offshore drilling rig!

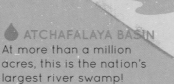

ATCHAFALAYA BASIN
At more than a million acres, this is the nation's largest river swamp!

LOUIS ARMSTRONG
1901–1971
This world-famous, gravelly-voiced trumpet player began his career by singing on the streets of New Orleans.

JEAN LAFITTE
c.1780–c.1823
Smuggler and war hero Lafitte used New Orleans as the base of his piratical operations.

GULF OF MEXICO

isiana

ELLEN DeGENERES
b.1958
DeGeneres began her entertainment career as a stand-up comic in New Orleans. She voiced Dory in *Finding Nemo* and hosts her own talk show.

PEYTON MANNING
b.1976
Super-Bowl champion and five-time NFL MVP, this superstar quarterback was born in New Orleans.

RUBY BRIDGES
b.1954
Bridges was one of the South's first black children in a white school. As an adult, she has created a foundation aimed at ending racism through education.

HUEY P. LONG, JR.
1893–1935
Long served as a governor and senator, calling the country to "Share Our Wealth." He was assassinated in 1935.

MARDI GRAS
This colorful carnival is famous the world over.

PADDLE STEAMERS
travel up and down the Mississippi from New Orleans.

LOUISIANA STATE MUSEUM

ABITA MYSTERY HOUSE
If it's strange, then you'll find it here at Louisiana's most eccentric museum.

LAKE PONTCHARTRAIN CAUSEWAY
This 24-mile long engineering wonder is one of the longest bridges in the world.

LAKE PONTCHARTRAIN

MARDI GRAS WORLD
Take a tour through the studios where the carnival floats are built.

LAKE BORGNE

THE LITTLE BILOXI STATE WILDLIFE MANAGEMENT AREA
is a favorite hangout for horse riders.

NEW ORLEANS

CHALMETTE BATTLEFIELD & NATIONAL CEMETERY

JEAN LAFITTE NATIONAL PARK
Here you can watch a gator catch a fish, meet a soldier from 1815, float down the bayou, and more.

MISSISSIPPI RIVER DELTA

MOMENTS TO REMEMBER

APRIL 30, 1803: The United States purchases the Louisiana territory from the French leader Napoleon Bonaparte for $15 million.

APRIL 30, 1812: Louisiana becomes the 18th state.

JANUARY 8, 1815: General Andrew Jackson defeats British troops in the Battle of New Orleans.

FEBRUARY 28, 1838: The first official Mardi Gras parade takes place in New Orleans.

1843: Norbert Rillieux invents the sugar processing evaporator, greatly improving sugar production.

AUGUST 4, 1901: One of the world's best-loved jazz musicians, Louis Armstrong, is born.

MAY 21, 1928: Huey P. Long, Jr., becomes Louisiana's 40th governor and goes on to champion vital services for the poor.

FEBRUARY 5, 1940: The best-selling song by Jimmie Davis and Charles Mitchell, "You Are My Sunshine," is recorded. It later becomes an official state song.

NOVEMBER 14, 1960: Ruby Bridges and five other six-year-olds are the first black children to attend all-white elementary schools in New Orleans.

NOVEMBER 2, 1977: Ernest "Dutch" Morial is elected the first black mayor of New Orleans.

AUGUST 29, 2005: Hurricane Katrina pounds the Gulf Coast, destroying parts of Louisiana.

KEY FACTS

CAPITAL
Baton Rouge

LARGEST CITIES
Baton Rouge
New Orleans
Shreveport

BIRD
Brown pelican

NAMED FOR
King Louis XIV of France

STATEHOOD DATE
April 30, 1812

STATEHOOD ORDER
18

FLOWER
Magnolia

POSTAL CODE
LA

REGION
Deep South

MAIN TIME ZONE
Central

TREE
Bald cypress

"UNION, JUSTICE, AND CONFIDENCE"

DOROTHEA DIX
1802–1887
Born in Hampden, Dix was an important campaigner for mental health reform.

HENRY WADSWORTH LONGFELLOW
1807–1882
This Portland-born poet is famous for his works "Paul Revere's Ride" and *Evangeline*.

LEON LEONWOOD (L.L.) BEAN
1872–1967
L.L. Bean's outdoor-wear company began in a small room in Freeport.

M

BAXTER STATE PARK
Baxter Peak in this park marks the north end of the Appalachian Trail.

MOUNT KATAHDIN
is the tallest mountain in Maine. Some Native Americans believe it to be the home of the storm god Pamola.

ROBERT EDWIN PEARY
1856–1920
Raised and educated in Portland, this explorer was the first person to reach the North Pole.

E. B. WHITE
1899–1985
This author's first children's book, *Stuart Little*, came from stories told to his nieces and nephews.

MOOSEHEAD LAKE
This area is home to many majestic moose, some weighing nearly 1,000 pounds.

JOAN BENOIT SAMUELSON
b.1957
In 1984 Benoit became the first winner of the Olympic Women's Marathon. She was raised in Cape Elizabeth.

CANADA

MAINE LOBSTER
Maine is famous for its lobster. In 2014 Maine fishermen caught a bright blue lobster, making headlines.

SKOWHEGAN INDIAN
This 62-foot-tall sculpture is a tribute to the Abenaki people.

STEPHEN KING
sets many of his spooky stories in this, his home state.

EAR MUFFS
15-year-old Chester Greenwood grew up ice-skating and invented "ear protectors" to keep himself warm.

PAUL BUNYAN
Maine's lumber capital, Bangor, boasts a 31-foot statue of this giant lumberjack of legend.

37 MILES TO MEXICO
Mexico, Maine, that is! A signpost in Lynchville gives distances to Paris and China . . . both places in Maine!

NORWAY	14MI
PARIS	15MI
DENMARK	23MI
NAPLES	23MI
SWEDEN	25MI
POLAND	27MI
MEXICO	37MI
PERU	46MI
CHINA	94MI

HAYSTACK
is a famous craft school offering courses in metalwork, woodwork, ceramics, and more.

THE MUSEUM IN THE STREETS©
is a walking-tour company celebrating Maine's rich shipbuilding history.

MAINE STATE HOUSE
The architect of the state house also designed the U.S. Capitol in Washington.

BANGOR

THE 1998 ICE STORM
Residents in and around Bridgton put antifreeze in their toilets to stop them from freezing solid!

AUGUSTA

ANDRE THE SEAL
once spent his winters at an aquarium in Boston, swimming back to his human "family" in Rockport, Maine, every spring.

ACADIA NATIONAL PARK

LEWISTON

MAINE COON
The Maine coon is the official state cat and one of the oldest natural breeds in the U.S.

WINSLOW HOMER
painted *Eight Bells* and other maritime paintings at Prouts Neck.

BEAN BOOT
L.L. Bean started his boot company in his brother's basement in Freeport.

PORTLAND

GULF OF MAINE

NEW HAMPSHIRE

EARTHA
The town of Yarmouth has the world's largest spinning globe, Eartha. California is 3 1/2 feet tall!

BATH IRON WORKS
is a major ship-building yard. Some 70,000 gallons of paint, 3,000 light fixtures, and 33 miles of pipe go into building a navy destroyer!

THE TROLLEY MUSEUM
is the largest electric railway museum in the world.

PORTLAND HEAD LIGHT
Whale-oil lamps were once used to light Maine's oldest lighthouse.

AINE

WELCOME TO THE PINE TREE STATE

You could easily have read about Maine before you even knew it was a state: generations of children have followed the adventures of a young girl from Maine in Robert McCloskey's well-loved picture book *Blueberries for Sal*. Once older, many of these same readers have devoured E. B. White's book *Charlotte's Web*, which was in part inspired by his life in rural Maine.

Legions of others have also found inspiration in the Pine Tree State: Winslow Homer's masterful oil paintings show the maritime landscapes that are so vital to the business and pleasure of the state. The many tribes of Native Americans in Maine's past created and shared legends and folktales that grew from the land's unique and beautiful features.

The nation's easternmost state is as beautiful and enriching as these artworks lead us to believe. Once you visit, you may create a masterpiece of your own!

MOMENTS TO REMEMBER

3,800–4,500 YEARS AGO: The Red Paint People, one of the first American maritime cultures, skillfully hunted dangerous swordfish.

1860: Milton Bradley introduces The Game of Life—one of the U.S.'s first board games.

JUNE 10, 1861: Dorothea Dix is made superintendent of women nurses for the Union army, and later goes on to create the first American hospitals for the mentally ill.

1912: L.L. Bean launches his outdoor clothing company. Problems with his early boots meant that 90 out of the first 100 pairs were returned as faulty, but today the company is famous for quality and customer satisfaction.

1923: While still a medical student, Charles Best receives a share of the Nobel Prize in Medicine for the discovery of insulin.

JANUARY 1953: Robert McCloskey wins a Caldecott Honor for his picture book *One Morning in Maine*, set in Brooksville.

OCTOBER 1980: President Carter signs the Maine Indian Land Claims agreement.

DECEMBER 1982: 10-year-old Samantha Smith writes to a Soviet leader about nuclear war concerns and becomes America's youngest goodwill ambassador.

JANUARY 1998: The Ice Storm—the worst storm in Maine's history—arrives, and half of the state's homes lose power.

2009: The Moxie Bottle House museum opens, featuring a 33-foot-tall bottle of the state's official beverage.

ATLANTIC OCEAN

THUNDER HOLE
Waves here can reach 40 feet!

BLUEBERRIES FOR SAL
Kuplink, kuplank, kuplunk! The mother and child in Robert McCloskey's award-winning book are modeled on his wife and daughter.

PROJECT PUFFINS
Interns summer on Eastern Egg Rock, helping to band and feed seabirds.

CADILLAC MOUNTAIN
Visitors come here early to see the "nation's first sunrise."

LOBSTER BOAT RACES
With speeds of 60 mph, these races are the NASCAR of Winter Harbor!

KEY FACTS

CAPITAL
Augusta

LARGEST CITIES
Portland
Lewiston
Bangor

BIRD
Black-capped chickadee

NAMED FOR
Possibly a nautical term, "the main"

STATEHOOD DATE
March 15, 1820

STATEHOOD ORDER
23

FLOWER
White pine cone and tassel

POSTAL CODE
ME

REGION
New England

MAIN TIME ZONE
Eastern

TREE
White pine

"I LEAD"

WELCOME TO THE OLD LINE STATE

although it is one of the smallest states in terms of area, Maryland is big in personality. Often described as "America in Miniature," Maryland has it all, from the pine groves and mountains of the west to the sandy beaches of the east, and from quiet fishing villages serving delicious blue crabs to the bustling city of Baltimore.

Steeped in history, Maryland has the oldest continuously used capitol building in the country. The 7th state got its nickname, the Old Line State, during the Revolutionary War, when a group of only 400 Maryland soldiers opposed a huge British force, holding the line so that George Washington's soldiers could escape.

Maryland is a state of many firsts: it was home to the first American passenger railroad, the first telegraph line, the first umbrella factory, and even the first ice cream factory! Plus, in the 17th century, Mistress Margaret Brent was America's first female lawyer, first female landowner, and first female taxpayer!

PHILIP GLASS
b.1937
An influential pianist and composer, Glass has created operas, symphonies, and film scores.

THURGOOD MARSHALL
1908–1993
A civil rights activist and lawyer, Marshall became the first African American justice of the Supreme Court.

CATOCTIN MOUNTAIN PARK
has been home to Camp Greentop since 1937. Here, campers with disabilities can fish, canoe, and have fun.

THE FROSTBURG DEPOT TURNTABLE
Find out how this rotating bridge allows just two people to change the direction of a massive steam engine.

DISCOVERY STATION
See the innards of a giant Mack truck engine—and its bulldog mascot—at this Hagerstown science museum.

C&O CANAL
The lock gates used to lift or lower boats on this canal were based on a design by Leonardo da Vinci from the 1400s!

FREDERICK ←

GERMANTOWN

COMMUNITY BRIDGE
Thousands of people submitted ideas for artist William Cochran and his volunteers to paint onto a concrete bridge in Frederick.

MARIE BOYD, BASKETBALLER
In 1924 a Lonaconing high school forward makes sports history—and a Guinness World Record—by scoring 156 points in one game.

WEST VIRGINIA

CHARLES F. MERCER
Take a trip back to the 1870s and ride this replica packet boat, drawn by mules, on the C&O canal.

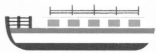

VIRGINIA

LAURA AMY SCHLITZ
b.1955
The award-winning children's book author of *Good Masters! Sweet Ladies!* was born in Baltimore.

HARRIET TUBMAN
c.1820–1913
After escaping slavery herself, Tubman helped more than 300 others to freedom on the Underground Railroad.

FREDERICK DOUGLASS
1818–1895
Douglass escaped slavery to become a world-renowned antislavery activist and adviser to President Lincoln.

PISCATAWAY PARK
is home to bald eagles and ospreys, who sometimes fight for fish.

MARYLAN

PENNSYLVANIA

BABE RUTH BIRTHPLACE MUSEUM
This baseball Hall of Famer was born in Baltimore in a house that is now just a long fly ball away from Oriole Park.

B&O RAILROAD MUSEUM
Passenger cars once resembled horse-drawn stagecoaches.

THE MUSEUM OF CIVIL WAR MEDICINE
houses curiosities such as early prosthetic legs made from wood and leather.

ENCHANTED FOREST
This fairy-tale themed amusement park was abandoned in the 1980s.

EDGAR ALLAN POE
Visit the home and grave of the author of the spooky story "The Tell-Tale Heart."

FORT McHENRY
A replica of the 15-star flag at Fort McHenry that inspired "The Star-Spangled Banner" is flown 24 hours a day.

NATIONAL AQUARIUM
Here you can see the starry puffer fish, which eats hard-shelled shrimp to wear down its teeth!

MARYLAND STATE HOUSE
The state house is topped by a 28-foot lightning rod constructed according to Benjamin Franklin's instructions!

ASSATEAGUE ISLAND
is home to a famous herd of wild ponies.

BALTIMORE

DELAWARE

ANNAPOLIS

COLUMBIA

LACROSSE
The state team sport is popular at the University of Maryland.

CALICO CAT
Only three states have a state cat; Maryland's was chosen because the cat's multi-colored fur matches the flag.

CLARA BARTON HOUSE
Was home to the founder of the American Red Cross.

THE CALVERT CLIFFS STATE PARK
has a sandy beach, Miocene-era fossils, a recycled tire playground, and fishing.

CHESAPEAKE BAY

SMITH ISLAND CAKE
This eight-layer cake has pencil-thin layers of fudge frosting and is often covered in crushed candy bars.

MATTHEW HENSON
This Charles County native was one of the first people to reach the Geographic North Pole.

THE ARK AND THE DOVE
Farmers, carpenters, and brickmakers were among the passengers of these ships: Maryland's first English settlers.

SKIPJACK BOAT
The traditional boat used on Chesapeake Bay for oyster dredging is named after a fish that leaps in and out of water.

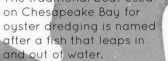

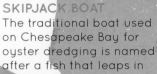

CAL RIPKEN, JR.
b.1960
Baseball Hall of Famer Ripken spent his entire 21-year career with the Baltimore Orioles.

MOMENTS TO REMEMBER

MARCH 25, 1634: The first English settlers in Maryland arrive at St. Clement's Island on two boats: the *Ark* and the *Dove*.

OCTOBER 18, 1767: Astronomer Charles Mason and surveyor Jeremiah Dixon determine the boundary between Pennsylvania and Maryland. This line divides the northern and southern states.

1791: Maryland donates a chunk of land that will become part of the new U.S. capital, Washington, D.C.

SEPTEMBER 13, 1814: Maryland-born lawyer and poet Francis Scott Key writes America's future national anthem, "The Star-Spangled Banner."

1844: The world's first telegraph line is set up between Baltimore and Washington, D.C.

MAY 23, 1922: Ragtime pianist Eubie Blake's show *Shuffle Along* opens, featuring the song "I'm Just Wild About Harry." Blake goes on to receive the Presidential Medal of Freedom.

1947: Marguerite Henry publishes the book *Misty of Chincoteague*, about the ponies of Assateague Island.

SEPTEMBER 4, 1987: Johns Hopkins University's neurosurgeon Ben Carson and a 70-person surgical team work for 22 hours to successfully separate twins who had been joined at the head.

SEPTEMBER 6, 1995: Baltimore Orioles shortstop Cal Ripken, Jr., plays in his 2,131st consecutive game, breaking "Iron Horse" Lou Gehrig's record for most consecutive games played.

JANUARY 28, 2013: The illustrator Bryan Collier wins his fifth Coretta Scott King Award with his illustrations for the book *I, Too, Am America*.

KEY FACTS

CAPITAL
Annapolis

LARGEST CITIES
Baltimore
Columbia
Germantown

BIRD
Baltimore oriole

NAMED FOR
Henrietta Maria, the English King Charles I's wife

STATEHOOD DATE
April 28, 1788

STATEHOOD ORDER
7

FLOWER
Black-eyed Susan

POSTAL CODE
MD

REGION
Mid-Atlantic

MAIN TIME ZONE
Eastern

TREE
White oak

"STRONG DEEDS, GENTLE WORDS"

I If you're someone who likes to be the first at something, then the Bay State is the place for you. A land of innovation, Massachusetts truly is a state of firsts: it was the first state to celebrate Thanksgiving, as well as the place where life-changing inventions such as Morse code were born . . . and it was even home to America's first public basketball game, in 1891! The historic sixth state has always had a pioneering spirit, from its early days as a place of religious freedom, to its later years as a key player in the iron and steel industries. Literary pioneers such as Emily Dickinson have made Massachusetts a stronghold of the arts world—indeed, her hometown of Amherst is still awash with writers and artists today.

In summer, the Bay State welcomes vacationers looking for beaches with a difference: where the coffee, cheese, and wine are as spectacular as the cool water, white sand, and lip-smacking seafood!

EMILY DICKINSON
1830-1886
One of America's most important poets was born in Amherst, where there is now a museum about her.

BARBARA WALTERS
b.1929
This Boston-born Emmy Award–winning journalist has interviewed some of the world's most famous people.

TONY DITERLIZZI
b.1969
This author and illustrator who co-created *The Spiderwick Chronicles* series now lives in Amherst.

THE SALEM WITCH TRIALS MEMORIAL honors the many people who were unfairly executed for witchcraft in 1692.

IN MEMORY OF THOSE INNOCENTS WHO DIED DURING THE SALEM VILLAGE WITCHCRAFT HYSTERIA OF 1692

SAUGUS IRON WORKS
The birthplace of the U.S. iron and steel industry still boasts working waterwheels and hot forges.

NEW HAMPSHIRE

WALDEN POND
This lake in Concord inspired the writings of conservationist and philosopher Henry David Thoreau.

VERMONT

METACOMET RIDGE
is named for the Wampanoag chief who tried to drive out the colonists and preserve native lands.

JOHNNY APPLESEED
Born in Leominster as John Chapman, this nature lover traveled across the Midwest planting thousands of apple seeds.

WATERTOWN
Famous graduates of the Perkins School for the Blind include Anne Sullivan, who taught Helen Keller.

BOSTON

Perkins

SUSAN B. ANTHONY BIRTHPLACE MUSEUM
This museum in Adams celebrates the antislavery and women's rights campaigner who was the first woman to appear on a U.S. coin.

LIBERTY 1980

SMITH COLLEGE
Gloria Steinem, the founder of the magazines *Ms.* and *New York*, is one of the graduates of this all-women's college.

ERIC CARLE
The author and illustrator of *The Very Hungry Caterpillar* founded a museum to celebrate picture book art in Amherst, near where he once lived.

WORCESTER

WILL YOU BE MINE?
In the mid-1800s, 19-year-old Worcester artist Esther Howland was the first person to sell Valentine's Day cards in the U.S.

BOSTON TERRIER
The friendly state dog is a good watchdog—and a loud snorer!

NEW YORK

KINDERGARTEN GAMES
Games maker Milton Bradley set up his board game company in Springfield. He was a supporter of the U.S.'s first kindergartens, giving them games for free!

JAMES NAISMITH
This physical education teacher organized the first basketball game, using a peach basket as a hoop, at the Springfield YMCA in 1891.

SPRINGFIELD

CONNECTICUT

RHODE ISLAND

MASSACHUSETTS

BENJAMIN FRANKLIN
1706–1790
Often called "The First American," this scientist, diplomat, and humorist was born in Boston.

AMY POEHLER
b.1971
Famous for her work on *Saturday Night Live*, this comedian grew up in Burlington.

THEODOR SEUSS GEISEL
1904–1991
Best known as Dr. Seuss, this Springfield-raised author-illustrator has helped generations learn to read.

TEAM HOYT
This father and son duo raced—one on foot, one on wheels—in 32 Boston Marathons.

ATLANTIC OCEAN

NECCO WAFERS
These candy wafers (made in Revere) don't melt, so they made excellent treats to send overseas to WWII troops!

FENWAY PARK
The home of the Boston Red Sox is Major League Baseball's oldest ballpark.

MASSACHUSETTS STATE CAPITOL
The state house was built on Beacon Hill, a former cow pasture owned by revolutionary leader John Hancock.

MORSE CODE
This communicative code, where dots and dashes are used in place of letters, was co-invented by Samuel Morse of Charlestown.

PUBLIC GARDEN
The swan boats at America's first botanic garden appear in Robert McCloskey's book *Make Way for Ducklings*.

IRISH ROOTS
The seaside town of Scituate was named the "most Irish town in the U.S." in 2011!

CAPE COD
is well known for its cranberries: one of just three fruits native to North America!

CAPE COD BAY

THE MAYFLOWER
This ship sailed from England to Cape Cod in 1620, carrying 102 passengers, the "Pilgrims," who hoped to start a new life in the New World.

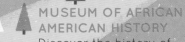
CAPE COD

MUSEUM OF AFRICAN AMERICAN HISTORY
Discover the history of African Americans on Nantucket, including how many became mariners and whalers after slavery was abolished here in 1773.

WHALING MUSEUM
Find a sperm whale skeleton and more at this New Bedford museum.

NANTUCKET

NANTUCKET SOUND

BUZZARDS BAY

VINEYARD SOUND

WAMPANOAG TRIBE
Some Native Americans, such as those on Martha's Vineyard, once used lobsters to fertilize crops.

MARTHA'S VINEYARD

MARIA MITCHELL
After discovering a comet in 1847, Mitchell became the first U.S. woman to work as an astronomer, earning $300 a year as a "celestial observer."

APRIL 1, 1621: Wampanoag tribal leader Chief Massasoit visits John Carver, first governor of the Plymouth Colony; they exchange gifts and agree on a peace treaty that will last some 50 years. Later that year, the settlers and the Wampanoag celebrate the First Thanksgiving.

DECEMBER 16, 1773: Samuel Adams and the Sons of Liberty throw 342 chests of tea into the Boston Harbor, protesting against an unfair British tax.

MAY 24, 1844: Samuel Morse, born in Charlestown, sends one of the world's first telegraphs from Washington, D.C., to Baltimore, bringing a new age in long-distance communication.

JUNE 28, 1904: With the help of teacher Anne Sullivan, 24-year-old Helen Keller graduates Radcliffe College with honors, becoming the first deaf and blind person to earn a college degree.

DECEMBER 21, 1937: Dr. Seuss has his first book published after being rejected 27 times!

MARCH 1, 1961: Massachusetts-born president John F. Kennedy creates the Peace Corps. Since then, some 220,000 Americans have volunteered to help in communities abroad.

APRIL 21, 1975: Bob Hall finishes the Boston Marathon in 2 hours, 58 minutes—in a wheelchair; Boston is the first major marathon to include a wheelchair division.

JANUARY 12, 2004: Mo Willems wins his first Caldecott Honor for his hilarious picture book *Don't Let the Pigeon Drive the Bus!*

KEY FACTS

CAPITAL
Boston

LARGEST CITIES
Boston
Worcester
Springfield

BIRD
Black-capped chickadee

NAMED FOR
The Massachusett people, whose name means "near the great hill"

STATEHOOD DATE
February 6, 1788

STATEHOOD ORDER
6

FLOWER
Mayflower

POSTAL CODE
MA

REGION
New England

MAIN TIME ZONE
Eastern

TREE
American elm

"BY THE SWORD WE SEEK PEACE, BUT PEACE ONLY UNDER LIBERTY"

LAKE SUPERIOR

MIC

ISLE ROYALE NATIONAL PARK
is a great place for moose-spotting.
At 5 feet tall or more, moose prefer to
munch tall grasses, because lowering
their heads is tricky!

CANADA

ROOT BEER FALLS
The massive Tahquamenon
waterfalls' nickname comes
from tannins that turn the
water a brownish-gold.

SKI HALL OF FAME MUSEUM
Learn the gripping story of the
Norwegian Birkebeiners—some
of the world's first skiers.

MACKINAC BRIDGE
The center deck of
this suspension
bridge can move
35-feet in
severe winds!

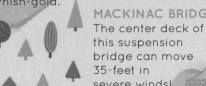

PETOSKEY STONES
These distinctive
pebble-shaped
fossils found in the
area are named for
the Ottawa Indian
Chief Pet-O-Sega.

KEY FACTS

CAPITAL
Lansing

LARGEST CITIES
Detroit
Grand Rapids
Warren

BIRD
American robin

NAMED FOR
The Chippewa Indian
word *Michigana*,
meaning
large lake

STATEHOOD DATE
January 26, 1837

STATEHOOD ORDER
26

FLOWER
Apple
blossom

POSTAL CODE
MI

REGION
Great Lakes

MAIN TIME ZONE
Eastern

TREE
Eastern
white pine

SLEEPING BEAR DUNES
Legend has it that a mother
bear waited atop this then
200-foot bluff for her missing
cubs.

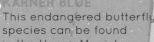

CHERRY-PICKING
The U.S. is among
the world's top
cherry producers.
At many Michigan
farms you can pick
your own fruit.

MUSHROOM HOUSES
Earl Young built 30 of
these quirky Hobbit-like
homes in Charlevoix.

MICHIGAN STATE CAPITOL
The capitol is built with brick
from Lansing, stone from Ohio,
cast iron from Pennsylvania, and
marble from Vermont.

"IF YOU SEEK A PLEASANT PENINSULA, LOOK AROUND YOU"

KARNER BLUE
This endangered butterfly
species can be found
in the Huron-Manistee
National Forest.

SUB SLEEPOVER
You can camp in the
tight quarters of the
USS Silversides at this
submarine museum in
Muskegon.

WISCONSIN

ANNA SUI
b.1964
This Detroit-born designer is
one of the most celebrated
names in American fashion.

JORDYN WIEBER
b.1995
Wieber, who began her
gymnastics training in DeWitt,
won a team gold at the 2012
London Olympics.

LANSING

GRAND RAPIDS

TULIP TIME
Catch a Dutch
dance in the city
of Holland's annual
festival.

AIR ZOO
Flying fanatics
at this museum
in Portage fawn
over the SR-71B
Blackbird—the
fastest plane ever
built!

HOME ALONE
Funny movie-
maker John
Hughes grew
up in Lansing.

LAKE MICHIGAN

HENRY FORD
1863-1947
Founder of the Ford Motor
Company, Ford introduced the
mass-production techniques that
revolutionized the car industry.

STEVIE WONDER
b.1950
Musician Stevie Wonder signed
with Detroit's Motown label at
age 11. His pop and R&B talents
have won him 25 Grammys.

FROZEN PIER
Winter waves crash
and freeze against the
St. Joseph North Pier.

CEREAL CITY
Kellogg's, founded
in Battle Creek, was
the first company
to include prizes in
their cereal boxes.

INDIANA

HIGAN

DRUMMOND DISASTERS
Fishing tug *Alice C* is one of 17 shipwrecks off the coast of Drummond Island.

LAKE HURON

TURNIP ROCK
20-foot-high trees grow atop this remote rock shaped by thousands of years of wave erosion.

SANILAC PETROGLYPHS
These Native American carvings were made 300–1,000 years ago in the Late Woodland Period.

OLYMPIC FLINT
Flint is the home of Claressa Shields, the youngest boxer to win the Olympic middleweight gold.

16

WARREN ◄ - - - -

LAKE ST. CLAIR

► DETROIT

LUCKY STAR
A straight-A student, Madonna got a scholarship to the University of Michigan dance program.

LAKE ERIE

OHIO

WELCOME TO THE GREAT LAKES STATE

Which state has the longest freshwater coastline in the U.S., is made up of two peninsulas, and has a bottom half shaped like a mitten? Michigan!

Its most famous city, Detroit, is known not only for the Model T—the first mass-produced car in history—but also for Motown, the record label that helped Diana Ross and Michael Jackson into the musical spotlight. But there's more to the 26th state than Motor City.

With wolf habitats, Native American rock engravings, and one-of-a-kind fossil finds, natural wonders abound in the "Wolverine State." Half of the state is covered in forest and, wherever you are in Michigan, you're not more than 6 miles from the nearest body of water. Which makes sense, considering it's bordered by four of the five Great Lakes. No wonder they call it the "Great Lakes State"!

HENRY FORD MUSEUM
Tour this complex of historical items documenting the Industrial Revolution.

PICKLE POWER
Michigan is well known for its pickled cucumbers.

MOON MIST & REDPOP
Faygo drinks are based in Detroit. The first flavors were based on cake frosting!

Redpop!

MOTOWN MUSEUM
celebrates music-history makers like the Miracles, Gladys Knight and the Pips, and the Supremes.

JOE LOUIS MONUMENT
This civil monument celebrates a gentle national hero and weighs 8,000 pounds!

MOMENTS TO REMEMBER

1622: French explorers Étienne Brûlé and his companion Grenoble are probably the first white men to see Lake Superior.

1812: Lewis Cass is appointed governor of the Michigan Territory.

OCTOBER 7, 1913: Henry Ford's car-production plant uses one of the world's first moving assembly lines to reduce Model T assembly time from 12 1/2 hours to 93 minutes within a year.

JUNE 17, 1940: A musical bell tower is opened in Belle Isle Park, dedicated to the much-loved advice columnist Nancy Brown; it was paid for with pennies donated by her loyal readers during the Depression.

NOVEMBER 1, 1957: The 5-mile-long Mackinac Bridge opens, finally connecting the Upper and Lower Peninsulas of Michigan.

1959: Berry Gordy, Jr., founds Motown Records in Detroit.

AUGUST 26, 1982: After his death, world heavyweight boxing champion Joe Louis is awarded the Congressional Gold Medal for bolstering the spirits of the nation.

1989: Pediatric neurosurgeon Dr. Alexa Canady becomes a member of the Michigan Women's Hall of Fame.

1998: Michigan University graduate Larry Page launches a new project with his colleague Sergey Brin; they give it the name "Google." Today Page is considered a pioneer in computer science and artificial intelligence.

DECEMBER 3, 2006: Smokey Robinson, the "King of Motown" and the founder of the Miracles, is given a Kennedy Center Honor for his contribution to arts and culture.

CHRISTOPHER PAUL CURTIS
b.1953
Curtis is a children's author born in Flint. His book *Bud, Not Buddy* won the Newbery Award.

MALCOLM X
1925–1965
Malcolm X spent some of his youth in Michigan. A controversial figure in the human rights movement, his views are still influential.

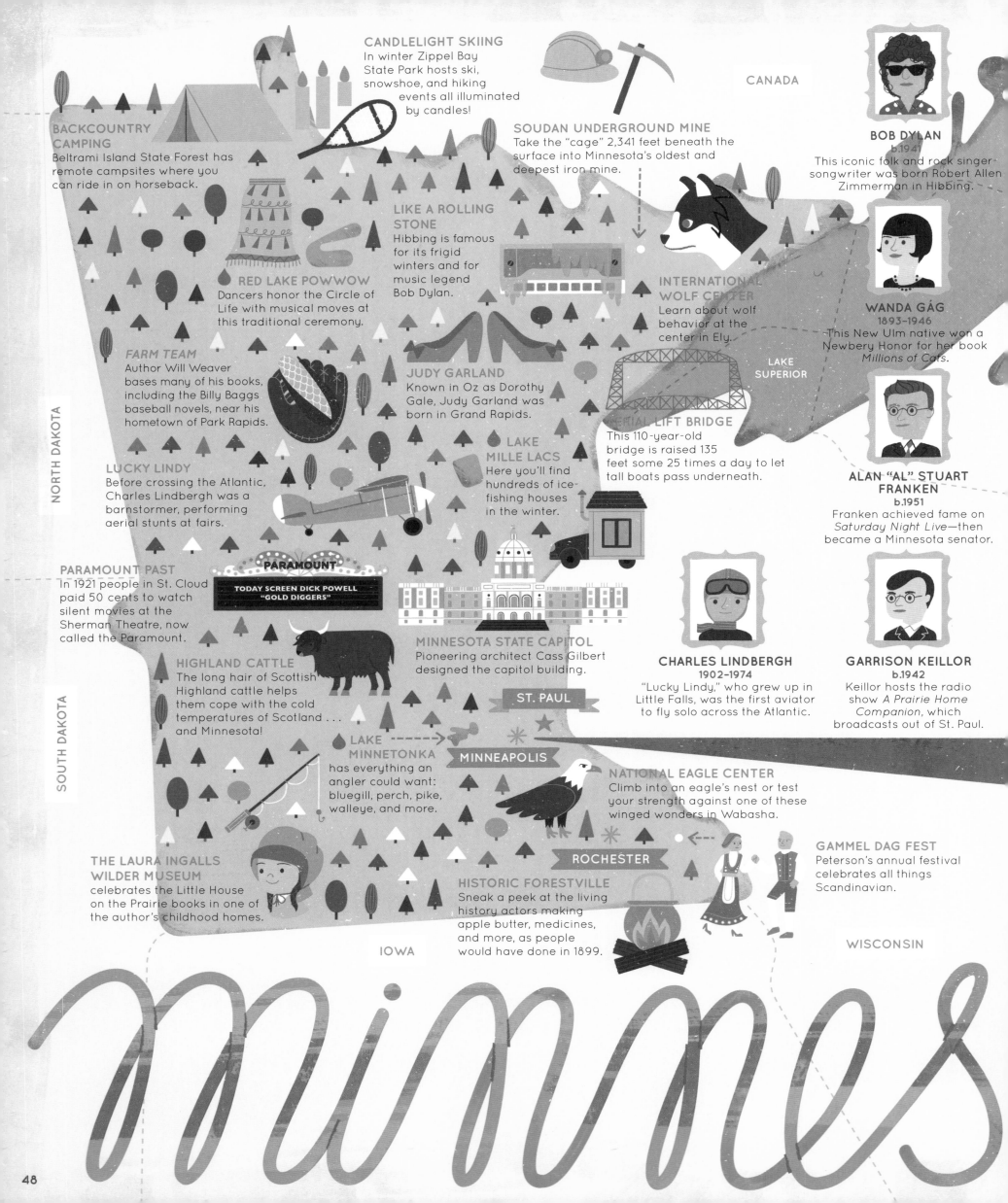

CANDLELIGHT SKIING
In winter Zippel Bay State Park hosts ski, snowshoe, and hiking events all illuminated by candles!

CANADA

BOB DYLAN
b.1941
This iconic folk and rock singer-songwriter was born Robert Allen Zimmerman in Hibbing.

BACKCOUNTRY CAMPING
Beltrami Island State Forest has remote campsites where you can ride in on horseback.

SOUDAN UNDERGROUND MINE
Take the "cage" 2,341 feet beneath the surface into Minnesota's oldest and deepest iron mine.

LIKE A ROLLING STONE
Hibbing is famous for its frigid winters and for music legend Bob Dylan.

RED LAKE POWWOW
Dancers honor the Circle of Life with musical moves at this traditional ceremony.

INTERNATIONAL WOLF CENTER
Learn about wolf behavior at the center in Ely.

WANDA GÁG
1893–1946
This New Ulm native won a Newbery Honor for her book *Millions of Cats*.

LAKE SUPERIOR

FARM TEAM
Author Will Weaver bases many of his books, including the Billy Baggs baseball novels, near his hometown of Park Rapids.

JUDY GARLAND
Known in Oz as Dorothy Gale, Judy Garland was born in Grand Rapids.

AERIAL LIFT BRIDGE
This 110-year-old bridge is raised 135 feet some 25 times a day to let tall boats pass underneath.

ALAN "AL" STUART FRANKEN
b.1951
Franken achieved fame on *Saturday Night Live*—then became a Minnesota senator.

NORTH DAKOTA

LUCKY LINDY
Before crossing the Atlantic, Charles Lindbergh was a barnstormer, performing aerial stunts at fairs.

LAKE MILLE LACS
Here you'll find hundreds of ice-fishing houses in the winter.

PARAMOUNT PAST
In 1921 people in St. Cloud paid 50 cents to watch silent movies at the Sherman Theatre, now called the Paramount.

PARAMOUNT
TODAY SCREEN DICK POWELL "GOLD DIGGERS"

MINNESOTA STATE CAPITOL
Pioneering architect Cass Gilbert designed the capitol building.

CHARLES LINDBERGH
1902–1974
"Lucky Lindy," who grew up in Little Falls, was the first aviator to fly solo across the Atlantic.

GARRISON KEILLOR
b.1942
Keillor hosts the radio show *A Prairie Home Companion*, which broadcasts out of St. Paul.

HIGHLAND CATTLE
The long hair of Scottish Highland cattle helps them cope with the cold temperatures of Scotland . . . and Minnesota!

ST. PAUL

SOUTH DAKOTA

LAKE MINNETONKA
has everything an angler could want: bluegill, perch, pike, walleye, and more.

MINNEAPOLIS

NATIONAL EAGLE CENTER
Climb into an eagle's nest or test your strength against one of these winged wonders in Wabasha.

THE LAURA INGALLS WILDER MUSEUM
celebrates the Little House on the Prairie books in one of the author's childhood homes.

ROCHESTER

HISTORIC FORESTVILLE
Sneak a peek at the living history actors making apple butter, medicines, and more, as people would have done in 1899.

GAMMEL DAG FEST
Peterson's annual festival celebrates all things Scandinavian.

IOWA

WISCONSIN

minnes

WELCOME TO THE NORTH STAR STATE

The land of 10,000 lakes, as it is often called, actually has closer to 12,000. This water world is where three American rivers begin their long journeys: the Red River of the North, the St. Lawrence, and even the mighty Mississippi. Beautiful lakeside resorts make the area popular with tourists during the summer, but the North Star State has much to offer all year round.

Fans of outdoor adventuring will love canoeing in the Boundary Waters, biking, horseback riding, snowshoeing, skiing, snowboarding, hiking, or just marveling at the scenery and camping under the stars in the off-the-beaten-track Voyageurs National Park.

City slickers will enjoy the sights and sounds of Minneapolis and St. Paul, with their museums, galleries, music venues, cool restaurants, and coffee shops.

Minnesota is the birthplace of a lot of famous Americans, from the skier Lindsey Vonn and the musician Bob Dylan to the celebrated author of *The Great Gatsby*, F. Scott Fitzgerald.

MOMENTS TO REMEMBER

MAY 17, 1673: French explorers Jacques Marquette and Louis Joliet explore the upper Mississippi Valley.

1776: Chief Tamaha, also known as Chief Standing Moose, of the Mdewakanton Sioux, is born. He becomes a powerful orator, famed for his diplomacy and peacemaking.

MAY 21, 1927: Charles Lindbergh (who grew up in Little Falls) completes the first solo flight across the Atlantic, from New York City to Paris.

JUNE 16, 1931: "Minnesota Woman," a 10,000-year-old skeleton of a 15-year-old girl, is discovered by a road repair crew near Pelican Rapids.

AUGUST 3, 1983: The Minneapolis-born musician Prince records his album *Purple Rain*.

OCTOBER 25, 1987: The Minnesota Twins win the World Series for the first time since moving from Washington in 1961. They win again in 1991.

FEBRUARY 2, 1996: Minnesota records its coldest temperature ever: a chilly 60 degrees below zero!

JANUARY 5, 1999: Jesse Ventura, a former Navy SEAL, bodyguard for the Rolling Stones, and professional wrestler, is sworn in as governor.

JANUARY 12, 2004: Kate DiCamillo wins the Newbery Medal for *The Tale of Despereaux*, the story of a mouse who falls in love with a princess.

APRIL 7, 2008: Bob Dylan, singer of "Blowin' in the Wind," wins a special Pulitzer Prize Citation for his "profound impact on music and American culture."

JULY 15, 2014: Rochester's Mayo Clinic is ranked top in the U.S. News List of Best Hospitals.

MICHIGAN

WALKER ART CENTER
At this Minneapolis museum you'll find Claes Oldenburg and Cooseje van Bruggen's enormous cherry and spoon sculpture.

SHAKOPEE'S MEMORIAL PARK
houses ancient burial mounds of the Dakota people, who lived in buffalo-hide tipis during winter.

FITZGERALD THEATER
This St. Paul venue hosts Garrison Keillor's radio show.

GREAT GATSBY
F. Scott Fitzgerald's childhood home, Summit Terrace, in St. Paul, has been preserved as a historic landmark.

TARGET FIELD
This Minneapolis stadium is home to the Minnesota Twins baseball team.

BULLSEYE
The Target Corporation has its HQ in Minneapolis, although its celebrity doggie mascot actually lives on a ranch in California.

LINDSEY VONN
b.1984
The women's World Cup skiing record holder was born in St. Paul.

KEY FACTS

CAPITAL
St. Paul

LARGEST CITIES
Minneapolis
St. Paul
Rochester

BIRD
Common loon

NAMED FOR
A Dakota Sioux word meaning "sky-tinted water"

STATEHOOD DATE
May 11, 1858

STATEHOOD ORDER
32

FLOWER
Pink and white lady's slipper

POSTAL CODE
MN

REGION
Great Lakes

MAIN TIME ZONE
Central Standard

TREE
Red pine

"THE STAR OF THE NORTH"

MISSISSI

WELCOME TO THE MAGNOLIA STATE

The 20th state is named for the largest and most important river in North America: the Mississippi. The name is apt—it comes from the Algonquin word *messipi*, meaning "great river."

The 2,340-mile-long "Big Muddy" begins in Lake Itasca in Minnesota, flows through ten states, then empties into the Gulf of Mexico. It forms the western border of the Magnolia State, Mississippi. Its overflow creates the fertile soil that provides the country with a bounty of cotton, rice, and soybeans, which are best eaten with southern staples such as catfish, turnip greens, fried dill pickle, and a slice of chocolate meringue pie.

Floating down Ol' Man River, you'll see important civil rights movement locations as well as the Delta, the heart of gospel and soul music. The river is as much a hero of Mark Twain's *Huckleberry Finn* as Huck and Jim themselves, and symbolizes freedom and possibility, making proud the residents of this great state.

ROBERT JOHNSON
1911–1938
Known as the "King of Delta Blues," Johnson's guitar techniques still influence blues and rock musicians today.

BEAUTY SHOP POLITICS
Vera Mae Pigee's salon in Clarksdale was a hub of civil rights activity in the 1950s and '60s.

COTTON
One bale of cotton can be used to make 313,600 $100 bills or 2,104 pairs of boxers!

PO' MONKEY'S LOUNGE
In Merigold, this is where you go to dance to some classic blues.

ARKANSAS

THE B.B. KING MUSEUM
in Indianola celebrates the life of musician B.B. King and the musical history of the Delta.

BLUES BIRTHPLACE
Blues musicians Muddy Waters, Lead Belly, and Charley Patton were all born in the Delta.

THE TEDDY BEAR
was invented after President Teddy Roosevelt refused to shoot an injured bear near Onward.

CATFISH CAPITAL OF THE WORLD
Every year, Mississippi produces over 350 million pounds of catfish!

LOUISIANA

KEY FACTS

CAPITAL
Jackson

LARGEST CITIES
Jackson
Gulfport
Southaven

BIRD
Mockingbird

NAMED FOR
The Algonquin word for "great river"

STATEHOOD DATE
December 10, 1817

STATEHOOD ORDER
20

FLOWER
Magnolia

POSTAL CODE
MS

REGION
Deep South

MAIN TIME ZONE
Central

TREE
Magnolia

IF THE SHOE FITS
In 1884, a Vicksburg shoe shop was the first to sell a *pair* of shoes, instead of just one at a time!

THE MIGHTY MISSISSIPI
At 21, Mark Twain fulfilled a childhood dream—becoming a steamboat pilot on the river.

THE VICTORY OF VICKSBURG
was a turning point for the Union Army in the Civil War.

NATCHEZ INDIANS
farmed, fished, and built ceremonial mounds in Mississippi from AD 700 until the 1730s.

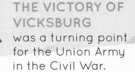

"BY VALOR AND ARMS"

PPI

WILLIAM FAULKNER
1897–1962
Nobel- and Pulitzer-Prize-winning writer Faulkner set many of his works in Mississippi.

TENNESSEE

The Sound and the Fury

JET

CORINTH PRINTS
Jet magazine was printed in the city of Corinth for 63 years.

**PUSHMATAHA,
THE "PANTHER'S CLAW"**
c.1764–1824
Known as the "greatest of Choctaw chiefs," Pushmataha was an exemplary diplomat.

**WILLIAM
FAULKNER**
was born in the city of New Albany and went on to win a Nobel Prize.

A KING IS BORN
Elvis was born in a two-room house in Tupelo . . .
and died in the 23-room mansion Graceland, in Tennessee.

THE NATCHEZ TRACE
was first a footpath forged by wild animals, then an Indian trade trail. Part of the trail is now a national parkway.

FRIENDSHIP CEMETERY
In 1866 the women of Columbus laid flowers on the graves of Civil War soldiers. This is said to be the origin of Memorial Day.

THE MISSISSIPPI UNIVERSITY FOR WOMEN
was the first state-sponsored women's college in the country, founded in 1884.

COLUMBUS

QUEEN OF CHICAGO
Oprah Winfrey was born in Kosciusko.

CHOCTAW BASKETS
are made by collecting, drying, dying, then weaving swamp cane.

JACKSON

MISSISSIPPI STATE CAPITOL
The first capitol building cost $3,500 to build in 1822 and was a mere 40 by 30 feet! This, the third building, is a touch grander.

ANDREW JACKSON.
The state's capital was named for Andrew Jackson, the future president, after he became a hero of the War of 1812.

ALABAMA

CRANK IT UP, MAN!
Meridian is the home of Peavey amplifiers, the largest amp maker in the world.

STAR
The town of Star, near Jackson, is childhood home of Grammy winner Faith Hill.

F.U.N.

WORD PLAY
The Jackson Children's Museum has a giant Scrabble board.

BILOXI LIGHTHOUSE
has weathered many hurricanes, including one of the fiercest, Katrina.

GULFPORT

GULF OF MEXICO

10,000 BC: Paleo-Indians arrive in the Mississippi Delta and hunt bison and mastodon with stone-tipped wooden spears.

AD 700: Natchez Indians conduct trade with tribes in other regions using a trail now called the Natchez Trace.

MAY 8, 1541: Hernando de Soto is one of the first Europeans to set eyes on the Mississippi river.

NOVEMBER 28, 1821: Jackson becomes state capital.

1861: Classes at the University of Mississippi in Oxford are suspended when most of the students enlist to fight in the Civil War.

LATE 1800s: Blues music begins in the Mississippi Delta. Rooted in the songs sung by slaves working in the fields and in African spiritual music, the blues offered a means of expression for many African Americans.

1907: Mississippi suffers from a plague of beetles called the boll weevil, which destroys much of the state's cotton crop.

MARCH 26, 1911: Playwright Tennessee Williams, author of *A Streetcar Named Desire,* is born in a church rectory in Columbus.

1927: The Mississippi river breaks its banks, flooding 27,000 square miles of land across ten states and leaving thousands homeless. It is the most destructive river flood in the nation's history.

DECEMBER 1938: Historian and folklorist Alan Lomax travels to the Mississippi Delta to record legendary blues musician Lead Belly.

MEDGAR WILEY EVERS
1925–1963
A civil rights activist, Evers fought against segregation in education. He was assassinated in 1963.

IDA B. WELLS
1862–1931
A former slave from Holly Springs, Wells became a campaigner for racial equality and women's right to vote.

HERNANDO DE SOTO
1496–1542
In 1539 this Spanish explorer discovered the territory that became Mississippi.

MAYA ANGELOU
1928-2014
The Pulitzer Prize–nominated author of *I Know Why the Caged Bird Sings* was born in St. Louis.

CHARLIE PARKER
1920–1955
One of the inventors of bebop music, saxophonist "Bird" was raised in Kansas City, Missouri.

SUSAN ELIZABETH BLOW
1843-1916
The "Mother of Kindergarten" opened the first public kindergarten in St. Louis.

IOWA

THE ICE CREAM CONE
was invented when a waffle vendor and an ice cream seller teamed up at the 1904 St. Louis World's Fair.

ST. LOUIS ABBEY
The Benedictine monks here pray five times daily and celebrate mass in English and Latin.

THE SCOTT JOPLIN HOUSE
honors the pianist and composer known as the "King of Ragtime Writers."

THE WORLD CHESS HALL OF FAME
in the Central West End neighborhood celebrates the game's history and great players.

THE GATEWAY ARCH
It takes four minutes for the tram inside this 63-story monument to reach the top.

OLD COURTHOUSE
In a famous 1846 case, a slave named Dred Scott sued unsuccessfully for his freedom.

GRANT'S FARM
in Grantwood Village is home to Clydesdale horses, which can grow to over 18 hands (6 feet) tall!

BLACK WALNUT
The official state nut is not just a yummy snack—its shells are used to make dynamite!

THE HOME OF SLICED BREAD
is Chillicothe, where Otto Rohwedder designed his 5-foot-long slicing machine in 1928.

NEBRASKA

EXCELSIOR SPRINGS
The natural spring water bubbling up here is said to have healing properties.

MARK TWAIN'S BOYHOOD HOME
is in Hannibal. This author's pen name is a riverboat term meaning "mark two," or a depth of two fathoms.

KANSAS

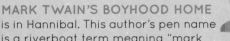

KANSAS CITY

THE MUSEUM OF ANTHROPOLOGY
in Columbia contains artifacts like these Sioux moccasins, made from leather and glass beads.

ILLINOIS

AMERICAN JAZZ MUSEUM
Kansas City native Charlie Parker's unusual plastic saxophone is on display here.

JEFFERSON CITY.

ST. LOUIS

MISSOURI STATE CAPITOL
This building is the third capitol to be built in Jefferson City and the sixth in state history!

BONNE TERRE MINES
This abandoned lead ore mine contains 17 miles of underground scuba diving paths!

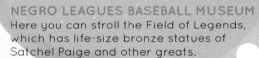

LEILA'S HAIR MUSEUM
in Independence has wreaths and jewelry all made from human hair—including that of Marilyn Monroe and Michael Jackson!

NEGRO LEAGUES BASEBALL MUSEUM
Here you can stroll the Field of Legends, which has life-size bronze statues of Satchel Paige and other greats.

MARK TWAIN
National Forest

JOHNSON'S SHUT-INS STATE PARK
This natural water park has slides and pools created by years of wind and water erosion.

THE TIGER SANCTUARY
in Ste. Genevieve enriches the tigers' environment with tasty pumpkins and meatball treats, and even box forts to play with.

WILSON'S CREEK NATIONAL BATTLEFIELD
Civil War cannons, like this one in Republic, had teams of eight soldiers to operate them!

FANTASTIC CAVERNS
This cave in Springfield was once a concert hall. Now you can take a ride-through tour to check out the stalactites and cave pearls.

SPRINGFIELD

THE MARK TWAIN NATIONAL FOREST
has over 5,000 caves, as well as streams, forests, and mountains.

THE OZARK HELLBENDER
is a rare species of giant salamander found in the Ozark National Scenic Riverways park.

OKLAHOMA

THE *TITANIC* MUSEUM
in Branson is a replica ship half the size of the doomed original, where "passengers" are given boarding passes and enter through an iceberg.

THE HEART OF THE OZARKS BLUEGRASS FESTIVAL
in West Plains features a Harmonica Howl and Fiddle Fest.

ARKANSAS

SAMUEL LANGHORNE CLEMENS (MARK TWAIN)
1835-1910
The humorous author of *The Adventures of Huckleberry Finn* was born in Florida, Missouri.

DOLLY PARTON'S DIXIE STAMPEDE
See acrobats and horse stunts during dinner at this Branson attraction.

BRAD PITT
b.1963
This world-famous movie actor and philanthropist grew up in Springfield.

KATE KLISE
b.1963
The award-winning author of *Regarding the Sink* now lives near Norwood.

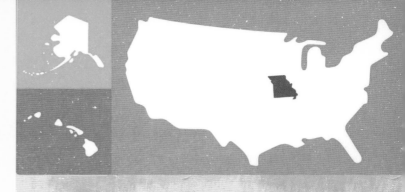

WELCOME TO THE SHOW ME STATE

You'll find the world's tallest monument in Missouri. The 630-foot gleaming Gateway Arch in St. Louis celebrates the city's significance as the Gateway to the West, the starting point for many pioneers and settlers heading out to new frontiers in the 1800s.

Now, of course, Missouri is as much a destination as it is a starting point. Country music lovers vacation in Branson, where there are some 50 theaters putting on music, magic, and comedy shows—with more seats than you'll find in New York's Broadway district! Heading north from here, visitors will want to explore the wilds of the Ozark Plateau, reveling in the forest ridges and rugged mountains. And you can even find a way of enjoying nature in Missouri's second-largest city, as St. Louis is home to the beautiful Forest Park, created in 1876 and beloved by residents ever since. Its name rings true: the Show Me State has plenty to show!

KEY FACTS

CAPITAL
Jefferson City

LARGEST CITIES
Kansas City
St. Louis
Springfield

BIRD
Bluebird

NAMED FOR
The Missouri River, which was named after the Missouri tribe

STATEHOOD DATE
August 10, 1821

STATEHOOD ORDER
24

FLOWER
White hawthorn blossom

POSTAL CODE
MO

REGION
Midwest

MAIN TIME ZONE
Central

TREE
Flowering dogwood

"THE WELFARE OF THE PEOPLE SHALL BE THE SUPREME LAW"

MOMENTS TO REMEMBER

MAY 21, 1804: Lewis and Clark set out from St. Charles, beginning their two-year-long exploration of the American West.

JANUARY 11, 1865: Slavery is abolished in Missouri in a near-unanimous vote.

FEBRUARY 18, 1885: Mark Twain, who grew up in Hannibal, publishes *The Adventures of Huckleberry Finn*—often called the "great American novel"—about a young boy's journey down the Mississippi.

APRIL 30, 1904: The World's Fair in St. Louis opens; highlights include the first tea served with ice and a water slide for elephants!

APRIL 15, 1912: Hannibal-born Molly Brown survives the sinking of the *Titanic*.

FEBRUARY 14, 1920: Superstar baseball pitcher Rube Foster sets up the Negro National League; the first game is played on May 2.

1923: The Country Club Plaza opens: it is the world's first shopping center for customers arriving by car—instead of on foot.

JULY 7, 1928: A Chillicothe baker takes a chance and puts the first sliced bread on his grocery store's shelves . . . it's a hit!

NOVEMBER 28, 1955: Kay Thompson (born in St. Louis) and Hilary Knight publish *Eloise: a Book for Precocious Grownups*.

SEPTEMBER 29, 1963: Baseball record-breaker Stan Musial of the St. Louis Cardinals plays his last game.

OCTOBER 28, 1965: Workers in St. Louis complete the 630-foot-high stainless steel Gateway Arch.

KENTUCKY

TENNESSEE

MISSOURI

MON

Montana is often called "Big Sky Country," and with its huge rolling plains stretching out beneath vast blue skies, it's not hard to see why. And the stunning scenery doesn't end there: the fourth-largest state also has towering mountains, ice-blue lakes, majestic cliffs, and cascading waterfalls. The locals call it "The Last Best Place" for its millions of acres of unspoiled wilderness.

It is also known as the Treasure State because its famous mountains are rich in gold, silver, and other precious minerals.

And Montana is rich in something else as well: wildlife. This state has more different species of mammals than any other state—in fact, its elk, deer, and antelope populations outnumber its humans! And you may also be able to spot wolves, moose, grizzly bears, swans, eagles, snow geese, pelicans, and more under the wide, pine-scented skies of the 41st state.

GLACIER NATIONAL PARK
In 1910 some 150 glaciers existed. Today, there are only around 25.

CANADA

FLATHEAD NATIONAL FOREST
Keep the grizzlies away by storing all your food in a bear-proof container.

OLD SHEP
For nearly 6 years this faithful dog stood vigil at the train station in Fort Benton, waiting for his dead master.

GREAT FALLS

GARNET GHOST TOWN
Ghost hunters visiting this 1800s gold-mining town claim to hear mysterious footsteps.

MISSOULA

MONTANA STATE CAPITOL
Paintings of four early Montanans grace the walls of the state house: a Native American, an explorer, a gold miner, and a cowboy.

LEWIS AND CLARK NATIONAL FOREST
spans seven mountain ranges. It is full of high peaks, grassy meadows, and great hiking.

NATIONAL BISON RANGE
When a bison's tail hangs down it is calm, but a tail held straight up means the bison is ready to charge!

THE GARDEN OF 1,000 BUDDHAS
near Arlee is a spiritual site where people come to pray and meditate.

SAPPHIRES
found in Montana come in all sorts of colors, from blue to green, pink, and yellow.

HELENA

CHARLEY PRIDE
This baseball pitcher turned country singer lived for a while in Helena.

GALLATIN RIVER
Thrill seekers ahoy! This is prime white-water rafting territory.

A RIVER RUNS THROUGH IT
Blackfoot River is prime water for trout fly-fishing.

BUTTE

EVEL KNIEVEL
This motorcyclist jumped rattlesnakes, mountain lions, sharks, and Greyhound buses!

BOZEMAN

MUSEUM OF THE ROCKIES
The research lab here is the base of *Jurassic Park* science adviser Jack Horner.

COOKE CITY
Fly-fishing abounds at this gateway to Yellowstone National Park.

ROBERT CRAIG "EVEL" KNIEVEL
1938–2007
A motorcycle daredevil, this Butte-native has a Guinness record for the most broken bones in a lifetime.

MUSEUM OF MINING
Don your hard hat and cap lamp for an underground tour of the Orphan Girl Mine.

BERKELEY PIT
This former copper mine now houses a lake so toxic it could kill you.

CHRISTOPHER PAOLINI
b.1983
The youngest author of a best-selling series, the *Inheritance Cycle*, Paolini lives in Paradise Valley.

MICHELLE WILLIAMS
b.1980
Born in Kalispell, Williams starred in *Dawson's Creek* and won an Oscar for *Brokeback Mountain*.

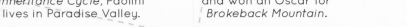
IDAHO

ROBERT YELLOWTAIL
1889–1988
Born in Lodge Grass, Yellowtail was a lawyer and a leader of the Crow Nation.

FROZE-TO-DEATH MOUNTAIN
Only experienced hikers dare climb this beautiful but deadly mountain—the name will give you a clue why.

54

tana

UPPER MISSOURI RIVER BREAKS NATIONAL MONUMENT
Much of the Breaks region is as unspoiled as it was when Lewis and Clark's party passed through in 1805.

THE LEWIS AND CLARK INTERPRETIVE CENTER
Find out about Lewis and Clark's famous journey to explore the American West.

COWBOY ARTIST
See C. M. Russell's paintings of cowboys, Native Americans and sweeping landscapes in Great Falls.

CASH CROP
Montana's many wheat farms make it the nation's third largest wheat producer.

PICTOGRAPH CAVE
Over 2,000 years ago prehistoric hunters made paintings on these walls.

LITTLE BIGHORN BATTLEFIELD
Sitting Bull and Lt. Colonel Custer fought here in one of the most famous battles of American history.

PRONGHORN ANTELOPES
The fastest mammal in North America can only be outrun by a cheetah!

BILLINGS

TEPEE CAPITAL OF THE WORLD
Some 1,200 tepees are set up during the annual Crow Fair.

THE CUSTER NATIONAL FOREST
is named for the cavalry commander who met his end in Montana.

WYOMING

"STAGECOACH" MARY FIELDS
1832–1914
The second woman and first African American mail coach driver, Mary drove the Cascades route.

JACK HORNER
b.1946
Raised in Shelby, this award-winning paleontologist was a technical adviser on the *Jurassic Park* films.

NORTH DAKOTA

SOUTH DAKOTA

MOMENTS TO REMEMBER

JULY 28, 1862: Gold is discovered at Grasshopper Creek, sparking Montana's first gold rush.

1895: At 60 years old, "Stagecoach Mary" becomes the second woman and the first African American to become a mail carrier for the U.S. Postal Service. She gets the job because she is the fastest applicant to hitch a team of six horses.

JUNE 2, 1924: Thanks in part to the work of Robert Yellowtail, a leader of the Crow Nation, Native Americans are given full U.S. citizenship and the right to vote.

MAY 2, 1932: Montana's Glacier National Park and Canada's Waterton Lakes National Park combine to make the world's first International Peace Park.

AUGUST 5, 1949: A team of 15 wildland firefighters, called smokejumpers, parachute from a military aircraft to battle the massive Mann Gulch wildfire. Only three of them survive.

MAY 1951: The first Miles City Bucking Horse Sale is held. This annual auction of rodeo stock is now a major annual event.

AUGUST 17 1959: An earthquake strikes southwestern Montana, killing 28 people and creating a 6-mile long lake.

MAY 1, 1993: Charley Pride, who once played baseball in Helena, joins the Grand Ole Opry, becoming the first black Opry regular in the show's long history.

2003: 19-year-old Christopher Paolini becomes a best-selling author with his dragon novel *Eragon*.

KEY FACTS

CAPITAL
Helena

LARGEST CITIES
Billings
Missoula
Great Falls

BIRD
Western meadowlark

NAMED FOR
The Spanish word for "mountains"

STATEHOOD DATE
November 8, 1889

STATEHOOD ORDER
41

FLOWER
Bitterroot

POSTAL CODE
MT

REGION
Rocky Mountain

MAIN TIME ZONE
Mountain Standard

TREE
Ponderosa pine

"GOLD AND SILVER"

MARLON BRANDO
1924–2004
This legendary method actor, star of *On the Waterfront* and *The Godfather*, was born in Omaha.

RED CLOUD
1822–1909
This Nebraska-born Lakota chief helped protect native lands from government takeover.

JANICE N. HARRINGTON
b.1956
This award-winning author wrote about her childhood experience of moving from Alabama to Nebraska in her picture book *Going North*.

ANDY RODDICK
B.1982
Omaha was the starting point for champion tennis player "A-Rod."

NEBRASKA

SOUTH DAKOTA

THE NEBRASKA NATIONAL FOREST
includes the 20,000-acre Bessey Nursery—the largest hand-planted forest in the U.S.

THE AGATE FOSSIL BEDS
are rich with fossils of long-extinct animals like the carnivorous bear dog.

SCOTTS BLUFF
Rock climbers beware! The crumbly clay of this 800-foot-tall landmark makes an ascent very dangerous.

BLUE AGATE
Some believe the official state gem has a calming effect that can help public speakers.

THE PONY EXPRESS
used a relay system to pass mail from rider to rider, from Missouri to California.

MONOWI
The sole resident of this town is also its mayor, librarian, and bartender!

NIOBRARA STATE PARK
Float Nebraska's longest river by canoe, tube, kayak, or raft.

CHIMNEY ROCK
This was a vital landmark to Native Americans and those traveling the Oregon and Mormon trails.

DOWSE SOD HOUSE
Early settlers built homes out of turf—not wood—because trees and stones were rare on the prairies.

PRESTON McDANIELS
The illustrator of *A Perfect Snowman* lives in Aurora.

PIONEERING PILOT
Evelyn Sharp, from Ord, made a living as a barnstormer, performing aerial stunts.

WYOMING

PANORAMA POINT
To visit Nebraska's highest point you must pass through a bison range!

 UNION PACIFIC

AIR MAIL

AIRMAIL FLIGHT
The first nighttime airmail flight, in 1921, flew between North Platte and Omaha.

BAILEY YARD
The world's largest train yard can repair up to 20 cars an hour.

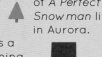

JOHNNY CARSON
1925–2005
The Emmy-winning host of *The Tonight Show* made his TV debut in Omaha—interviewing pigeons!

EVELYN SHARP
1919–1944
At 15, this Ord-raised pioneer of women's aviation became the youngest female pilot in the nation.

BILLIONS OF BUGS
Terrifying swarms of grasshoppers ate farmers' entire crops—and even their clothes—in the mid-1800s.

PIONEER VILLAGE
At this Minden museum you can see some 100 early tractors, among other historical curiosities.

WILLA CATHER
This Pulitzer Prize winner wrote novels about life on the Great Plains in the 1800s. Her childhood home is in Red Cloud.

HASTINGS MUSEUM
Kool-Aid was born in Hastings, with the original name "Fruit Smack!" Find out more at this museum.

COLORADO

KANSAS

WELCOME TO THE CORNHUSKER STATE

If you have ever met a Nebraskan, then you will know that the warmhearted people of this Midwest state are part of what makes it so special. Famous Nebraskans include performers such as Marlon Brando and Fred Astaire; writers such as Willa Cather and Raymond Chandler; the 38th president, Gerald Ford; and many more notable figures: athletes, scientists, educators . . . and even fictional characters, like the Wizard of Oz!

Nebraska's natural beauty can be seen in landmarks such as Chimney Rock—the 325-foot-tall geological wonder that has served as an important landmark for travelers throughout history—and the Bessey Nursery—the nation's largest hand-planted forest! In 1872 J. Sterling Morton proposed a holiday to promote the planting of trees in Nebraska. On the first "Arbor Day," about one million trees were planted, and today, the whole nation has adopted Nebraska's green-thumbed holiday with enthusiasm and pride.

MOMENTS TO REMEMBER

MAY 20, 1862: The Homestead Act allows any American to claim up to 160 acres of federal land—for free. As a result, many settlers head to Nebraska.

APRIL 10, 1872: Newspaper editor and nature lover J. Sterling Morton's dream of an Arbor Day comes true: more than a million trees are planted in a day!

MAY 12, 1879: Ponca chief Standing Bear wins an important court case, where a federal judge recognizes the right of Native Americans to legal protection under the constitution.

JANUARY 12, 1888: During one of Nebraska's most punishing blizzards, 19-year-old teacher Minnie Freeman links her 13 students together with twine to lead them safely home from school.

FEBRUARY 22, 1921: Pilot Jack Knight makes the U.S.'s first nighttime airmail flight, following a path of bonfires lit by farmers.

DECEMBER 10, 1958: After studying eye color and bread mold, Wahoo-born George Beadle is awarded a Nobel Prize for his genetics research.

JANUARY 22, 1997: The Nebraska Cornhuskers make college football history by winning their third national championship in four years.

SEPTEMBER 6, 2003: Omaha-born tennis star Andy Roddick wins the U.S. Open.

JANUARY 2005: A. LaFaye wins the Scott O'Dell award for *Worth*, a novel about the Orphan Train set in 1870s Nebraska.

JUNE 25, 2006: The "Wizard of Omaha," billionaire businessman Warren Buffett pledges history's largest charitable donation to the Gates Foundation.

CORNHUSKER STATE
The state nickname honors the University of Nebraska's Lincoln football team.

NEBRASKA STATE CAPITOL
The state house is topped with a 19-foot-tall statue, *The Sower*, who tosses seeds into the wind.

OMAHA

BELLEVUE

LINCOLN

FRED ASTAIRE
Born in Omaha, this tap-dancing star started young, performing with his sister, Adele, when he was only seven.

THE DURHAM MUSEUM
has its home in Omaha's Art Deco Union Station.

THE WORLD'S LARGEST BALL OF STAMPS
is a 600-pound ball made of 4,655,000 postage stamps on display in Boys Town.

IOWA

WIND POWER
Nebraska's flat landscape makes for a windy state—perfect for windmills!

HOMESTEAD NATIONAL MONUMENT
Hear stories of some of the nearly 4 million homesteaders who settled the U.S. over 123 years.

MISSOURI

NATIONAL MUSEUM OF ROLLER SKATING
The first roller skates didn't change direction—you could only skate forward!

KEY FACTS

CAPITAL
Lincoln

LARGEST CITIES
Omaha
Lincoln
Bellevue

BIRD
Western meadowlark

NAMED FOR
The Otoe Indian words meaning "flat water"

STATEHOOD DATE
March 1, 1867

STATEHOOD ORDER
37

FLOWER
Goldenrod

POSTAL CODE
NE

REGION
Midwest

MAIN TIME ZONE
Central

TREE
Cottonwood

"EQUALITY BEFORE THE LAW"

OREGON

TONY MENDEZ
b.1940
Born in Eureka, Mendez designed gadgets for the CIA and rescued six diplomats from Iran in 1980. He was played by Ben Affleck in the 2012 movie *Argo*.

WAYNE NEWTON
b.1942
Also known as Mr. Las Vegas, this singer is one of the most well-known entertainers there.

BRADLEY WATCH
Reno-born Paralympic swimmer Brad Snyder has a watch for the blind named after him.

CALIFORNIA

PHANTOM STALLION BOOKS
The horses of Terri Farley's best-selling series are based on the wild horses of the Calico Mountains.

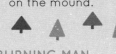

FLY GEYSER
This strange-looking geyser spouts boiling-hot water. It is constantly growing because minerals from the water build up on the mound.

BURNING MAN
A 50-foot figure is burned every year in the Black Rock Desert's annual festival.

PYRAMID LAKE
Pelicans and cutthroat trout can be found in this beautiful lake on a Paiute reservation.

BASQUE FESTIVAL
Traditional competitions at Elko's annual celebration include wood chopping, sheep hooking, and high-kick dancing.

NE

SARAH WINNEMUCCA
1844–1891
Born in Humboldt Sink, this Native American activist and writer established a school for Paiute students.

RENO

CARSON CITY

DUCK DECOYS
In 1924 nearly a dozen 2,000-year-old duck models were found in Lovelock Cave. They were probably used by hunters to attract real ducks.

WESTERN SKINK
This lizard, found in the Great Basin Desert, has a blue tail that can snap off if caught!

BERLIN-ICHTHYOSAUR STATE PARK
These ancient marine reptiles swam through Nevada 225 million years ago! See their fossils here.

GREAT BASIN NATIONAL PARK
You can see the Milky Way from here, a favorite spot for stargazers.

NEVADA STATE CAPITOL
A time capsule was buried under the capitol's cornerstone when it was built in 1870.

DAT SO LA LEE
This celebrated Native American Washoe basket weaver lived in Carson City.

THE V&T RAILROAD
connected the Comstock Lode silver mines in Virginia City to Carson City.

THE COMSTOCK LODE
This silver deposit under Mount Davidson has produced huge amounts of silver since 1859.

LAKE TAHOE
The largest alpine lake in the country, near Carson City, is a great spot for stand-up paddle boarding.

THE CARSON VALLEY
was named for legendary explorer and mountain man Kit Carson.

RHYOLITE GHOST TOWN
This abandoned gold mining town near Beatty now boasts beautiful ruins and outsider art.

MICHAEL HEIZER
This "land artist" has been working on *City*—an enormous sculpture in Garden Valley—for more than 40 years!

AREA 51
is a top-secret military base where the F-117 Nighthawk and other stealth planes were developed.

UTAH

DEVILS HOLE
The endangered pupfish lives in the hot underground water-filled caves of Death Valley.

LAKE MEAD
This man-made lake is surrounded by desert where some plants, such as the Joshua tree, thrive, despite the low rainfall.

LAS VEGAS

ANDRE AGASSI
b.1970
This Grand Slam champion and Olympic gold medalist started playing tennis in Las Vegas.

PAT NIXON
1912–1993
Passionate about education, volunteering, and the arts, this First Lady was born in Ely.

SAMMY DAVIS, JR.
1925–1990
A winner of the Grammy Lifetime Achievement Award, this performer was a Las Vegas star.

HENDERSON

ARIZONA

NEVADA

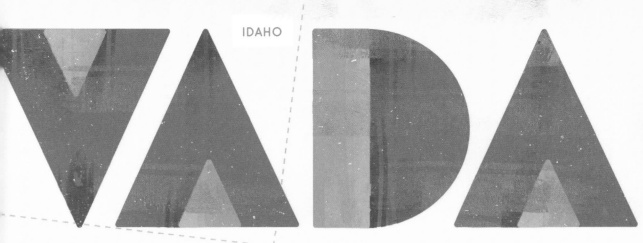

WELCOME TO THE SILVER STATE

nevada's nickname comes from the silver rush of the mid-1800s, when there was such an abundance of the precious metal that you could shovel it right off the ground! These days, Nevada is still a top producer of silver, along with gold, livestock, onions . . . and the all-you-can-eat buffet, which began in Las Vegas in the 1940s!

The 36th state is a place of interesting contradictions: while it is the seventh-largest state, it is also among the least populated for its size. And while Las Vegas is one of the top tourist destinations in the entire world, with some 41 million people stopping by each year, just 150 miles north is Area 51, a top-secret air force base where NO visitors are allowed.

So whether you come to experience the vast solitude of the open desert, the heights of the snowy mountains, or the thrill and crush of people on the 4-mile-long Las Vegas Strip, just make sure you visit!

MOMENTS TO REMEMBER

225 MILLION YEARS AGO: Prehistoric marine reptiles such as the ichthyosaur swim in the ocean that covers Nevada.

JUNE 1859: The Comstock Lode, the richest-known deposit of silver in the country, is discovered. In its lifetime, it produced (in today's prices) $4.5 billion of silver!

MARCH 1, 1869: Nevada is the first state to ratify the 15th Amendment, giving African American men the right to vote.

MARCH 1, 1936: The Hoover Dam is completed two years ahead of schedule; over the course of five years 21,000 men worked on the dam.

JANUARY 27, 1951: Nuclear weapons testing begins at the Nevada Test Site when a 1-kiloton nuclear device is dropped on Frenchman Flat.

1960: Frank Sinatra, Dean Martin, and Sammy Davis, Jr., take part in the original *Ocean's 11* movie, set in Las Vegas.

2005: Las Vegas–born Paralympic snowboarder Amy Purdy co-founds Adaptive Action Sports, helping those with disabilities take part in snowboarding, skateboarding, and other sports.

SEPTEMBER 2009: Junior astronomers stay up late for the Great Basin's first annual Astronomy Festival.

APRIL 18, 2010: Suzanne Morgan Williams wins the National Cowboy & Western Heritage Award for her novel *Bull Rider*.

DESERT BIGHORN SHEEP
The horns of the state animal never stop growing: male horns can weigh as much as 30 pounds!

RED ROCK CANYON
Outstanding hiking and picnicking await just 17 miles from the Vegas Strip.

LAS VEGAS STRIP
With its bright lights, glamorous casinos, and live shows, Vegas is known as the "Entertainment Capital of the World."

HOOVER DAM
You could pave a highway from San Francisco to New York with all the concrete used in this famous Colorado River dam, near Boulder City.

PINBALL HALL OF FAME
Grab your quarters and play more than 200 classic games; all proceeds go to charity.

KEY FACTS

CAPITAL
Carson City

LARGEST CITIES
Las Vegas
Henderson
Reno

BIRD
Mountain bluebird

NAMED FOR
The Spanish word for "snowy," referring to the mountains in the west

STATEHOOD DATE
October 31, 1864

STATEHOOD ORDER
36

FLOWER
Sagebrush

POSTAL CODE
NV

REGION
Southwest

MAIN TIME ZONE
Pacific

TREE
Single-leaf pinyon

"ALL FOR OUR COUNTRY"

CANADA

MAINE

VERMONT

MASSACHUSETTS

SKIING
is the state sport, and New Hampshire is the only state that offers ski jumping as a high school sport!

THE CANNON MOUNTAIN AERIAL TRAMWAY
Enjoy the view from this cable car, which whizzes up the mountain to 4,080 feet.

FIDDLEHEAD FERNS
flourish for a short spring season in the rich river soil of towns like Gorham.

THE OLD MAN OF THE MOUNTAIN
was a series of cliff ledges that looked like a face. It collapsed in 2003 but still exists on the state quarter!

THE FLUME GORGE
Here you can follow a boardwalk that winds between huge granite walls and past waterfalls.

CORNISH-WINDSOR BRIDGE
At 449 feet long, this is the longest 19th-century covered bridge in America.

LAKE WINNIPESAUKEE
Here the *Sophie C.*, the U.S.'s oldest floating post office, carries mail to the lake's islands.

MOUNT WASHINGTON
is 6,288 feet tall and the highest mountain in the northeast.

WHITE MOUNTAIN NATIONAL FOREST
Forests cover more than 80% of New Hampshire's landscape.

THE CHINOOK TRAIL
This route is named after Arthur Walden's famous mastiff-husky cross, Chinook, from which he bred other sled dogs.

McAULIFFE-SHEPARD DISCOVERY CENTER
This science museum is dedicated to the high school teacher chosen to be the first American in space.

NEW HAMPSHIRE STATE CAPITOL
Fittingly, the state house of the Granite State is built from local granite.

SAINT-GAUDENS HISTORIC SITE
This site preserves the home of one of the country's top sculptors. In 1907 he designed the $20 gold coin.

CONCORD COACHES
These 1800s wagons were pulled by horses that were swapped every 10–15 miles.

CONCORD

THE MEETINGHOUSE BELL
in historic Hancock was made by Revolutionary War hero Paul Revere.

MANCHESTER

CARLETON ELLIS
This chemist, born in Keene, invented better-tasting margarine and a new type of paint remover.

THE MACDOWELL COLONY
is a haven for artists. Lunch is delivered to each studio door in picnic baskets to make sure that the workers aren't disturbed!

NASHUA

ANDRES INSTITUTE OF ART
This outdoor museum in Brookline has some 75 sculptures nestled along walking trails.

AMERICA'S STONEHENGE
These mysterious stone structures may be an ancient calendar, a colonial root cellar, or a tourist-trapping hoax!

KEY FACTS

CAPITAL
Concord

LARGEST CITIES
Manchester
Nashua
Concord

BIRD
Purple finch

NAMED FOR
Hampshire, England

STATEHOOD DATE
June 21, 1788

STATEHOOD ORDER
9

FLOWER
Purple lilac

POSTAL CODE
NH

REGION
New England

MAIN TIME ZONE
Eastern

TREE
White birch

"LIVE FREE OR DIE"

BODE MILLER
b.1977
The winner of a record-breaking six Olympic medals first donned skis in Franconia.

TOMIE DEPAOLA
b.1934
The author and illustrator of some 200 books, including *Strega Nona*, lives in New London.

AMOSKEAG MILLYARD
In the 1800s the Amoskeag Company was the largest cotton producer in the world. Mill girls made $2 a week working 14-hour days.

DEKA'S ARM
This robotic arm, from Manchester-based company DEKA, is so smart it can hold a grape!

HART'S TURKEY FARM
boasts more than 60 different turkey items on its menu . . . it's Thanksgiving every day!

GREAT BAY

BLACK JACK MARINERS
Black sailors made up 25% of some crews in the 1800s, but many stories are lost. Find out more on the Portsmouth Black Heritage Trail.

PISCATAQUA RIVER
Tugboats guide tankers up the U.S.'s third-fastest tidal river.

GUNDALOWS
are flat-bottomed barges once common in New England. The replica *Piscataqua* is based in Portsmouth.

GREAT BAY ESTUARY
The waters here are rich in horseshoe crabs.

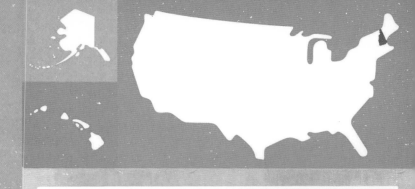

WELCOME TO THE GRANITE STATE

Where will you find some of the largest ski mountains on the East Coast, the shortest ocean coastline, and buckets and buckets of sweet maple syrup? You've got it: New Hampshire!

The 9th state is a natural wonderland, boasting stunning scenery and outdoor adventures all year round. Skiing is a major draw, of course: if the dazzling slopes of Cannon Mountain are good enough for Olympic talents Bode Miller and Leanne Smith, they should be good enough for you!

You'll want to stick around come spring, when the sun comes out, and hundreds of frozen waterfalls start to melt. And, of course, spring is the season for hunting the elusive fiddlehead fern, which, for generations, has been turned into scrumptious buttery dishes. With famous fall foliage and spectacular summers, every season is worth exploring in New Hampshire, so get out and enjoy the great Granite State!

JANUARY 5, 1776: New Hampshire is the first state to declare independence from Britain—six months before the Declaration of Independence is signed.

DECEMBER 30, 1828: Around 400 mill girls walk out of the Dover Cotton Factory, becoming the first U.S. women to strike for better working conditions.

APRIL 9, 1833: The U.S.'s first free public library is founded in Peterborough.

MARCH 1870: New Hampshire's first female lawyer, Marilla Ricker, is the state's first woman to attempt to vote; she keeps trying for the next 50 years.

1907: Edward and Marian MacDowell found the MacDowell Colony, the U.S.'s first artists' colony.

1922: One of the moon's craters is named after the inventor, engineer, and astronomer Ambrose Swasey, who was born in Exeter.

MARCH 1926: Adventurer Arthur Walden, along with his team of dogs, is the first musher to reach the summit of Mount Washington.

MAY 5, 1961: Aboard the *Freedom 7*, Alan Shepard is the first American in space. Ten years later, he is the first American to play golf on the moon.

1989: Dean Kamen founds FIRST, a youth organization that operates the FIRST robotics competition, designed to inspire students in engineering. In 2014 it gives out $20 million in college scholarships.

JANUARY 10, 2011: Children's librarians award New London resident Tomie dePaola the Laura Ingalls Wilder Award for his lifetime contribution to American children's literature.

KEN BURNS
b.1953
This award-winning documentary director lives in Walpole.

DEAN KAMEN
b.1951
The entrepreneurial inventor of the Segway lives in Bedford.

ED MOODY
c.1911–1994
This legendary Tamworth sled maker has crafted dog sleds for mushers from Alaska to Japan.

SETH MEYERS
b.1973
This Emmy-winning *Saturday Night Live* funnyman grew up in Bedford.

New Hampshire

ATLANTIC OCEAN

CLARA BARTON
1821–1912
Before founding the American Red Cross, Barton opened a school in Bordentown.

WILLIAM CARLOS WILLIAMS
1883–1963
Born in Rutherford, Williams was a doctor and a modernist poet. He was awarded a Pulitzer Prize after his death.

PENNSYLVANIA

NEW JERSEY STATE CAPITOL
NJ schoolkids raised money to pay for the 48,000 pieces of gold leaf on the capitol building's dome—$1 for each piece!

NEW JERSEY STATE MUSEUM
features a version of Alexander Calder's sculpture *El Sol Rojo*, created for the 1968 Olympic Games.

BORDENTOWN
American Red Cross founder Clara Barton opened the state's first free school here.

CAMDEN

PAUL ROBESON
1898–1976
Born in Princeton, Robeson was an actor and singer who became involved in the civil rights movement.

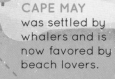

BRUCE SPRINGSTEEN
b.1949
"The Boss" draws on his New Jersey roots to inspire his music, for which he has won 20 Grammys.

GLOWING ROCKS
The Rainbow Tunnel at the Sterling Hill Mining Museum houses huge fluorescent minerals.

PATERSON

NEWARK

JERSEY CITY

NEW YORK

KID FROM RED BANK
The Count Basie Theatre in Red Bank was named after the great jazz pianist William "Count" Basie.

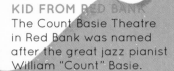

ASBURY PARK
The carousel in Asbury Park was built in the 1920s.

WOLF WATCH
Lucky visitors to the Lakota Wolf Preserve will hear a happy, or haunting, howl!

LIVIN' ON A PRAYER
Perth Amboy is the birthplace of Jon Bon Jovi.

The lighthouse at Sandy Hook has served sailors since the 1700s.

SANDY HOOK

FARM HAND
Plough a field like an 18th-century pro at Howell Living History Farm.

SHARK ATTACK!
The Matawan Creek shark attacks served as inspiration for the movie *Jaws*.

TRENTON

U.S. NAVY

LAND OF THE LOST
In Farmingdale, you can visit a collection of dinosaurs made from old car parts.

BLIMP BASE
During WWI the U.S. Navy sent out airships from Lakehurst to patrol for submarines.

WIGWAM
The Lenni Lenape people, New Jersey's native inhabitants, made wigwams from birch bark.

ATLANTIC CANDY
Legend has it that saltwater taffy was created when a storm flooded an Atlantic City candy store in 1883.

CAMDEN CHILDREN'S GARDEN

HADROSAURUS HUZZAH
In 1858, geologist William Foulke discovers America's first near-complete dinosaur skeleton.

LUCY THE ELEPHANT
In 1881 the U.S. Patent Office granted inventor James Lafferty the right to make animal-shaped buildings for 17 years. His first creation, Lucy, still stands in Margate, Atlantic City.

BRAINY BLUEBERRIES
NJ's tasty state fruit helps prevent memory loss!

DELAWARE

CAPE MAY
was settled by whalers and is now favored by beach lovers.

DELAWARE BAY

MARBLE CHAMPIONSHIPS
Marble shooters compete for college scholarships and more at the National Marbles Tournament in Wildwood!

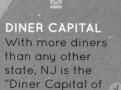

HEAVY METAL
The George Washington Bridge contains 43,000 tons of steel!

DINER CAPITAL
With more diners than any other state, NJ is the "Diner Capital of the World"!

THE DOCTOR POET
Rutherford was long home to William Carlos Williams, author of "The Red Wheelbarrow."

BRIGHT IDEA
In West Orange you can visit inventor Thomas Edison's lab and house.

BASEBALL BATTLES
Many believe that organized baseball started in NJ in 1846.

JUDY BLUME
b.1938
This best-selling, award-winning author for children and teens spent her childhood in Elizabeth.

THOMAS EDISON
1847–1931
Inventor of the lightbulb and motion-picture camera, Edison was known as the "Wizard of Menlo Park" (the site of his laboratory).

NEW JERSEY

WELCOME TO THE GARDEN STATE

ATLANTIC OCEAN

With a nickname like the Garden State, it's no surprise that New Jersey has more than 10,000 farms and produces an incredible 100 varieties of fruits and vegetables, including the famous Jersey blueberries, peaches, and cranberries. In fact, cranberries have been harvested in New Jersey since the 1500s when Native Americans used these versatile berries, or ibimi, to make food, dyes, and medicines.

Whereas the Lenni Lenape people would have picked this tart superfruit by hand, today's cranberry bogs are flooded to make the ripe berries float to the top, where they are skimmed off by special machines. Come October, you can visit many a New Jersey farm to see this strange harvesting method for yourself.

New Jersey is the most densely populated state in the country and, as the third state in the Union, it has a rich cultural history, as well as many beautiful landscapes—mountains, seashores, and forests.

MOMENTS TO REMEMBER

DECEMBER 26, 1776: George Washington crosses the Delaware River and enters the Battle of Trenton, one of the 100 battles fought in NJ during the Revolutionary War.

JUNE 28, 1778: Mary Ludwig, nicknamed Molly Pitcher, carries pitchers of water to soldiers during the Battle of Monmouth. Legend has it that she also takes part in the fighting, loading cannons, and has a near miss when an enemy cannonball flies between her legs and rips through her skirt.

NOVEMBER 6, 1869: The first intercollegiate football game (Rutgers v. Princeton) is played in New Brunswick.

1870: The world's first boardwalk is built in Atlantic City. It remains the longest on Earth—stretching for 6 miles.

1876: The inventor Thomas Edison opens his research laboratory in Menlo Park.

OCTOBER 1879: Thomas Edison invents one of the world's first lightbulbs.

FEBRUARY 1913: Silk workers in Paterson begin a six-month-long strike for better working conditions.

JUNE 6, 1933: The first drive-in movie theater in the country opens in Camden, NJ.

1947: Larry Doby, from Paterson, becomes the second African American to play Major League Baseball.

1965: The "Sultan of Swoon" Frank Sinatra, born in Hoboken, receives a Grammy Lifetime Achievement Award.

KEY FACTS

CAPITAL
Trenton

LARGEST CITIES
Newark
Jersey City
Paterson

BIRD
Eastern goldfinch

NAMED FOR
The island of Jersey in the English Channel

STATEHOOD DATE
December 18, 1787

STATEHOOD ORDER
3

FLOWER
Violet

POSTAL CODE
NJ

REGION
Mid-Atlantic

MAIN TIME ZONE
Eastern

TREE
Red oak

"LIBERTY AND PROSPERITY"

JEFF BEZOS
B.1964
The founder of Amazon was born in Albuquerque and loved computers as a kid.

NEIL PATRICK HARRIS
b.1973
A Ruidoso native, this Tony Award winner's first big hit was playing a teenage doctor on TV.

FRANCISCO VÁZQUEZ DE CORONADO
c.1510–1554
In search of the Seven Golden Cities of Cibola, this Spanish noble explored New Mexico.

COLORADO

NEW MEXICO STATE CAPITOL
The glass skylight that tops the Santa Fe Roundhouse displays a Native American basket weaving pattern.

PET PARADE
In the annual *Desfile de Los Niños*, about 2,000 kids parade with their pets, in costume!

UTAH

NAVAJO NATION
This is the country's largest Native American territory, covering part of Arizona, Utah, and New Mexico. The squash blossom necklace is an important type of Navajo jewelry.

AZTEC RUINS NATIONAL MONUMENT
Explore a 900-year-old settlement with over 400 rooms! The ruins were named mistakenly in the 1920s—they are not actually Aztec.

GEORGIA O'KEEFFE MUSEUM
This artist painted flowers and southwestern landscapes even after her eyesight failed in her later years.

RA PAULETTE CAVES
This self-taught sculptor carves elaborate caves into the cliffs around San Jose.

ARIZONA

THE ENCHANTED MESA
This jutting sandstone rock rises 430 feet above the surrounding landscape.

AEOLIAN HARP
In Budaghers you'll find a 3,000-pound harp that is played by the wind!

WHEELWRIGHT MUSEUM OF THE AMERICAN INDIAN
This museum was set up in the 1930s to showcase Navajo art.

OKLAHOMA

MINING MUSEUM
Visit the only uranium mining museum in the world, in Grants.

LAGUNA PUEBLO
This Native American tribe is famous for its pottery.

PETROGLYPH NATIONAL MONUMENT
The Pueblo people made petroglyphs by chiseling the rock. Here you'll find more ancient carvings than almost anywhere else in the country.

SANTA FE

RIO RANCHO

ALBUQUERQUE BALLOON FIESTA
Hot-air balloons are usually about 7 stories tall and use 90,000 cubic feet of heated air!

ALBUQUERQUE

LIGHTNING FIELD
Walter De Maria's outdoor sculpture has 400 steel poles that capture lightning in a storm!

TRINITY ATOMIC BOMB SITE
Twice a year visitors can tour the site where the first nuclear explosion made a half-mile-wide crater in 1945.

SADIE ORCHARD
This "wild woman of the West" was one of few female stagecoach owners and drivers.

RATTLESNAKE MUSEUM
This museum has the world's largest collection of different species of live rattlesnakes!

SACAGAWEA MODEL
While studying at the University of New Mexico, Shoshone woman Randy'L Teton posed as Sacagawea for the millennium $1 coin.

HATCH CHILI FESTIVAL
The town of Hatch, the "Chili Capital of the World," hosts an annual festival. The state grows more than 50,000 tons of chilies a year!

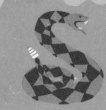

THE ROSWELL UFO MUSEUM
explores all things extraterrestrial: crop circles, alien abductions, and, of course, the Roswell crash.

GILA CLIFF DWELLINGS
Mummified bodies and handprints of the 13th-century Puebloan builders have been discovered here.

WHITE SANDS NATIONAL MONUMENT
These stunning white sand dunes are made of gypsum crystals, which are used in blackboard chalk.

SIDNEY GUTIERREZ
b.1951
The first Hispanic American astronaut to command a space flight logged 488 space hours and lives in Albuquerque.

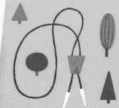

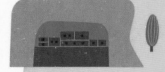

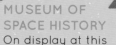
LAS CRUCES

MUSEUM OF SPACE HISTORY
On display at this Alamogordo museum is the *Little Joe II* rocket, which was used in tests for the Apollo missions.

THE BOLO TIE
The state's official tie—a piece of leather with metal tips—may originate in Zuni, Hopi, or Navajo traditions.

THE NEW MEXICO SPADEFOOT TOAD
smells like peanuts when it is handled!

CARLSBAD CAVERNS
In 1898 16-year-old Jim White discovered these huge caves, made when sulfuric acid dissolved the surrounding rock.

MEXICO

WELCOME TO THE LAND OF ENCHANTMENT

*I*f you know anything about the Southwest, you probably know that much of it is covered by a vast, dry desert. So it will be no surprise to you that New Mexico has the lowest water-to-land ratio of all 50 states: lakes and rivers cover just 0.002% of it!

But just because water is scarce it doesn't mean the wildlife or history is. Carlsbad Caverns in the Guadalupe Mountains is home to tens of thousands of bats that swoop down each evening in search of dinner. And Clayton Lake State Park is a destination for dinosaur detectives, with a fossilized track of 100-million-year-old dinosaur footprints! For budding archaeologists, New Mexico offers around 25,000 ancient Ancestral Puebloans and Hisatsinom sites, such as the magnificent sandstone ruins found in the Chaco Culture National Historical Park.

Today, New Mexicans are proud of their diverse roots and modern advancements in the aerospace, science, and engineering industries . . . as well as their unique Hatch chile culinary delights!

NEW MEXICO

TEXAS

MOMENTS TO REMEMBER

1610: Santa Fe is founded by the Spanish. Its original name is a bit of a mouthful: *La Villa Real de la Santa Fé de San Francisco de Asis* ("Royal City of the Holy Faith of St. Francis of Assisi").
SEPTEMBER 16, 1712: The first Santa Fe Fiesta is held. The fiesta still takes place today—a highlight is the burning of Zozobra, where "Old Man Gloom" is set alight to make way for a new, better year.
JULY 16, 1945: Deep in the New Mexico desert, the world's first nuclear device was exploded by the U.S. army as part of the Manhattan Project (which produced the first atomic bombs during WWII).
JULY 4, 1947: An alien UFO (or maybe just a weather balloon) crash-lands near Roswell.
MARCH 31, 1950: The town of Hot Springs changes its name to "Truth or Consequences" as part of a publicity scheme for a popular radio show.
APRIL 8, 1972: The first International Balloon Fiesta is held in Albuquerque. Today, the festival takes place every October with over 500 hot-air balloons a year, making it the world's largest balloon event.
SEPTEMBER 2, 1972: Swimmer Cathy Carr bags two golds at the Munich Olympics, becoming New Mexico's first Olympic gold medal swimmer.
1996: New Mexico's state question, "Red or Green?" becomes official. It refers to whether you prefer red or green chile with your meal.
JANUARY 28, 2013: Author Benjamin Alire Sáenz wins the Pura Belpré Award and a Printz Honor for his book *Aristotle and Dante Discover the Secrets of the Universe.*

KEY FACTS

CAPITAL
Santa Fe

LARGEST CITIES
Albuquerque
Las Cruces
Rio Rancho

BIRD
Greater
roadrunner

NAMED FOR
Mexico, by the Spanish

STATEHOOD DATE
January 6, 1912

STATEHOOD ORDER
47

FLOWER
Soaptree
yucca

POSTAL CODE
NM

REGION
Southwest

TIME ZONE
Mountain

TREE
Pinyon
pine

BENJAMIN ALIRE SÁENZ
b.1954
Born in Las Cruces, this award winner was named one of the "Fifty Most Inspiring Authors in the World."

GEORGIA O'KEEFFE
1887–1986
A celebrated painter of flowers, O'Keeffe was inspired by, and lived in, Abiquiú.

"IT GROWS AS IT GOES"

NEW YORK

DEREK JETER
b.1974
Jeter's 20-year baseball career with the New York Yankees included five World Series championships.

LENA DUNHAM
b.1986
NYC-born Dunham is an Emmy Award–winning writer, director, producer, and actress.

JOHN D. ROCKEFELLER
1839–1937
Rockefeller made a huge fortune in the oil industry. He spent his later life giving money to many charities.

CANADA
You may not cross the border into Canada with dog food, potatoes, or minnows!

LAKE ONTARIO

ELIZABETH CADY STANTON
helped break barriers at the first women's suffrage convention, held in Seneca Falls.

NIAGARA FALLS
Ten tightrope walkers have crossed the 165-foot-tall waterfalls. One cooked an omelet halfway across!

ROCHESTER

WINGS OF PROGRESS
The four aluminum wings of Rochester's Times Square Building weigh 12,000 pounds each!

CANADA

WELCOME TO THE EMPIRE STATE

LAKE ERIE

BUFFALO
is famous for its tasty chicken wings.

THE FINGER LAKES
are made up of 11 long, thin lakes.

IROQUOIS ATHLETICS
An early form of lacrosse was played by the Iroquois nations.

New York was America's capital before it was a nation, and still a British colony. After the Americans won their independence, George Washington—the first president—was sworn in on the steps of New York City's Federal Hall.

With a population of more than 8 million, New York City is the largest city by far in the country. In fact, "the City that Never Sleeps" has more people than 40 of the U.S.'s 50 states! This mighty metropolis is one of the only places where the price of a slice of pizza and the cost of a single ride on the subway have been equal for over 50 years!

One visit is all it takes to fall in love with this historic, culture-filled state—from the jaw-dropping awesomeness of Niagara Falls or the rugged beauty of the Adirondacks to the cheesecake, hot dogs, and clam chowder of the Big Apple.

I LOVE LUCY
Dress up like comedian Lucille Ball and act out scenes from her hit show at the Desilu Studios in Jamestown.

PENNSYLVANIA

KEY FACTS

CAPITAL
Albany

LARGEST CITIES
New York City
Buffalo
Rochester

BIRD
Bluebird

FLOWER
Rose

NAMED FOR
The 17th-century English Duke of York

STATEHOOD DATE
July 26, 1788

STATEHOOD ORDER
11

POSTAL CODE
NY

REGION
Mid-Atlantic

MAIN TIME ZONE
Eastern

TREE
Sugar maple

"EVER UPWARD"

FRANKLIN AND ELEANOR ROOSEVELT
1882–1945 • 1884–1962
The Roosevelts were raised and educated in New York before becoming president and First Lady.

ALL ABOUT APPLES
New York is big on apples: it grows the most of any state after Washington.

CHATEAUGUAY RIVER
Trout are plentiful here, in one of New York's many rivers.

DUTCH HISTORY
The Dutch settled here in 1624.

TICONDEROGA
Lead Mountain, near Ticonderoga, has been mined for pencil lead since 1815.

VERMONT

WRESTLING HALL OF FAME
This Amsterdam museum celebrates the outrageous acrobatics of many theatrical mat men.

BOLDT CASTLE
Multimillionaire George Boldt began building this castle in 1900 but stopped when his wife died in 1904.

ADIRONDACK MOUNTAINS
When leaves take a break from photosynthesizing in the fall, nature lovers celebrate the colorful result.

ERIE CANAL
In the 1800s horses pulled freighters full of produce along this 363-mile canal.

SYRACUSE
experiences the highest average snowfall of any American city.

NEW YORK STATE CAPITOL
The "Million Dollar Staircase" in the capitol building has 77 stone faces, including those of Washington, Lincoln, and strangers from the street!

CHITTENANGO
The birthplace of the *Wizard of Oz* author L. Frank Baum has an actual yellow brick road!

COOPERSTOWN
is home to the National Baseball Hall of Fame and Museum.

ALBANY

SAGAN PLANET WALK
Walk to Mars in moments on this scale model of the solar system in Ithaca.

CATSKILL MOUNTAINS
Found here, the timber rattlesnake grows a new segment of rattle each time it sheds its skin.

WOODSTOCK
was one of the most famous music and arts festivals of the 20th century.

THE ALBANY SYMPHONY ORCHESTRA
has been making music since 1930.

CHINATOWN
One of the largest Chinese populations outside of Asia lives here.

BROADWAY
More than 1,500 theater performances are held here each year.

GUGGENHEIM MUSEUM
Frank Lloyd Wright made over 700 sketches of this famous building while designing it.

Theater District

SOJOURNER TRUTH
was one of America's best known antislavery and gender-equality speakers.

CONNECTICUT

MASSACHUSETTS

JIMMY FALLON
b.1974
Brooklyn-bred Fallon starred in *Saturday Night Live* and now hosts *The Tonight Show*.

STATUE OF LIBERTY
This huge sculpture was completed in 1886. Representing freedom, it has become an icon of New York and the U.S. as a whole.

LONG ISLAND SOUND

WORLD TRADE CENTER
The new Freedom Tower opened in 2014.

SUBWAY
NYC has 722 miles of subway track!

NEW YORK CITY

ATLANTIC OCEAN

MANHATTAN

CONEY ISLAND
has long been known for its seaside amusement parks.

NEW JERSEY

STATEN ISLAND

SEPTEMBER 10, 1609: Exploring for the Dutch, Englishman Henry Hudson sails a mighty river, and names it after himself!

JULY 8, 1779: General George Washington moves his Revolutionary War headquarters to West Point, which later becomes the United States Military Academy.

MARCH 15, 1820: Washington Irving publishes "The Legend of Sleepy Hollow," making Tarrytown "Headless Horseman" territory.

JULY 19–20, 1848: Votes for women! The first suffrage convention is held in Seneca Falls.

MAY 24, 1883: The Brooklyn Bridge opens and 21 elephants cross to test its strength!

JANUARY 1, 1892: "Give me your tired, your poor." The first 700 immigrants pass through Ellis Island immigration station.

APRIL 15, 1947: Batter up! Jackie Robinson starts on first base with the Brooklyn Dodgers, becoming the first African American to play Major League Baseball.

AUGUST 15–18, 1969: 400,000 people come together in the name of peace at the Woodstock festival.

SEPTEMBER 11, 2001: Tragedy strikes in New York City as the World Trade Center's twin towers are struck by terrorists. Many people lose their lives.

JOHN COLTRANE
1926–1967
The "Trane" grew up in High Point and became one of the world's most innovative saxophonists and jazz composers.

FRANCES O'ROARK DOWELL
b.1964
The award-winning author of *Dovey Coe* graduated from Wake Forest University.

INDIE ROCK
Merge Records has helped fans rock out to bands like Arcade Fire and the Mountain Goats.

SOCCER SUPERSTAR
Soccer star Mia Hamm started a bone marrow foundation in Chapel Hill in memory of her brother.

ANDY GRIFFITH
1926–2012
Born in Mount Airy, Griffith was an actor and singer best known for the sitcom *The Andy Griffith Show*.

BASKETBALL BATTLE
The rivalry between the Tar Heels and the Blue Devils is one of the most intense in sporting history.

SWEET POTATO SUPERSIGHT!
The vitamin A found in the state's most abundant crop helps keep your vision healthy.

NORTH CAROLINA STATE CAPITOL
The state capitol building was completed in 1840.

VIRGINIA

OLD FARMER'S BALL
Dance the Georgia Rang Tang and the Shoo-Fly Swing in Swannanoa.

GREENSBORO

RALEIGH

UNTO THESE HILLS
On summer evenings at the 2,800-seat Mountainside Theater, you can watch an outdoor drama of the story of the Cherokee people.

CHAPEL HILL

DOC WATSON
In Boone, fans decorate this local musician's statue with flowers.

NEED FOR SPEED
The NASCAR Hall of Fame celebrates the story of car racing.

TENNESSEE

MUSEUM OF ART
The *Cloud Chamber* sculpture in the Museum Park projects the sky outside onto the floor inside.

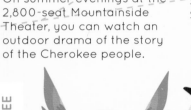

CHARLOTTE

BARNSTORMERS
Graffiti artists such as David Ellis have transformed these barns in Cameron.

NINA SIMONE
Tryon is the birthplace of the legendary pianist, singer, and civil rights spokesperson.

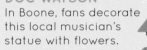

TOWN CREEK INDIAN MOUND
Arrowheads and other stone tools are some of the ancient Pee Dee treasures found here.

MICHAEL JORDAN
This basketball superstar moved from New York to Wilmington when he was a toddler.

NORTH 23 CAROLINA

JUDACULLA ROCK
Cherokee legend says a seven-fingered and seven-toed giant created the carvings in this soapstone boulder.

LI'L DAN, THE DRUMMER BOY
The artist and writer Romare Bearden, born in Charlotte, created this picture book about the Civil War.

THE NANTAHALA NATIONAL FOREST
is home to black bears, bobcats, and the highest waterfall east of the Rockies.

SOUTH CAROLINA

NORTH CAROLINA

MIA HAMM
b.1972
Before winning two Olympic gold medals, soccer star Hamm played for the North Carolina Tar Heels.

GERTRUDE BELLE ELION
1918–1999
A Nobel Prize winner for her work in pharmacology, Elion was a research professor at Duke University.

JOSEPH McNEIL
b.1942
In 1960 McNeil and three other black students sat at a "whites only" counter in Greensboro, protesting against racial segregation.

SUGAR RAY LEONARD

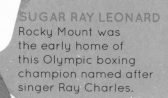

Rocky Mount was the early home of this Olympic boxing champion named after singer Ray Charles.

FIRST FLIGHT

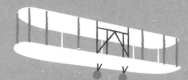

The Wright brothers took their bike smarts and invented a plane! Their first flight took place at Kill Devil Hills on the Outer Banks.

ROANOKE ISLAND & DARE MAINLAND

GRAVEYARD OF THE ATLANTIC

Many ships, like the USS *Monitor*, have been wrecked in these treacherous waters.

NORTHERN BEACHES

ALBEMARLE SOUND

CAPE HATTERAS

In 1999, preservationists moved this 208-foot-tall brick lighthouse half a mile!

HATTERAS ISLAND

THE EDENTON TEA PARTY

was a political protest of 1774 where 51 women vowed to give up tea and other British products to oppose British taxes.

PAMLICO SOUND

BANKER HORSES

Ocracoke Island is home to a breed of wild horse—the original horses may have swum to shore following a 1585 shipwreck!

OCRACOKE ISLAND

PLOTT HOUNDS

Courageous and determined, these dogs were first bred in North Carolina to protect farms from wildcats.

BLACKBEARD'S BATTLE

This savage pirate terrorized ships along the Ocracoke Inlet and met his demise here.

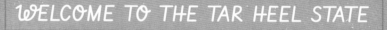

BLUE CRABS

The scientific name for these 10-legged crustaceans is *Callinectes sapidus*, meaning "savory beautiful swimmer!"

WELCOME TO THE TAR HEEL STATE

ATLANTIC OCEAN

I f you can get into a heated conversation about the best type of barbecue or the most impressive college basketball team, and can sing along to James Taylor's "Carolina in My Mind," then chances are you've been bitten by the North Carolina bug!

Natives are fiercely proud of the Old North State's innovations, which include Krispy Kreme donuts (cooked at 360 degrees), Cheerwine cherry-flavored soda (family-owned for almost 100 years), and even the bar code!

Visitors are impressed by the diversity of wildlife found in the Great Smoky Mountains National Park, the prime surfing to be had around the Outer Banks islands, and the majesty of the Appalachian Mountains. Whether you were born in the 12th state or simply have the good fortune to visit, you will undoubtedly be charmed by all that North Carolina has to offer.

MOMENTS TO REMEMBER

AUGUST 18, 1587: Virginia Dare is born on Roanoke Island, making her the first child born to English settlers in the Americas.

SPRING 1799: 12-year-old Conrad Reed goes fishing and finds a 17-pound rock . . . made of gold! The Reed Gold Mine becomes the first commercial gold mine in the country.

1861: Antislavery campaigner Harriet Ann Jacobs publishes *Incidents in the Life of a Slave Girl*.

MARCH 3, 1865: Congress establishes the Freedmen's Bureau to provide food, medical aid, and schooling to former slaves, as well as helping search for lost relatives.

DECEMBER 17, 1903: The Wright brothers fly the first powered airplane at Kill Devil Hills. The flight lasts 12 seconds and covers 120 feet.

FEBRUARY 1, 1960: The Greensboro Four—a group of African American students—sit at a segregated Woolworth's lunch counter in protest.

1964: Folk legend Doc Watson releases his first album. He goes on to win seven Grammys and a Lifetime Achievement Award.

JANUARY 7, 1985: Bruce Brooks wins a Newbery Honor for *The Moves Make the Man*, a story of friendship and basketball.

1990: The Romare Bearden Foundation is established to support young artists and writers. This celebrated artist was born in Charlotte.

JULY 1, 1997: President Clinton calls to congratulate Robey Morgan, the winner of annual Hollerin' Contest held in Spivey's Corner.

KEY FACTS

CAPITAL
Raleigh

LARGEST CITIES
Charlotte
Raleigh
Greensboro

BIRD
Northern cardinal

NAMED FOR
From *Carolus*, the Latin for Charles, after King Charles I of England

STATEHOOD DATE
November 21, 1789

STATEHOOD ORDER
12

FLOWER
Dogwood

POSTAL CODE
NC

REGION
South

MAIN TIME ZONE
Eastern Standard

TREE
Longleaf pine

"TO BE, RATHER THAN TO SEEM TO BE"

CANADA

PEGGY LEE
1920–2002
The 12-time Grammy nominated singer of "Fever" was born in Jamestown.

LAWRENCE WELK
1903–1992
Born in Strasburg, this TV bandleader has two stars on the Hollywood Walk of Fame.

PHIL JACKSON
b.1945
This star NBA coach of the Bulls and the Lakers played college ball in Grand Forks.

THE SQUARE DANCE
is North Dakota's official folk dance. A caller might say, "Ace of Diamonds, Jack of Spades, meet your partner and all promenade!"

SCANDINAVIAN HERITAGE
Find a Norwegian stave church and a 25-foot-tall Swedish Dala horse in Minot.

MYSTICAL HORIZONS
See an amazing sunset at the granite-built "Stonehenge of the Prairie."

DURUM WHEAT
68% of the country's durum wheat (used to make pasta) is grown in North Dakota.

THE INTERNATIONAL PEACE GARDEN
lies on the border between the U.S. and Canada. The Peace Tower represents the ambition of early immigrants to these countries.

FORT UNION TRADING POST
Northern Plains tribes traded buffalo hides and clothing for blankets and beads in 1800s Williston.

THE GEOGRAPHICAL CENTER OF NORTH AMERICA
in Rugby is marked by the flags of Canada, Mexico, and the U.S.

THE W'EEL TURTLE
in Dunseith, made from 2,000 wheel rims, is 18 feet high and 40 feet long!

GRAND FORKS

THE PAUL BROSTE ROCK MUSEUM
in Parshall has a tree made from rainbow-colored rock spheres.

THE KNIFE RIVER INDIAN VILLAGE
displays a painted buffalo robe, a common cold-weather garment for the Hidatsa people.

SUNFLOWERS
Native to the Americas, these flowers can remove harmful toxins from soil.

MEDICINE WHEEL PARK
in Valley City has an enormous horizon calendar based on Native American traditional structures.

THE UKRAINIAN CULTURAL INSTITUTE
in Dickinson displays traditional decorated Easter eggs.

LADY BUG
The state insect can lay more than 1,000 eggs in its lifetime!

THE ANNE CARLSEN CENTER
Here in Jamestown, the center's therapy dog, Champ, lends a paw to children with autism.

BISMARCK

MONTANA

NOKOTA HORSE
Some of the wild state horses running free in the badlands may be descendants of Chief Sitting Bull's own herd.

THE ENCHANTED HIGHWAY
near Regent has seven huge metal sculptors built by retired teacher Gary Greff.

FARGO

VALLEY CITY
is known for the Hi-Line Railroad Bridge, built over the Sheyenne River.

THE NATIONAL BUFFALO MUSEUM
in Jamestown is home to White Cloud, a rare white buffalo.

SOUTH DAKOTA

THEODORE ROOSEVELT NATIONAL PARK
President Roosevelt's love of the rugged grasslands and sandstone landscapes here inspired a nature park.

MR. BUBBLE
This bath-time buddy was first made in 1961 Bismarck.

UNITED TRIBES INTERNATIONAL POWWOW
Bismarck's annual powwow brings together drummers and dancers from around the world.

ARBORETUM TRAIL
75 species of plants can be found along this city-center nature trail—along with a 60-million-year-old tree stump!

THE PLAINS ART MUSEUM
in Fargo has traditional Native American art, folk art, contemporary art, and a hip-hop-themed graffiti mural!

THE FIVE NATIONS GALLERY
in Mandan has Native American crafts, including dream catchers to protect sleepers from bad dreams.

NORTH DAKOTA STATE CAPITOL
Every New Year's Eve, the rooms of the capitol are lit up to spell out the numbers of the new year.

DR. ANNE CARLSEN
1915–2002
Born without forearms or lower legs, this educator—who settled in North Dakota—devoted her career to serving people with disabilities.

CHARLES EASTMAN (OHÍYE S'A)
1858–1939
This Santee Dakota advocate and doctor helped set up the Boy Scouts and lived in northern North Dakota.

70

On a fall day in 1889, both North Dakota and South Dakota were admitted to the union as the 39th and 40th states. Although North Dakota is recognized as the 39th state because it comes first alphabetically, we don't actually know which state was admitted first. When he was signing the proclamation papers, President Benjamin Harrison shuffled them and had the state names hidden from him so there would be no argument about which was first!

This rugged and majestic Midwestern state is the country's 19th largest, and is also one of its least populated, which means locals and visitors alike have the chance to get away from it all, enjoying the peace of the wide prairies and rolling hills. Even North Dakota's large cities, such as Fargo, have a small-town feel that makes everyone feel welcome. But get outside the cities and the landscape feels the opposite of small; in the expansive Theodore Roosevelt National Park, you can catch glimpses of bison, elk, and wild horses roaming their natural habitat.

NORTH DAKOTA

MOMENTS TO REMEMBER

9,500 BC: Paleo-Indian people hunt mammoths and giant bison on the Northern Plains.

1781: The first known North Dakota business, a fur trading post, opens near the Souris River.

SEPTEMBER 17, 1851: The Treaty of Fort Laramie is signed, allocating nearly 12 million acres of the Dakota, Montana, and Wyoming territories to Native tribes. However, white settlers still travel across and settle on the lands set aside for the tribes, causing much conflict.

JULY 14, 1932: The International Peace Garden, which celebrates the peace between Canada and the United States, is opened.

MARCH 16, 1941: A severe and sudden blizzard hits North Dakota; it provides the backdrop for Phyllis Reynolds Naylor's later novel, *Blizzard's Wake*.

OCTOBER 1, 1961: Roger Maris, from Fargo, sets a baseball record by hitting 61 home runs for the New York Yankees, breaking Babe Ruth's 1927 record.

JANUARY 17, 1985: Beryl Levine becomes the first female Justice of the North Dakota Supreme Court.

1989: The North Dakota Legislative Assembly rejects a call to allow the state to drop the "North" from its name and be renamed "Dakota."

NOVEMBER 17, 1999: Louise Erdrich's novel *The Birchbark House*, which tells the story of an Ojibwa girl, becomes a National Book Award Finalist.

2006: Oil is discovered near Parshall, contributing to the North Dakota oil boom.

MINNESOTA

LOUISE ERDRICH
b.1954
The author of *The Birchbark House* grew up in Wahpeton and is a member of the Turtle Mountain Band of Chippewa Indians.

KEY FACTS

CAPITAL
Bismarck

LARGEST CITIES
Fargo
Bismarck
Grand Forks

BIRD
Western
meadowlark

NAMED FOR
The Dakota tribe;
Dakota meaning "friend"

STATEHOOD DATE
November 2, 1889

STATEHOOD ORDER
39

FLOWER
Wild prairie
rose

POSTAL CODE
ND

REGION
Midwest

MAIN TIME ZONE
Central

TREE
American
elm

"LIBERTY AND UNION, NOW AND FOREVER, ONE AND INSEPARABLE"

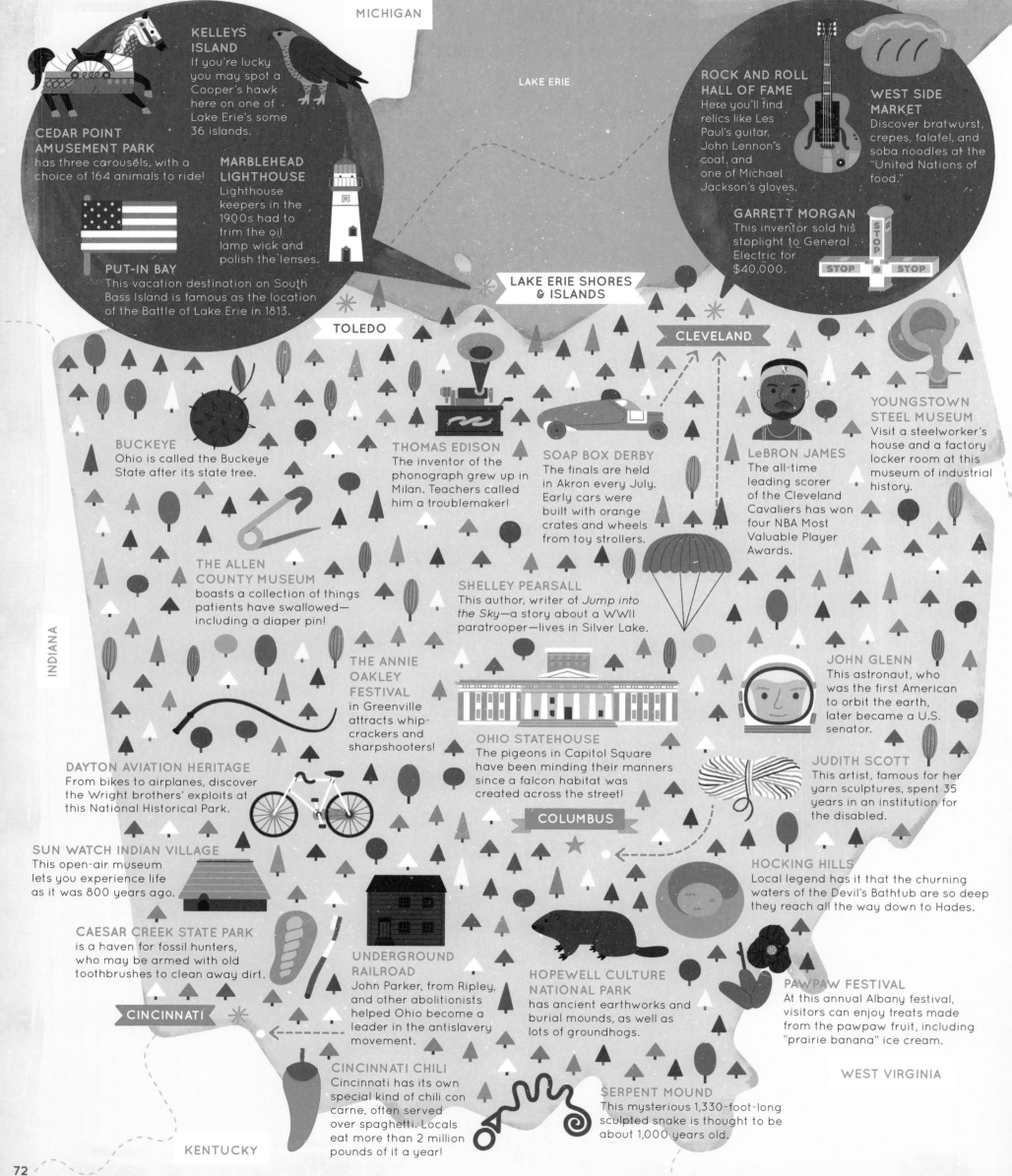

KELLEYS ISLAND
If you're lucky you may spot a Cooper's hawk here on one of Lake Erie's some 36 islands.

CEDAR POINT AMUSEMENT PARK
has three carousels, with a choice of 164 animals to ride!

MARBLEHEAD LIGHTHOUSE
Lighthouse keepers in the 1900s had to trim the oil lamp wick and polish the lenses.

PUT-IN BAY
This vacation destination on South Bass Island is famous as the location of the Battle of Lake Erie in 1813.

MICHIGAN

LAKE ERIE

ROCK AND ROLL HALL OF FAME
Here you'll find relics like Les Paul's guitar, John Lennon's coat, and one of Michael Jackson's gloves.

WEST SIDE MARKET
Discover bratwurst, crepes, falafel, and soba noodles at the "United Nations of food."

GARRETT MORGAN
This inventor sold his stoplight to General Electric for $40,000.

STOP

LAKE ERIE SHORES & ISLANDS

TOLEDO

CLEVELAND

YOUNGSTOWN STEEL MUSEUM
Visit a steelworker's house and a factory locker room at this museum of industrial history.

BUCKEYE
Ohio is called the Buckeye State after its state tree.

THOMAS EDISON
The inventor of the phonograph grew up in Milan. Teachers called him a troublemaker!

SOAP BOX DERBY
The finals are held in Akron every July. Early cars were built with orange crates and wheels from toy strollers.

LeBRON JAMES
The all-time leading scorer of the Cleveland Cavaliers has won four NBA Most Valuable Player Awards.

THE ALLEN COUNTY MUSEUM
boasts a collection of things patients have swallowed—including a diaper pin!

SHELLEY PEARSALL
This author, writer of *Jump into the Sky*—a story about a WWII paratrooper—lives in Silver Lake.

INDIANA

THE ANNIE OAKLEY FESTIVAL
in Greenville attracts whip-crackers and sharpshooters!

JOHN GLENN
This astronaut, who was the first American to orbit the earth, later became a U.S. senator.

DAYTON AVIATION HERITAGE
From bikes to airplanes, discover the Wright brothers' exploits at this National Historical Park.

OHIO STATEHOUSE
The pigeons in Capitol Square have been minding their manners since a falcon habitat was created across the street!

JUDITH SCOTT
This artist, famous for her yarn sculptures, spent 35 years in an institution for the disabled.

COLUMBUS

SUN WATCH INDIAN VILLAGE
This open-air museum lets you experience life as it was 800 years ago.

HOCKING HILLS
Local legend has it that the churning waters of the Devil's Bathtub are so deep they reach all the way down to Hades.

CAESAR CREEK STATE PARK
is a haven for fossil hunters, who may be armed with old toothbrushes to clean away dirt.

UNDERGROUND RAILROAD
John Parker, from Ripley, and other abolitionists helped Ohio become a leader in the antislavery movement.

HOPEWELL CULTURE NATIONAL PARK
has ancient earthworks and burial mounds, as well as lots of groundhogs.

PAWPAW FESTIVAL
At this annual Albany festival, visitors can enjoy treats made from the pawpaw fruit, including "prairie banana" ice cream.

WEST VIRGINIA

CINCINNATI

CINCINNATI CHILI
Cincinnati has its own special kind of chili con carne, often served over spaghetti. Locals eat more than 2 million pounds of it a year!

SERPENT MOUND
This mysterious 1,330-foot-long sculpted snake is thought to be about 1,000 years old.

KENTUCKY

WELCOME TO THE BUCKEYE STATE

What's round on the ends and "hi" in the middle? Ohio, of course! Eight American presidents and a whole host of inventors have called Ohio home. Many useful objects—for example, the cash register, the pop-top soda can, the airplane, and even the hot dog—were invented in Ohio, and world-famous innovator Thomas Edison was born here. Today, the National Inventors Hall of Fame has its headquarters in Ohio, along with the Rock and Roll Hall of Fame and the Pro Football Hall of Fame.

At one point, Ohio was America's western frontier. Since becoming the 17th state in 1803, it has been key to America's development into a modern nation, in part due to its geography: Ohio's canals connected Lake Erie and the Northeast to the Ohio River and Midwest, putting it at the center of industry and transport. Located squarely in the thick of things, it's no wonder that great things have grown up in Ohio!

MOMENTS TO REMEMBER

MAY 29, 1851: Women's rights activist Sojourner Truth delivers her famous "Ain't I A Woman?" speech at the Woman's Convention in Akron.

MAY 21, 1862: Mary Jane Patterson graduates from Oberlin College, becoming the first African American woman to gain a bachelor's degree.

1895: The Wright brothers begin designing and making bicycles. They use the profits from the Wright Cycle Co. to fund their flight experiments.

FEBRUARY 17, 1900: Teacher Joseph Oppenheim patents the first manure spreader. He designed it to keep his students from missing school to help their families spread manure.

JULY 25, 1916: The gas mask—invented by Garrett Morgan—saves the lives of 32 Cleveland men who are trapped underground, exposed to toxic fumes. Morgan also invented the smoke detector, a traffic signal, and a hair-straightening cream.

AUGUST 1936: Sprinter Jesse Owens wins four gold medals at the Olympics in Germany. He was previously a track star in high school in Cleveland.

APRIL 8, 1992: Highly acclaimed children's author Virginia Hamilton, from Yellow Springs, is announced as the Hans Christian Andersen Award winner.

MAY 27, 1995: Woodpeckers delay the launch of the *Discovery* space shuttle by pecking holes in its foam insulation. The shuttle finally departs in July, with an all-Ohio crew.

FEBRUARY 18, 2002: Akron-born basketball forward LeBron James appears on the cover of *Sports Illustrated* while he is still in high school.

MAYA LIN
b.1959
This sculptor won a competition to design the Vietnam Veterans Memorial while at college.

GARRETT MORGAN
1877–1963
This Cleveland inventor's devices included a gas mask and a traffic signal.

CHIEF PONTIAC
c.1720–1769
Chief of the Ottawa Tribe, Pontiac led a revolt against the British.

ANNIE OAKLEY
1860–1926
"Little Miss Sure Shot" starred in Buffalo Bill's Wild West Show.

GLORIA STEINEM
b.1934
Born in Toledo, this journalist is a leader of the feminist movement.

PAUL NEWMAN
1925–2008
This Oscar-winning actor also raced cars and started a food company.

KEY FACTS

CAPITAL
Columbus

LARGEST CITIES
Columbus
Cleveland
Cincinnati

BIRD
Northern cardinal

NAMED FOR
The Seneca Indian word meaning "beautiful river"

STATEHOOD DATE
March 1, 1803

STATEHOOD ORDER
17

FLOWER
Scarlet carnation

POSTAL CODE
OH

REGION
Great Lakes

MAIN TIME ZONE
Eastern Standard

TREE
Ohio buckeye

"WITH GOD, ALL THINGS ARE POSSIBLE"

JIM THORPE (BRIGHT PATH)
1888–1953
This Native American football, basketball, and track-and-field athlete was born on a farm in Prague.

BILL AND CAROL WALLACE
1947–2012 • b.1948
As a team and individually, this children's book duo has authored some 55 books; both grew up in Chickasha.

ELIZABETH WARREN
b.1949
This U.S. senator was born in Oklahoma City and was her family's first college graduate.

KRISTIN CHENOWETH
b.1968
This performer started out singing gospel in Broken Arrow and has since starred in *Wicked*, *Glee*, and more.

COLORADO

OKLAHOMA

NEW MEXICO

BLACK MESA STATE PARK
Horned lizards now roam where outlaws once hid!

BEAVER DUNES STATE PARK
Dune buggy riders flock to the 300 acres of sand hills in Oklahoma's panhandle.

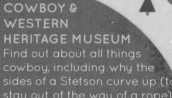

COWBOY & WESTERN HERITAGE MUSEUM
Find out about all things cowboy, including why the sides of a Stetson curve up (to stay out of the way of a rope).

PARKING PIONEER
In 1935, Oklahoma City installed the world's first parking meter—it cost a nickel an hour.

WELCOME TO THE SOONER STATE

OKLAHOMA STATE CAPITOL
This is the world's only state house surrounded by working oil wells!

FIRE AND DUST INTERPRETIVE TRAIL
A rock dugout house and a working windmill show what life was like for homesteaders in the Black Kettle Grassland.

O f all the nine "panhandle" states, Oklahomans would argue that theirs most closely resembles the handle of a cooking pan! And Okies sure know how to cook. The lip-smacking official state meal includes chicken-fried steak, fried okra, squash, cornbread, barbecue pork, biscuits, sausage and gravy, grits, corn on the cob, black-eyed peas, strawberries . . . and pecan pie!

Oklahoma is home to the second-largest Native American population of any state. With headquarters for 39 of America's tribal nations, as well as 25 different Native American languages spoken, the 46th state has the largest diversity of tribes in the country.

The Sooner State boasts outdoor marvels of all kinds, including the lava rocks of the Black Mesa State Park, and seemingly endless prairies, which today are covered in wind farms. It's not rare to hear the phrase "hold on to your hat" in Oklahoma, where, in the words of the state song, the wind comes sweeping down the plain!

WICHITA MOUNTAINS WILDLIFE REFUGE
The free-roaming buffalo here are descendants of those bred in a zoo in New York!

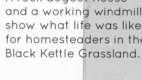

WIND FARM
In 2013 Oklahoma generated enough energy from wind to power 1 million homes!

NAVAJO CODE TALKERS

THE COMANCHE NATIONAL MUSEUM
celebrates the heroics of WWII "Code Talkers," who sent secret battle messages based on their tribal language.

TEXAS

MARIA TALLCHIEF
1925–2013
Born in Fairfax, this skilled dancer was the first Native American prima ballerina.

WOODY GUTHRIE CENTER
The political folksinger of "This Land is Your Land" was born in Okemah.

GOLDEN DRILLER
The state monument is dedicated to the people of the petroleum industry.

GILCREASE MUSEUM
Allan Houser's sculpture *Sacred Rain Arrow* greets visitors to this massive museum.

PRICE TOWER ARTS CENTER
Frank Lloyd Wright designed this, his only skyscraper, to look like a tree that escaped the forest!

KANSAS

PIONEER WOMAN MONUMENT
This 17-foot-tall, 12,000-pound bronze statue in Ponca City celebrates the women who helped build Oklahoma.

TOTEM POLE PARK
The centerpiece of this folk art collection stands 90 feet tall and rests on a concrete turtle!

MISSOURI

THE NATIONAL ROD & CUSTOM CAR HALL OF FAME
in Afton features 50 custom-built cars by hot rod designer Darryl Starbird.

PRIMA BALLERINA
Maria Tallchief spent her early years on the Osage reservation.

TULSA

WHERE THE RED FERN GROWS
Author Wilson Rawls set this novel featuring two hunting dogs in the Ozark Mountains, where he grew up.

JASMINE MORAN CHILDREN'S MUSEUM
At this museum in Seminole kids can perform heart surgery . . . on a model!

OKLAHOMA CITY

OKMULGEE INVITATIONAL RODEO
Bull riding, calf roping, and steer wrestling abound at the nation's oldest African American rodeo.

TSA-LA-GI
ᏣᎳᎩ

CHEROKEE HERITAGE CENTER
This Park Hill museum celebrates Cherokee culture, history, and language.

NORMAN

TOY & ACTION FIGURE MUSEUM
WOW! 13,000 action figures, Bat Cave, and . . . superhero underwear! BAM!

THE SPIRO MOUNDS
are one of the most important Native American sites in the nation.

BIGFOOT CROSSING

SHOWMEN'S REST
The Mount Olivet Cemetery has a special section for circus performers who would spend the winter in the town of Hugo.

KIAMICHI MOUNTAINS
Local lore claims Bigfoot lives here—and nearby Honobia has an annual Bigfoot Festival!

TURNER FALLS
This 77-foot-tall waterfall is one of many geological wonders in the area.

MOMENTS TO REMEMBER

AD 500–1300: Spiro Indians build hundreds of complex burial mounds filled with artworks and artifacts of their powerful society.

APRIL 22, 1889: In the first Land Rush, some 50,000 white settlers race across "Unassigned Lands" to claim homesteads. Some settlers (called "Sooners") rush in before the official signal is given, leading to the state's nickname.

MAY 1909: The first Boy Scout troop in America is formed in Pawhuska. They rescue a "kitten" from under a rock ledge, which turns out to be a skunk!

NOVEMBER 4, 1938: David Randolph Milsten is inspired to write "Howdy Folks" about his friend, the actor and newspaper columnist Will Rogers. It later becomes the state poem.

MAY 25, 1973: To honor the Native American tribes of his home state Oklahoma, astronaut William Pogue (of Choctaw descent) carries a specially designed flag aboard NASA's *Skylab 2*.

DECEMBER 14, 1985: Wilma Mankiller becomes the first woman to serve as the Cherokee tribe's chief, improving the government, health care, and education systems.

DECEMBER 8, 1996: Ballerina Maria Tallchief receives a Kennedy Center Honor for lifetime achievements.

APRIL 2013: Oklahoma City opens the Century Chest time capsule, filled with items residents in 1913 paid $3 per inch to include!

MARCH 24, 2014: Cherokee Nation Remembrance Day is established to honor those forced from their homes during the 1838 Trail of Tears.

ARKANSAS

KEY FACTS

CAPITAL
Oklahoma City

LARGEST CITIES
Oklahoma City
Tulsa
Norman

BIRD
Scissor-tailed flycatcher

NAMED FOR
The Choctaw phrase *okla humma*, meaning "red people"

STATEHOOD DATE
November 17, 1907

STATEHOOD ORDER
46

FLOWER
Mistletoe

POSTAL CODE
OK

REGION
Southwest

MAIN TIME ZONE
Central

TREE
Redbud

"LABOR CONQUERS ALL THINGS"

WELCOME TO THE BEAVER STATE

Oregon is . . . original. Way back in 1971, the 33rd state passed the first ever Bicycle Bill, which said that all new roads must include areas for bikers and walkers. Usually a governor signs a new bill at an official-looking desk, but the Bicycle Bill was signed outdoors—on the seat of a bike!

It's no wonder that a bike-loving state overflows with natural beauty and outdoor adventuring. Indeed, the windswept Pacific coast was a fitting destination for the intrepid explorers of the Lewis and Clark Expedition.

But Oregon is not only about the great outdoors: cities such as Portland are bursting with cultural offerings to satisfy music and art lovers. Buzzing, vibrant Portland is overflowing with friendly, energetic, creative types, giving the metropolis a welcoming, small-town feel.

MARIE AIOE DORION
c.1786–1850
Dorion, from the Iowa tribe, was a guide on the Astor Expedition to find an overland route to the Pacific coast.

MATT GROENING
b.1954
The creator of *The Simpsons* was born in Portland.

BEVERLY CLEARY
b.1916
The "Ramona" author grew up in Yamhill: a town so small it didn't have a library—so her mom started one!

YAQUINA HEAD
At 93 feet tall, this is the tallest of Oregon's 11 lighthouses.

SEA LION CAVES
Just north of Florence, this is one of the largest sea caves in the world and a perfect place for sea lion spotting.

PETER IREDALE
Marvel at—but don't try sailing—this 1906 wreck!

CANNON BEACH
is famous for Haystack Rock.

GARIBALDI
Place your bets! The residents of Garibaldi have been racing crabs since 1985.

LINCOLN CITY'S KITE FESTIVAL
See some of the biggest kites in the world.

WASHINGTON

LEWIS & CLARK NATIONAL HISTORICAL PARK

COLUMBIA RIVER

BURNSIDE SKATEPARK
in Portland was built by the public, for the public.

PORTLAND

GRESHAM

OREGON STATE CAPITOL
Atop the Salem capitol building is a gold-plated statue of an ax-wielding pioneer.

WILLAMETTE RIVER

SALEM

COWS ON CAMPUS
Oregon State University (in Corvallis) is known as "Moo U" because of its agricultural program.

MOUNT HOOD
This volcano last erupted in 1805.

WARM SPRINGS INDIAN RESERVATION

EUGENE

UNIVERSITY OF OREGON
Olympic runner Steve Prefontaine was born in Coos Bay and starred in track at the UO in Eugene.

CRATER LAKE NATIONAL PARK
Find the deepest lake in the country here.

LAVA LANDSCAPES
Visit volcanic landscapes and lava caves at the Newberry National Volcanic Monument.

THE OREGON CAVES NATIONAL MONUMENT
has 15,000 feet of marble passages. That *rocks!*

OREGON SHAKESPEARE FESTIVAL
Nearly 700 volunteers work each year to bring the Bard's plays to life.

DAFFODILS
The town of Brookings is the nation's top producer of daffodils and Easter lilies.

CALIFORNIA

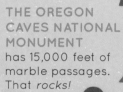
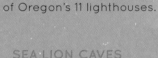

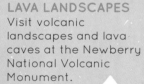

OREGON

TRYON CREEK
Search for slugs in these forested canyons.

POWELL'S
is the largest bookstore in the world!

POWELL'S BOOKS
USED & NEW BOOKS

FLIP A COIN
Two pioneers founded Portland: one from Boston, MA, and one from Portland, ME. They flipped a coin to decide the name of the city!

VOODOO DOUGHNUT
Here you can savor a bacon-maple doughnut bar and even get married!

HIN-MAH-TOO-YAH-LAT-KEKT (THUNDER ROLLING DOWN THE MOUNTAIN): CHIEF JOSEPH
1840–1904
Joseph's 1877 speech at the surrender of his Nez Perce tribe was a famous expression of hope for equality.

JOSEPH
This city is named for the Nez Perce chief who famously said, "It does not require many words to speak the truth."

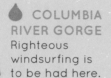

MULTNOMAH FALLS
Oregon has more than 200 waterfalls, but at 620 feet none are taller than this one.

COLUMBIA RIVER GORGE
Righteous windsurfing is to be had here.

YEE-HAW!
Bronco-rider George Fletcher wowed rodeo fans at the Pendleton Round-Up.

HAZELNUT
Oregon is the U.S.'s top producer of hazelnuts.

SHANIKO
Oregon has more ghost towns than any other state . . . and this is one of the best!

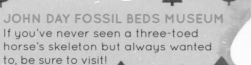

JOHN DAY FOSSIL BEDS MUSEUM
If you've never seen a three-toed horse's skeleton but always wanted to, be sure to visit!

PRESERVED SANDALS
Sandals found in a cave in Fort Rock Park are over 10,000 years old!

PAINTED HILLS
These hills, formed in ancient times, are named after their colorful layers of rock.

COFFEE
A recent study found over 1,000 coffee shops brewing in Oregon!

FLAG
Oregon has the only state flag with a different image on either side.

TABITHA MOFFATT BROWN
1780–1858
The "Mother of Oregon" trekked the Oregon Trail at age 66, then established a home and school for orphaned children.

LINUS CARL PAULING
1901–1994
This Portland native won two Nobel prizes: the first for Chemistry and the second for Peace.

NEVADA

IDAHO

KEY FACTS

CAPITAL
Salem

LARGEST CITIES
Portland
Eugene
Gresham

BIRD
Western meadowlark

NAMED FOR
Some think the name comes from the French word for hurricane, *ouragan*

STATEHOOD DATE
February 14, 1859

STATEHOOD ORDER
33

FLOWER
Oregon grape

POSTAL CODE
OR

REGION
Pacific

MAIN TIME ZONE
Pacific

TREE
Douglas fir

"SHE FLIES WITH HER OWN WINGS"

Pennsylvania

NEW YORK

NEW JERSEY

MAKING MUSIC
In Nazareth, learn how a guitar is made at the Martin Guitar Factory.

BETHLEHEM
is home to the Just Born candy factory, where marshmallow Peeps are made. On New Year's Eve, a giant Peeps chick is dropped from a crane!

WILLIAMSPORT
This city hosted the first World Series of Little League Baseball in 1947.

A FORK IN THE ROAD
Literally. A 9-foot dinner fork stands at an intersection in Centerport.

GOBBLER'S KNOB
is famous for furry resident Punxsutawney Phil: a groundhog who predicts how long winter will last.

COVERED BRIDGE
Pennsylvania has the most covered bridges of any state in the country!

NEW CASTLE
is home to the country's two largest fireworks factories!

PENNSYLVANIA STATE CAPITOL
President Teddy Roosevelt described Pennsylvania's capitol as "the handsomest building I ever saw."

ALLENTOWN

CITY LIFE
Forbes.com named Pittsburgh America's "Most Livable City" in 2014.

OHIO

HARRISBURG

PHILADELPHIA

LEAP-THE-DIPS
The world's oldest operating wooden roller coaster is in Lakemont Park in Altoona.

VALLEY FORGE
George Washington's soldiers spent a cold winter here in 1777.

EMOTICONS
The first two Internet emoticons, the smiley and frowny faces, were invented at Carnegie Mellon University in Pittsburgh.

PITTSBURGH

BANANA SPLIT
This famous sundae was first served in Latrobe in 1904.

GETTYSBURG
The famous site of the battle hailed as a turning point in the Civil War.

KENNETT SQUARE
The "Mushroom Capital of America" holds an annual Mushroom Festival.

SWEET STREETS
The streetlights in Hershey, "Chocolate Capital of America," are shaped like candy kisses.

FALLINGWATER
Frank Lloyd Wright designed this house, built over a waterfall in the Laurel Highlands.

WEST VIRGINIA

MARYLAND

CAPITAL CITY
Lancaster served as the nation's capital for one day!

DELAWARE

IN THE BAG
Six potato chip companies have factories along the Potato Chip Belt.

LANCASTER COUNTY
is known as the "Pretzel Basket of America."

ANDY WARHOL
1928–1987
Born in Pittsburgh, Warhol was a leading artist of the 1960s Pop Art movement.

BILLIE HOLIDAY
1915–1959
Philly native "Lady Day" was one of the most influential jazz singers of her time.

ROBERTO CLEMENTE
1934–1972
This National Baseball Hall of Famer broke batting records playing for the Pittsburgh Pirates.

TAYLOR SWIFT
b. 1989
The Grammy-winning music superstar was raised in Wyomissing and sang at a Philadelphia 76ers game at age 12.

JERRY PINKNEY
b.1939
This Philly-born book illustrator has won the Caldecott Medal, five Caldecott honors, and five Coretta Scott King Awards!

**"NELLIE BLY"
(ELIZABETH COCHRANE)**
1864–1922
This early feminist and investigative journalist made a record-breaking trip around the world in 72 days.

RINGING HILL PARK
The rocks of this 7-acre boulder field "ring" when they are struck by a hammer.

BOONE TOWN
The home of 18th-century pioneer Daniel Boone can be visited in Baumstown.

WELCOME TO THE KEYSTONE STATE

a keystone is the central wedge in an arch that locks all the other stones in place; and so Pennsylvania–The "Keystone State"–was the central state of the original 13 colonies, playing an important role in the history of the nation. As the birthplace of independence and the Constitution itself, Pennsylvania is something of a spiritual home for history lovers. There are plenty of chances to travel back in time: visitors can walk the Gettysburg Battlefield, see the iconic Liberty Bell, or venture within the hallowed walls of Liberty Hall, and that's just the tip of the iceberg!

Aside from history, the second state has a lot more to offer. Philadelphia and Pittsburgh are thriving university cities with big music, theater, and art scenes. Or, for a chance to get away from it all, you can head to Pennsylvania's stunning forests and mountains. And if you really want to escape the hustle and bustle, then take a trip to Lancaster County and discover the Amish community's simple, peaceful way of life.

MOMENTS TO REMEMBER

FEBRUARY 28, 1681: King Charles II of England pays a debt by granting the Quaker William Penn 45,000 acres of land in the New World. The king names the area Pennsylvania to honor Penn's father.

SEPTEMBER 5, 1774: The First Continental Congress, a meeting of representatives from 12 of the 13 original colonies, secretly assembles in Philadelphia's Carpenters' Hall to discuss their grievances against the British.

JULY 4, 1776: The Second Continental Congress signs the Declaration of Independence in what is now called Independence Hall, Philadelphia.

JULY 1–3, 1863: The Battle of Gettysburg takes place. This proves a turning point in the Civil War, with Union forces defeating the Confederates' plan to invade Pennsylvania and take the North.

MAY 1876: Philadelphia hosts the Centennial Exposition on the country's 100th anniversary. A showcase of manufacturing and technological marvels, it introduces the telephone and typewriter.

MARCH 2, 1903: Milton Hershey breaks ground in Derry Church for his new chocolate factory.

NOVEMBER 8, 1938: Crystal Bird Fauset becomes the first African American woman elected to the Pennsylvania House of Representatives.

JUNE 6, 1939: Carl Stotz puts together teams of neighborhood children for a summer baseball program that he names the "Little League."

MARCH 28, 1979: The most serious nuclear energy accident in the U.S. occurs when the Three Mile Island plant experiences a partial meltdown.

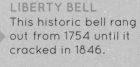

LIBERTY BELL
This historic bell rang out from 1754 until it cracked in 1846.

PHILLY FOOD
Hoagies, cheesesteaks, Cracker Jacks, Tastykakes, and soft pretzels were all invented here!

HISTORIC CAPITAL
Philly was the nation's capital for 10 years while a permanent capital was built.

THE PHILADELPHIA MINT
The oldest coin producer in the country, this mint can make more than 13 billion coins a year!

KEY FACTS

CAPITAL
Harrisburg

LARGEST CITIES
Philadelphia
Pittsburgh
Allentown

BIRD
Ruffed grouse

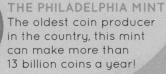

NAMED FOR
The father of the founder of the state, William Penn; the name means "Penn's Woodland"

STATEHOOD DATE
December 12, 1787

STATEHOOD ORDER
2

FLOWER
Mountain laurel

POSTAL CODE
PA

REGION
Mid-Atlantic

MAIN TIME ZONE
Eastern

TREE
Eastern hemlock

VIRTUE, LIBERTY, AND INDEPENDENCE

MASSACHUSETTS

HASBRO'S HOME
The makers of the Mr. Potato Head and My Little Pony toys first made doctors' kits!

SLATER MILL MUSEUM
Slater Mill was the U.S.'s first successful cotton mill, helping make Rhode Island a leader in textile production in the 1800s.

CORMAC McCARTHY
b.1933
This Pulitzer Prize–winning author wrote *No Country for Old Men*, which became an Oscar-winning movie.

WILD OYSTERS
help keep coastal waters clean—and taste great with lemon!

H. P. LOVECRAFT
This fantasy writer is famous for creating strange creatures, such as the octopus-headed Cthulhu.

BETSEY'S BONNET
In 1786 12-year-old Betsey Metcalf made hat-making history with her inexpensive straw hat, launching the American straw hat industry.

OLD SCHOOL
Portsmouth is home to the nation's oldest schoolhouse. Students in 1725 brought their lunch in a pail.

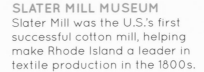

PROVIDENCE

RHODE ISLAND SCHOOL OF DESIGN
Graduates include Shepard Fairey, creator of the street-art OBEY Giant.

CRANSTON

BRISTOL

WARWICK

HOG

RHODE ISLAND STATE HOUSE
The state house is topped with an 11-foot-tall, 500-pound, gold-covered statue called "Independent Man."

THE GREEN ANIMALS TOPIARY GARDEN
has some 20 trees shaped to look like animals.

CONNECTICUT

NEUTACONKANUT PARK
offers spectacular views, a tangle of trails, and prime sledding.

QUONSET POINT
Quonset huts, used as temporary buildings in WWII, were made here.

QUAHOG SHELL
Tribes like the Narragansett used quahog shells to make wampum beads.

PRUDENCE

NARRAGANSETT BAY

AQUIDNECK

THE CONANICUT ISLAND LIGHTHOUSE
was used in the filming of Wes Anderson's *Moonrise Kingdom* as the home of Suzy Bishop.

CONANICUT

JANET TAYLOR LISLE
The award-winning author of *Afternoon of the Elves* writes in Little Compton.

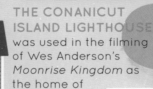

DUTCH ISLAND

NEWPORT

MASSASOIT OUSAMEQUIN
c.1581–1661
Massasoit was chief of the Wampanoag tribe. His alliance with the Pilgrims led to the first Thanksgiving.

MARATHON MAN
Charlestown was home to "Tarzan" Brown, called Deerfoot by the Narragansett people. He won the Boston marathon twice.

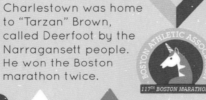

RHODE ISLAND SOUND

BOAT SCHOOL
Students at the IYRS (International Yacht Restoration School) learn how to build and restore boats.

HORSESHOE CRABS
Every spring these "living fossils" travel back to their breeding beaches to lay eggs: a female can lay some 90,000 eggs a season!

POINT JUDITH LIGHTHOUSE
This wooden lighthouse's beach is crowded with mysterious stacks of rocks.

HOUSE ON THE ROCKS
The eco-friendly Clingstone house sits on an island barely bigger than itself!

TOURO SYNAGOGUE
This 1763 synagogue, the oldest in the U.S., faces east toward Jerusalem.

ROGER WILLIAMS
c.1603–1683
Williams was the founder of the Rhode Island colony.

BLOCK ISLAND SOUND

TENNIS HALL OF FAME & MUSEUM
Q: What do you serve but not eat? A: A tennis ball!

THE BREAKERS MANSION
Some of the 20 bathrooms inside this historic mansion have tubs with extra faucets . . . for salt water!

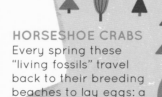

BLOCK

ANNIE SMITH PECK
1850–1935
Providence-born Peck was an early female mountaineer. She was one of the first women to scale the Matterhorn.

FLYING HORSE CAROUSEL
The horses of the nation's oldest carousel in Watch Hill swing from chains!

ENDANGERED INSECT
Block Island is one of the few places the carrion-eating burying beetle still survives.

IDA LEWIS
This heroic lighthouse keeper made her first rescue when she was just 17.

WELCOME TO THE OCEAN STATE

The nation's smallest state packs in 400 miles of coastline, and its fresh—and saltwater—beaches offer so much to see, do, and eat! For instance, there's Block Island to explore, Narragansett Bay to swim, the Beavertail Lighthouses to linger by, and in Newport, clam chowder, scallops, and littlenecks to savor.

For a chance to see a future Boston Red Sox star, sports enthusiasts won't want to miss the opening pitch of a Pawtucket Red Sox game. And history buffs will have a heyday in this, the Ocean State, where they can visit the beautiful mansions of the 1800s' elite, the oldest synagogue in the United States, and the first town established by a woman.

With so much to offer in Rhode Island, it's no wonder the Vanderbilts chose to spend their summers here . . . chances are, after just one visit, you'll wish you could live here all year round!

MOMENTS TO REMEMBER

MAY 13, 1636: Roger Williams founds Rhode Island with principles of religious toleration and political democracy—radical ideas at the time.

MAY 23, 1774: Newport hosts America's first circus: visitors pay $0.25 to see Christopher Gardner ride a horse—while standing on his head!

MARCH 1, 1784: The General Assembly of Rhode Island passes the Gradual Emancipation Act, which meant that children born to slaves would not be slaves. This followed the antislavery campaign led by the Quaker Moses Brown.

JULY 4, 1785: In Bristol, the Rev. Henry Wight organizes a gathering in support of independence. This is the birth of the oldest Fourth of July celebration in the country.

JULY 25, 1965: Bob Dylan shocks the crowd when he plays an electric guitar at the Newport Folk Festival.

FEBRUARY 5–7, 1978: 21 lives are lost in the Great Northeast Blizzard.

APRIL 11, 1983: The federal government acknowledges the Narragansett Nation.

JANUARY 15, 1991: The author known as Avi is awarded a Newbery Honor for *The True Confessions of Charlotte Doyle*, the story of a 13-year-old journeying to Providence.

DECEMBER 31, 1994: Barnaby Evans creates WaterFire: a piece of performance art where fires are lit along the rivers in Providence.

JULY 3, 2001: Ruth Simmons becomes president of Brown University; she is the first African American to head an Ivy League institution.

ATLANTIC OCEAN

ELIZABETH BUFFUM CHACE
1806–1899
Chace's home in Valley Falls was a stop on the Underground Railroad; she also fought for women's rights and prison reform.

MATILDA SISSIERETTA JOYNER JONES
1869–1933
A graduate of the Providence Academy of Music, this operatic soprano was the first African American to sing at Carnegie Hall.

KEY FACTS

CAPITAL
Providence

LARGEST CITIES
Providence
Warwick
Cranston

BIRD
Rhode Island Red

NAMED FOR
Its resemblance to the Greek island of Rhodes

STATEHOOD DATE
May 29, 1790

STATEHOOD ORDER
13

FLOWER
Violet

POSTAL CODE
RI

REGION
New England

MAIN TIME ZONE
Eastern

TREE
Red Maple

"HOPE"

81

HOW TO STEAL A DOG
The author Barbara O'Connor was born and raised in Greenville.

BOYKIN SPANIELS
Cheerful and energetic, these pooches were originally bred in this state to help turkey hunters.

CATAWBA CULTURAL CENTER
Catawba Indian pottery earns its distinctive coloring through wood firing.

DIZZY GILLESPIE
The bebop trumpeter famous for "Salt Peanuts" was born in Cheraw.

COTTON MUSEUM
In Bishopville, find out that a dollar bill is 75% cotton!

WILLIAM H. JOHNSON
The painter of *Street Musicians* got his start in Florence.

ROCK HILL

GREENVILLE

SUPER SOYBEAN
Soybeans are one of South Carolina's top crops. One acre of beans can be used to make more than 82,000 crayons!

LANE KIRKLAND
1922–1999
Camden-born Kirkland was president of the labor union AFL-CIO for 16 years.

NEVERBUST CHAIN
One night the artist Blue Sky installed this enormous chain sculpture between two office blocks—in secret!

SOUTH CAROLINA STATE HOUSE
Each of the capitol's 43-foot-high columns is cut from a single piece of stone.

THE CAROLINA CUP
is an annual horse race held in Camden.

TOPIARY GARDEN
Pearl Fryar's 3-acre garden has some 300 shrubs trimmed into amazing shapes.

WILD TURKEYS
The official state game bird can outrun a galloping horse!

COLUMBIA

THE POINSETTIA
is named for Joel Roberts Poinsett, a diplomat from Charleston, who brought the plant back from Mexico.

THE BLACK RIVER SWAMP
is home to the rare swallow-tailed kite, a lizard-eating raptor.

LION'S MANE
Found in Congaree National Park, this mushroom tastes like crab and may even improve memory.

JACQUELINE WOODSON
b.1963
The award-winning author of *Miracle's Boys* was influenced by time spent in Greenville during her youth.

JAMES BROWN
1933–2006
A founding father of funk music, the "Godfather of Soul" was born in Barnwell.

PEACH CAPITAL
South Carolina is known as the "Tastier Peach State" and Johnston calls itself Peach Capital of the World.

MONKEY ISLAND
Morgan Island is home to some 4,000 rhesus monkeys used in medical testing.

NORTH CHARLESTON

CHARLESTON

MARINE CORPS
Training for new recruits takes place on Parris Island.

HALLELUJAH SINGERS
Learn about the Gullah language and culture through music in Beaufort.

FORE!
Golf is played at the some 350 courses in South Carolina.

GEORGIA

SOUTH CAROLINA

RED THUNDER CLOUD (CARLOS WESTEZ)
1919–1996
The spoken language of the Catawba tribe died with its last speaker, a New England linguist named Red Thunder Cloud.

NORTH CAROLINA

ATOMIC ACCIDENT
In 1958 the air force made a 75-foot crater when they dropped 7,600 pounds of explosives on a house in Mars Bluff—by accident!

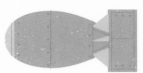

REGULAR, GOOFY, MONGO
Skate for free at the Matt Hughes Skate Park in Myrtle Beach.

MYRTLE BEACH
In 2007 the Guinness World Record for the Tallest Sand Castle was awarded to Myrtle Beach!

ATLANTIC OCEAN

CHADWICK BOSEMAN
b.1976
Born in Anderson, this actor and writer has played Jackie Robinson in *42* and James Brown in *Get on Up*.

CHARLES FERNLEY FAWCETT
1915–2008
Fawcett grew up in Greenville, then became a WWII resistance fighter, helping Jewish refugees leave Europe. He later became an actor and filmmaker.

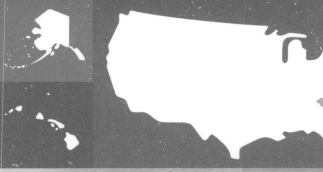

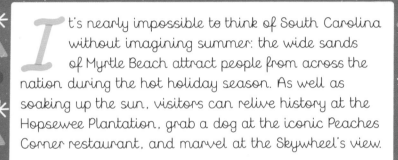

WELCOME TO THE PALMETTO STATE

It's nearly impossible to think of South Carolina without imagining summer: the wide sands of Myrtle Beach attract people from across the nation during the hot holiday season. As well as soaking up the sun, visitors can relive history at the Hopsewee Plantation, grab a dog at the iconic Peaches Corner restaurant, and marvel at the Skywheel's view.

There's plenty inland, as well, such as the vast Blue Ridge Mountains. Here, you can see beautiful vistas, cascading waterfalls, and some 680 species of wildflowers.

And of course there's Charleston, steeped in southern charm, tradition, and beautiful architecture. You can breathe deep here, enjoying the scents of jasmine and honeysuckle in the morning, and gumbo and deviled crab cakes in the evening. Summer can't last forever, but in South Carolina you can almost believe it will.

MOMENTS TO REMEMBER

1698: The first public library in the nation is established in Charleston.

JANUARY 17, 1781: As a result of his brilliant tactical plan, General Daniel Morgan defeats the British troops at the Battle of Cowpens during the Revolutionary War.

1954: The Pimento Cheeseburger, made with pimento cheese, or "Carolina caviar," is purportedly invented in Colombia.

JULY 6, 1957: Althea Gibson is the first black American to win Wimbledon; she goes on to win the U.S. Open in September.

APRIL 5, 1968: James Brown gives a rare televised live concert, hoping to prevent riots following Martin Luther King, Jr.'s assassination.

JANUARY 1974: Alice Childress wins a Coretta Scott King Award honor for her young-adult novel *A Hero Ain't Nothin' but a Sandwich*.

NOVEMBER 24, 1990: The Catawba people hold their first Yap Ye Iswa celebration. The day begins with a calling song and continues with traditional drumming and dancing.

1997: The National Endowment for the Arts presents famed Catawba potter Georgia Henrietta Harris with a National Heritage Award.

JANUARY 27, 2006: The Pee Dee Indian tribe of South Carolina obtains official state recognition.

2054: Myrtle Beach residents will open a time capsule that Horry County Elementary School students buried in 2004!

CITADEL MILITARY COLLEGE
New students at this famous college are called "knobs"—with their new military haircuts they look like doorknobs!

ANGEL OAK
This 65-foot-tall, 1,500-year old tree has survived hurricanes, floods, and earthquakes.

FORT SUMTER
Confederate forces fired the first shots of the Civil War from this sea fort.

KEY FACTS

CAPITAL
Columbia

LARGEST CITIES
Columbia
Charleston
North Charleston

BIRD
Carolina wren

NAMED FOR
King Charles I of England

STATEHOOD DATE
May 23, 1788

STATEHOOD ORDER
8

FLOWER
Yellow jessamine

POSTAL CODE
SC

REGION
South

MAIN TIME ZONE
Eastern

TREE
Palmetto tree

"WHILE I BREATHE, I HOPE"

83

and what a state it is! The pines and prairies of the nation's 17th-largest state have long beckoned ramblers and roamers, who come to marvel at the landscapes of America's Midwest.

The tree-covered mountains of the Black Hills are a big attraction. Holding a sacred place in the culture of the Lakota people, these hills were their home until the discovery of the gold in 1874. After this, miners rushed in and the Lakota were forced to move elsewhere. Gold mining continues today, and other underground riches have also been unearthed, such as Sue—the largest and most complete *Tyrannosaurus rex* skeleton ever discovered!

The hills are also home to two of the country's most important monuments, located just 17 miles apart. Mount Rushmore and the Crazy Horse Memorial are awe-inspiring in size and invite visitors to reflect on the diverse contributions of the founders of our nation.

KEY FACTS

CAPITAL
Pierre

LARGEST CITIES
Sioux Falls
Rapid City
Aberdeen

BIRD
Ring-necked pheasant

NAMED FOR
The Dakota tribe;
Dakota meaning "friend"

STATEHOOD DATE
November 2, 1889

STATEHOOD ORDER
40

FLOWER
Pasque flower

POSTAL CODE
SD

REGION
Midwest

MAIN TIME ZONE
Central

TREE
Black Hills spruce

"UNDER GOD, THE PEOPLE RULE"

NORTH DAKOTA

GRAND RIVER NATIONAL GRASSLAND
is home to antelopes, who can run in bursts of 53 mph!

STURGIS MOTORCYCLE RALLY
is the world's largest rally and attracts enthusiasts from across the globe.

THE DAYBREAK STAR
is a Native American symbol shown in quilts made by crafters such as Ina McNeil, born on the Standing Rock Reservation.

MONTANA

THE CENTER OF THE NATION
Including Alaska and Hawaii the geographic center of the country, in Belle Fourche, is marked with a monument and 50 state flags.

TERMESPHERE GALLERY
Instead of using a flat canvas, artist Dick Termes paints on spheres. Visit his gallery in Spearfish.

THE WALL DRUG STORE
is a tourist attraction offering everything from free ice water to an 80-foot dinosaur and a 6-foot jackalope!

MINUTEMAN MISSILE NATIONAL HISTORIC SITE
This Cold War nuclear missile complex can be toured by visitors.

GEORGE LEE "SPARKY" ANDERSON 1934–2010
Born in Bridgewater, this baseball manager won three World Series titles.

TOM BROKAW b.1940
This legendary journalist and news anchor was born in Webster.

RAPID CITY

MOUNT MORIAH CEMETERY
This graveyard in Deadwood is the resting place of Wild Bill Hickok, Calamity Jane, and other Wild West legends.

BADLANDS NATIONAL PARK
This strange landscape, filled with jutting spikes, was named *mako sica* ("bad land") by the Lakota people.

SITTING BULL c.1831–1890
The Hunkpapa Lakota chief known for his courage and resistance was born on the Grand River.

CRAZY HORSE MEMORIAL
Begun in 1948, this huge sculpture of Lakota chief Crazy Horse is due to have a final size of 641 feet wide by 563 feet high!

MOUNT RUSHMORE
Over 90% of this presidential monument near Keystone was carved using dynamite!

THE MAMMOTH SITE
near Hot Springs is an active paleontological dig site, where the bones of at least 61 mammoths have been unearthed.

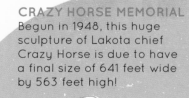

CHAPEL IN THE HILLS
This replica Norwegian church was built to house a Lutheran radio show.

CITY OF PRESIDENTS
On the streets of Rapid City you can find a bronze statue of each U.S. president.

FAIRBURN AGATE
is the official gemstone of South Dakota, found in the Black Hills. The more bands a stone has, the higher its value.

THE RED CLOUD INDIAN SCHOOL
The heritage center at this Lakota school in Pine Ridge has a top hat given to tribal leader American Horse by the government in the 1880s. It was decorated by his wife who found the original too plain!

NEBRASKA

WYOMING

SOUTH DAKOTA

MOMENTS TO REMEMBER

AUGUST 25, 1804: During their famous journey to investigate the American West, explorers Lewis and Clark reach Spirit Mound, a windy spot feared by the Sioux people.

c.1840: The Lakota war leader Crazy Horse is born near present-day Rapid City.

NOVEMBER 1875: Gold is discovered in Deadwood Creek and a town springs up to support the mining.

OCTOBER 31, 1941: Mount Rushmore National Memorial is completed; it took 14 years and 400 people to carve four presidents' faces into the rock.

MAY 1943: Future governor of South Dakota Joe Foss is awarded a Congressional Medal of Honor for his WWII air combat heroics.

JUNE 3, 1948: Lakota Chief Henry Standing Bear and sculptor Korczak Ziolkowski officially start work on the world's largest sculpture: the Crazy Horse Memorial.

1955: Rodeo superstar Casey Tibbs—from Fort Pierre—wins the World All-Around Rodeo Champion title for the second time.

1960: The Dakota Indian Oscar Howe is named the artist laureate of South Dakota.

JUNE 9, 1972: Heavy thunderstorms create flash floods throughout Rapid City, causing 238 deaths.

JANUARY 1979: Paul Goble wins a Caldecott Medal for his book *The Girl Who Loved Wild Horses*.

FEBRUARY 15, 2013: Olympic gold medalist Billy Mills receives the Presidential Citizens Medal for his work with the American Indian charity Running Strong, which he co-founded in 1986.

HONEYBEE
South Dakota is one of the U.S.'s top honey producers, and the honeybee is the official state insect!

ABERDEEN

MINNESOTA

THE SOUTH DAKOTA STATE CAPITOL displays dolls wearing miniature replica gowns worn by the state's First Ladies!

PIERRE

RODEO
The state sport grew out of the daily chores of cattle ranchers.

LAURA INGALLS WILDER HISTORIC HOMES
Visit eight locations in De Smet that appear in the famous *Little House* books.

PORTER SCULPTURE PARK
in Montrose has welded metal sculptures, including a 60-foot bull's head and a roaring dragon.

SIOUX HORSE EFFIGY
This 140-year-old wooden artifact can be found at the Cultural Heritage Center in Pierre.

SIOUX FALLS

MITCHELL CORN PALACE
The designs covering this building are made from some 3,000 bushels of corn—replaced each year!

IOWA

PIONEER AUTO MUSEUM
Marvel at over 300 vintage cars, including "General Lee" from the *Dukes of Hazzard* TV show.

1880 COWBOY TOWN
This Buffalo Ridge attraction brings the Wild West to life, using mechanical cowboys!

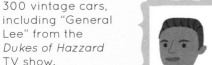

WILLIAM MERVIN "BILLY" MILLS
b.1938
This Oglala Lakota athlete, born in Pine Ridge, is the only American to win an Olympic gold in the 10,000-meter race.

ZITKALA-SA
This Sioux writer was one of the first to publish stories based on tribal legends; she was born on the Yankton Reservation.

ERNEST LAWRENCE
1901–1958
Born in Canton, this pioneering nuclear scientist won the 1939 Nobel Prize for Physics.

ROSE WILDER LANE
1886–1968
This journalist and novelist, born in De Smet, helped shape her mother's *Little House on the Prairie* books.

WELCOME TO THE VOLUNTEER STATE

Music is so essential to Tennessee that it has ten state songs—more than any other state! And for the best in country and blues music, the world turns to Nashville (called "Music City"), Memphis ("Home of the Blues"), and Bristol (known as the "Birthplace of Country Music").

Every year some 6,000 songs are performed during Nashville's Grand Ole Opry concerts, which are broadcast to the world. The Opry is America's longest-running radio show—not too shabby! Music guru Larry Nager heralds Memphis as the "most musical city on the planet," while country-music birthplace Bristol is home to a 70-foot-long guitar-shaped building!

For those looking to explore the great outdoors, Tennessee has lots to offer. The lush Smoky Mountains are the place to go hiking and rafting by day, while at night you can gather round a camp fire with good company and a handful of s'mores.

BESSIE SMITH
1894–1937
Born in Chattanooga, the "Empress of the Blues" was the highest-paid black singer of her time.

TENNESSEE STATE CAPITOL
Before the capitol building's architect William Strickland died, he asked to be buried within the walls . . . and he was!

BLUES HARP
DeFord Bailey, from Smith County, won nationwide fame as the "Harmonica Wizard."

THE GRAND OLE OPRY
is a weekly stage concert that launched the careers of some of country music's biggest stars.

MISSOURI

CLARKSVILLE

Clarksville athlete Wilma "Skeeter" Rudolph overcame polio to win three gold medals in the 1960 Rome Olympics.

NASHVILLE

LUCKY DUCKS
Ever seen a family of ducks march from a hotel penthouse to the lobby fountain? Those at the Peabody Hotel have—it's happened every day since the 1930s!

BBQ, I ♥ U
Tennessee holds supreme bragging rights to world class barbecue.

SUN STUDIO
From Johnny Cash to Roy Orbison, all the biggest rockabilly stars have recorded here.

THE KING
Graceland was the home of the hip-swiveling legend who changed the music world: Elvis Presley.

FISH FRY FIESTA
Fish lovers won't want to miss the "World's Biggest Fish Fry" every April in Paris.

HANDS UP!
If you take the Railway Museum's train from Nashville to Watertown, you may be part of a train robbery!

FATHER OF THE UNITED NATIONS
Born in a log cabin in 1871, Cordell Hull went on to help found the United Nations.

THE SEEING EYE
In 1929, Dorothy Eustis founded this school in Nashville to train dogs to help the blind.

FLYING SAUCER HOUSE
Spend your vacation in an out-of-this-world house on Signal Mountain!

ARKANSAS

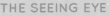

TENNESSEE RIVER

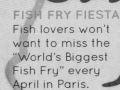

STROLLING JIM
The famous Tennessee Walking Horse, Strolling Jim, is buried outside the stables at the Walking Horse Hotel, Wartrace.

MEMPHIS

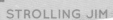

THE BATTLE OF SHILOH
was a major battle of the Civil War.

MISSISSIPPI RIVER

CHATTANOOGA
The chocolate-marshmallow cake that is the MoonPie was created in Chattanooga.

SEQUOYAH
c.1776–1843
A member of the Cherokee Nation, this silversmith created a system of writing for the Cherokee language.

ELVIS PRESLEY
1935–1977
A Tupelo native, this world famous singer and actor is known as the "King of Rock and Roll."

ALABAMA

HATTIE CARAWAY
1878–1950
Born and educated in TN, Caraway was the first woman elected to the U.S. Senate.

MISSISSIPPI

NESSEE

COWBOY TALES
Jonesborough's National Storytelling Festival is the place to hear ghost stories.

258,000 NAILS
At 97 feet tall, the Minister's House in Crossville is the world's tallest tree house. Guess how many nails it took to build it?

LEADING LEADERS
Civil rights leaders like Rosa Parks and Stokely Carmichael studied in New Market.

DAVID FARRAGUT
1801–1870
This Civil War naval hero was born in Knoxville. He joined the navy when he was only 9.

KNOXVILLE

BELOVED CHIEF
Oconostota, the Warrior of Chota and celebrated Cherokee diplomat, was buried at Chota in his canoe.

KING OF THE WILD FRONTIER
In Rutherford you can peek into a cabin modeled on the home of legendary pioneer, explorer, and politician Davy Crockett.

TENNESSEE RIVER

NORTH CAROLINA

AL GORE
b.1948
Gore served as the 45th Vice President. His environmental activism has won him a Nobel Peace Prize.

GEORGIA

DOLLYWOOD
is a theme park owned by country-music star Dolly Parton. Dare to ride the Mystery Mine roller coaster!

GREAT SMOKY MOUNTAINS
Otherwise known as the "Salamander Capital of the World," this national park hosts more than 30 different species.

SHARK SLEEPOVER
Don't forget your jammies! Fall asleep at Ripley's Aquarium with sharks swimming all around you.

MOMENTS TO REMEMBER

AUGUST 18, 1920: Tennessee casts the deciding vote to pass the 19th Amendment, giving women the right to vote.

1821: Sequoyah finishes his Cherokee alphabet, meaning that the Cherokee language can be written down for the first time. His first student is his six-year-old daughter.

JANUARY 1866: Fisk University is founded. Future graduates of this prestigious institution include anthropologist Johnnetta B. Cole, sociologist W.E.B. Du Bois, poet Nikki Giovanni, and suffragette Ida B. Wells.

AUGUST 1878: Memphis is struck by the deadly yellow fever. Instead of fleeing, a few brave volunteers led by Sister Constance stay to nurse the sick. Constance died on September 9 and is honored every year on this date.

NOVEMBER 28, 1925: The Grand Ole Opry—the radio show that made country music famous—is first broadcast, introducing fiddle player Uncle Jimmy Thompson.

NOVEMBER 1932: Highlander Folk School opens, training leaders such as Martin Luther King, Jr., Rosa Parks, and Stokely Carmichael.

JUNE 9, 1951: "Rocket 88" by Jackie Brenston and his Delta Cats tops the charts. Recorded at Sun Studio, it is famed as the first rock and roll record.

JANUARY 3, 1987: Aretha Franklin, the "Queen of Soul," one of the 100 Greatest Artists of All Time, becomes the first female performer in the Rock and Roll Hall of Fame.

KEY FACTS

CAPITAL
Nashville

LARGEST CITY
Memphis
Nashville
Knoxville

BIRD
Mockingbird

NAMED FOR
Tanasi was the name of a Cherokee village on the Tennessee River

STATEHOOD DATE
June 1, 1796

STATEHOOD ORDER
16

FLOWER
Iris

POSTAL CODE
TN

REGION
South

MAIN TIME ZONE
Central

TREE
Tulip poplar

"AGRICULTURE AND COMMERCE"

TEXAS

PALO DURO CANYON
Here, frost and rain have created colorful pillars of rock called hoodoos.

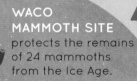

WELCOME TO THE LONE STAR STATE

Sometimes known as the Jumbo State, Texas is BIG! As the second-largest state in the country after Alaska, Texas is bigger than Germany and Great Britain combined. And everything about Texas is big as well: it is the nation's leading oil producer, the leading beef producer, the leading cotton producer, and, appropriately, it also has the largest capitol building in the country. The people of Texas are famously bighearted, too, known for their generosity and welcoming nature.

The Lone Star State is steeped in cowboy lore, proud of its riding-and-roping heritage. But it's not all broncs and buckaroos: from the bright lights of its big cities to its mountain ranges, white sandy beaches, and pine forests, Texas is extremely diverse. Whether you want to trek and raft in Big Bend National Park, check out some mouthwatering barbecue in Austin, or visit the historic site of the Battle of the Alamo in San Antonio, Texas has it all.

NEW MEXICO

WACO MAMMOTH SITE
protects the remains of 24 mammoths from the Ice Age.

DR. SEUSS HANDS
See bronze models of these and those of Disney, Eisenhower, and others at the Baylor University hand collection in Waco.

KERMIT OLIVER
This celebrated artist, who has designed several scarves for the fashion house Hermès, is a retired postman from Waco.

GUADALUPE MOUNTAINS PARK
This national park is home to the collard lizard, which can run on its hind legs!

FRIDAY NIGHT LIGHTS
High school football is so big in Odessa that it inspired a book, movie, and TV show.

THE LEGEND OF BLUEBONNET
A Comanche Indian legend describes how a little girl sacrificed her beloved doll to make the rains come.

MEXICO

CONGRESS AVENUE BRIDGE
is home to 1.5 million Mexican free-tailed bats; at dusk they exit en masse in search of food.

ALVIN AILEY
This groundbreaking choreographer and dancer was born in Rogers, north of Austin.

TEXAS STATE CAPITOL
The state house boasts a natural pink hue, thanks to the "Sunset Red" granite used to build it.

SOUTH BY SOUTHWEST
Austin's funky and creative music scene inspired this annual festival.

KEY FACTS

CAPITAL
Austin

LARGEST CITIES
Houston
San Antonio
Dallas

BIRD
Mockingbird

NAMED FOR
The Caddo Indian word *taysha*, meaning "friend"

STATEHOOD DATE
December 29, 1845

STATEHOOD ORDER
28

FLOWER
Bluebonnet

POSTAL CODE
TX

REGION
Southwest

MAIN TIME ZONE
Central Standard

TREE
Pecan

"FRIENDSHIP"

OKLAHOMA

LARRY McMURTRY
This writer grew up a rancher's son near Archer City, where he sets many of his stories.

FOSSIL RIM WILDLIFE CENTER
Here you can camp overnight close to endangered species such as rhinos and antelopes.

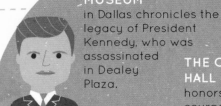

THE SIXTH FLOOR MUSEUM
in Dallas chronicles the legacy of President Kennedy, who was assassinated in Dealey Plaza.

THE COWGIRL HALL OF FAME
honors the extraordinary courage and pioneer spirit of trailblazers like Annie Oakley, Helen Groves, and Mary Walker.

WATER GARDENS
Thousands of gallons of water cascade down steps in this Fort Worth park.

BUREAU OF ENGRAVING AND PRINTING
Take a tour and learn how money is made!

ARKANSAS

D-BAT FACTORY
These bats are made from northern white ash or super-hard maple wood.

FORT WORTH
DALLAS

WACO

LOUISIANA

WES ANDERSON
Even in fifth grade the director of the *Fantastic Mr. Fox* movie loved making puppet shows.

NINE-BANDED ARMADILLO
This relative of the anteater and the sloth can run at up to 30 mph. Zoom!

OIL BOOM
The "gusher" at Spindletop was the most powerful oil geyser ever seen, shooting "black gold" 150 feet into the air.

AUSTIN

A·T·M

HOUSTON

TREE SCULPTURE TRAIL
Chainsaw sculptors in Galveston have transformed trees destroyed by Hurricane Ike into works of art.

SAN ANTONIO

TEXAS A&M UNIVERSITY
The football team here has a famous mascot: a rough collie named Reveille.

THE HOUSTON LIVESTOCK SHOW & RODEO
is the largest livestock show in the world!

GULF OF MEXICO

THE ALAMO
Here a band of Texans held out for 13 days against a Mexican army, before meeting their ends.

SPACE CENTER
The official visitor center of NASA's Johnson Space Center has an amazing collection of space hardware, including a lunar rover, or moonbuggy.

PADRE ISLAND
is a refuge for endangered Kemp's ridley sea turtles.

BESSIE COLEMAN
1892–1926
This pioneering aviator was a celebrated stunt flier.

WES ANDERSON
b.1969
This Houston-born film director made *Fantastic Mr. Fox* and *The Grand Budapest Hotel.*

BEYONCÉ KNOWLES
b.1981
A 20-time Grammy Award winner, this singer was born in Houston.

LARRY McMURTRY
b.1936
This author won a Pulitzer Prize for his novel *Lonesome Dove.*

WILLIE NELSON
b.1933
A Country & Western singer, activist, and actor, Nelson was born in Abbott.

EMMITT JAMES SMITH III
b.1969
This Football Hall of Famer played for the Dallas Cowboys for 12 years.

IDAHO

SPIRAL JETTY
Robert Smithson's huge spiral sculpture on the Great Salt Lake is often underwater.

THE GOLDEN SPIKE
represents the spot at Promontory Summit where the East and West Coast railroads were finally joined.

THE KENNECOTT COPPER MINE
is so big you can see it from space.

NEVADA

GREAT SALT LAKE
The lake is so salty that it's hard to sink— instead, you float like a cork!

GAME ON!
Nolan Bushnell's game *Pong* helped establish the video game industry.

SALTAIR
When this "Coney Island of the West" opened in 1893, bathers could rent suits for a quarter.

UTAH STATE CAPITOL
The capitol building houses several sculptures, including one of Unca Sam, an Utah Indian peace negotiator.

SALT LAKE CITY

WEST VALLEY CITY
hosted the ice hockey during the 2002 Winter Olympics.

WEST VALLEY CITY

BONNEVILLE SPEEDWAY
Several land speed records have been set at the Bonneville Salt Flats.

THE MUSEUM OF ANCIENT LIFE
houses the bones of a 120-foot-long Supersaurus.

AIR FORCE MUSEUM
Climb aboard a WWII warbird at the museum in Heber Valley.

JONES HOLE
is popular for trout fishing.

GRASSHOPPER GRUB
These protein- and calcium-rich insects were an important food source to the Goshute tribe of Utah.

THE SUNDANCE FILM FESTIVAL
was founded by actor, director, and environmentalist Robert Redford.

COLORADO

PROVO

FIND-A-FOSSIL
At U-Dig Fossils, a limestone shale quarry, you can search for your own 500-million-year-old trilobite.

THE DESERT BIGHORN SHEEP
is uniquely adapted to survive in hot, dry climates.

THE ARCHES NATIONAL PARK
is bursting with more than 2,000 stone arches shaped by wind and water.

THE MARS SOCIETY
runs a desert research station to prepare astronauts for a possible mission to Mars.

STUNT CITY
Daredevils flock to Moab for rock climbing and base jumping.

COVE FORT
This old stagecoach way station is now something of a ghost town, with heaps of abandoned buildings.

GRAND STAIRCASE-ESCALANTE
This spectacular and rugged landscape was the last place in the continental U.S. to be mapped.

NEWSPAPER ROCK
The symbols etched in sandstone act as a 2,000-year-old newspaper of native cultures such as the Ancestral Puebloans and Navajo peoples.

BUTCH CASSIDY
The notorious train robber was the eldest of 13 children in a ranching family in Beaver.

DIRTY DEVIL RIVER

LAKE POWELL
This dramatic resevoir was formed when a hydroelectric dam flooded beautiful Glen Canyon.

HOVENWEEP NATIONAL MONUMENT
Ruins of the Pueblo buildings can be found in many places in Utah.

UT CO
AZ NM

COLOROW IGNACIO OURAY WALKARA
c.1808–1855
This Ute warrior and chief negotiated several truces between his tribe and the Mormons.

BRIGHAM YOUNG
1801–1877
The second president of the Church of Jesus Christ of Latter-day Saints (Mormons) brought its worshippers to Utah to escape persecution.

FOUR CORNERS
This is the only place in the U.S. where four states meet!

ARIZONA

NEW MEXICO

WELCOME TO THE BEEHIVE STATE

Stunning scenery abounds in the 45th state's rainbow-colored canyons, bizarrely shaped rock formations, wide windswept plateaus, plunging cliffs, and petrified forests.

Through the ages, the unique landscape of Utah has inspired much art and architecture, from the ancient Ancestral Puebloan villages carved high into the cliffs up until AD 1200 to Robert Smithson's 1,500-foot sculpture, *Spiral Jetty*, built on the shore of the Great Salt Lake in 1970. Every year, the state hosts the internationally famous Sundance Film Festival to showcase groundbreaking American films.

"This is the place," said the leader of the Mormon Pioneers, Brigham Young, upon first seeing the Great Salt Lake Valley in 1847—and so Salt Lake City was founded. Since then, legions of people have been inspired to migrate west to this sun-kissed state.

UTAH

JAMES P. BECKWOURTH
c.1798–1866
A freed slave, mountain man Beckwourth spent time in Utah as an explorer and fur trapper.

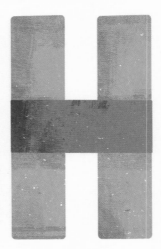

MARTHA HUGHES CANNON
1857–1932
Cannon had a successful medical career in Salt Lake City and won the first woman's seat in the Utah State Senate.

JOHN C. FRÉMONT
1813–1890
Southerner Frémont led many expeditions into Utah.

STEVE HOLCOMB
b.1980
This Park City native was driver for the 2010 Olympic gold medal-winning four-man bobsled team.

MOMENTS TO REMEMBER

SEPTEMBER 1776: A group of explorers led by Spanish priests Francisco Dominguez and Silvestre de Escalante travels through Utah, making maps that will be used by travelers in years to come.

JULY 24, 1847: Brigham Young and his group of Mormon pioneers arrive in the Salt Lake Valley after fleeing religious persecution in Illinois.

MAY 10, 1869: The Union and Central Pacific Railroads are finally joined at Promontory Summit, meaning that the railroad now stretches all the way across the continent.

FEBRUARY 14, 1870: Sarah Young is the first Utah woman to vote—50 years before Congress passed the Nineteenth Amendment.

NOVEMBER 1875: Ann Eliza Young publishes her autobiography, *Wife No. 19*, which details the "sorrows, sacrifices, and sufferings" of women in polygamy (where a husband takes many wives).

1957: Salt Lake City native Virginia Sorensen wins the Newbery Medal for *Miracles on Maple Hill*.

JUNE 27, 1972: Ogden inventor Nolan Bushnell founds video-game company Atari and lets one of the first arcade games, *Pong*, loose on the world.

JUNE 21, 1976: Sculptor Nancy Holt completes her *Sun Tunnels* in the Great Basin Desert.

OCTOBER 18, 1988: *Roseanne*, produced and starred in by Salt Lake City's Roseanne Barr, airs its first of 222 episodes.

FEBRUARY 8, 2002: Salt Lake City hosts the opening ceremony for the Winter Olympics; 202 Americans competed, winning a total of 34 medals.

KEY FACTS

CAPITAL
Salt Lake City

LARGEST CITIES
Salt Lake City
West Valley City
Provo

BIRD
California gull

NAMED FOR
The Ute Indians

STATEHOOD DATE
January 4, 1896

STATEHOOD ORDER
45

FLOWER
Sego lily

POSTAL CODE
UT

REGION
Rocky Mountain

MAIN TIME ZONE
Mountain

TREE
Quaking aspen

"INDUSTRY"

**BEN COHEN &
JERRY GREENFIELD**
b.1951 & b.1951
The childhood friends and
co-founders of Ben & Jerry's
Ice Cream started their company
in an old gas station
in Burlington.

ETHAN ALLEN
1738–1789
The Connecticut-born leader
of the Green Mountain Boys
played an important part in the
Revolutionary War. He was one of
the founders of Vermont.

ROBERT FROST
1874–1963
This poet won four Pulitzer
Prizes and in 1961 was named the
poet laureate of Vermont.

THE ABENAKI TRIBAL MUSEUM &
CULTURAL CENTER
in Swanton celebrates the Abenaki heritage
through clothing, craftwork, and maps.

**SMUGGLERS' NOTCH
STATE PARK**
Smugglers once hid out in
the caves of this beautiful
Stowe park.

**ST. ALBANS
MAPLE
FESTIVAL**
It takes
40 gallons of
maple sap to
make 1 gallon
of maple syrup!

COLCHESTER

BURLINGTON

SOUTH BURLINGTON

THE BREAD & PUPPET MUSEUM
in Glover has a huge collection of
puppets and masks used by the
Bread & Puppet Theater company.

BUG ART
The Fairbanks Museum in St. Johnsbury
has a collection of pictures created using
thousands of carefully positioned insects!

VERMONT STATE HOUSE
is topped with a statue of Ceres,
the Roman goddess of agriculture.

MONTPELIER

**NO BIG MACS
IN MONTPELIER**
The country's smallest
capital city is the
only one without a
McDonald's!

ROCK OF AGES
Most of the U.S.'s
granite headstones
come from this massive
quarry in Graniteville.

NEW YORK

BEN & JERRY'S ICE CREAM
is frozen to 10° below zero
before being shipped from
the Waterbury factory.

*JUSTIN MORGAN
HAD A HORSE*
This 1945 book
is based on the
state horse, bred in
Weybridge.

KNIGHT'S SPIDER WEB FARM
Here in Williamstown, spiders' webs
are preserved and sold as art!

**THE BREAD LOAF
WRITERS' CONFERENCE**
in Ripton is the oldest and most
prestigious in the country.

NEW HAMPSHIRE

ROBERT FROST WAYSIDE TRAIL
Several of this well-loved writer's
poems are mounted along this
woodland trail outside Ripton.

**MARSH-BILLINGS-ROCKEFELLER
NATIONAL HISTORICAL PARK**
Ramble among sugar maples and
explore the home of 19th century
environmentalist George Perkins Marsh.

KILLINGTON
The ski resort here is
called the "Beast of the East"
due to its 3,050 drop—the
largest in New England!

**THE OLD ROUND
CHURCH**
in Richmond was
made circular so the
devil would have no
place to hide—or
so says the legend!

CHAMP
This monster, called
Tatoskok by the
Abenaki people, lives
in Lake Champlain,
according to locals.

FLYING MONKEYS
made from steel
top several buildings
in Burlington.

**THE SHELBURNE
MUSEUM**
is home to a huge
collection of American folk
art collected by heiress
Electra Havemeyer Webb.

**HILDENE: A LINCOLN
FAMILY HOME**
Descendants of Abraham Lincoln
lived here from 1905 until 1975.

FLY FISHING
In 1856 Charles Orvis
set up the Orvis
company in Manchester,
selling fishing tackle.

**THE AMERICAN
PRECISION
MUSEUM**
in Windsor has a
massive collection
of the machine
tools that changed
American industry.

NEKO CASE
b.1970
This Grammy-nominated
singer-songwriter has
a home in Delaware's
Northeast Kingdom.

CHEDDAR CHEESE
from Vermont is usually
white; in Wisconsin they add
color to make it orange.

**HORATIO
NELSON JACKSON**
This Burlington businessman
and his dog, Bud, made the first
cross-country drive from San
Francisco to New York in 1903—
in a car with no windshield!

SNOWFLAKE BENTLEY
is a Caldecott-winning
picture book about
Jericho-born Wilson
Bentley, who figured out
a way to photograph
snowflakes.

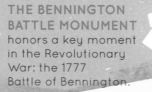

**THE BENNINGTON
BATTLE MONUMENT**
honors a key moment
in the Revolutionary
War: the 1777
Battle of Bennington.

KATHERINE PATERSON
b.1932
The award-winning
author of *Bridge
to Terabithia* now lives
in Barre.

MASSACHUSETTS

WELCOME TO THE GREEN MOUNTAIN STATE

Tucked into the northeastern corner of the U.S. is a state known for its skiing, syrup, and scoops of ice cream. The 14th state is blanketed in forests that are home to about 50 species of trees, key to the livelihood of many Vermonters.

In winter, the woodlands are transformed into a snowy wonderland. Skiers and snowboarders flock to one of the snowiest places in the Northeast, Jay Peak, which gets some 30 feet of the white stuff each year. Come spring, the state's many sugar maples take center stage, as they are tapped for the sweet sap that makes breakfasts across the nation so enjoyable.

Book lovers may be interested in *Witness*, a story told in poems by the Newbery Award winning Karen Hesse, about a small Vermont town in 1924. Robert Newton Peck tells the hilarious story of two mischievous boys growing up in rural Vermont in *Soup* and its many prank-filled sequels.

ATLANTIC OCEAN

KEY FACTS

CAPITAL
Montpelier

LARGEST CITIES
Burlington
South Burlington
Colchester

BIRD
Hermit thrush

NAMED FOR
The French words *mont vert*, meaning "green mountain"

STATEHOOD DATE
March 4, 1791

STATEHOOD ORDER
14

FLOWER
Red clover

POSTAL CODE
VT

REGION
New England

MAIN TIME ZONE
Eastern

TREE
Sugar maple

"FREEDOM AND UNITY"

MOMENTS TO REMEMBER

MARCH 4, 1791: Vermont becomes the first state to join the Union after the original 13 colonies.

JULY 9, 1793: Vermont is the first state to outlaw adult slavery in their state constitution.

1823: Alexander Twilight graduates from Middlebury College, becoming the first African American to receive a U.S. college degree.

OCTOBER 5, 1829: Future president Chester Arthur is born in Fairfield. On July 4, 1872 another future president is born in Vermont: Calvin Coolidge, the only president with an Independence Day birthday!

1893–1896: The British author Rudyard Kipling lives in Dummerston, writes *The Jungle Book*, and receives so much mail that the government authorizes a special post office for Kipling alone!

JANUARY 15, 1968: Vermont becomes the first state to ban billboards—so drivers can see the scenery.

DECEMBER 1, 1977: One of the inventors of the snowboard, Jake Burton Carpenter, sets up the Burton Snowboard company in a barn in Londonderry.

2006: Belmont-born Olympic gold snowboarding medalist Hannah Teter sets up her charity, Hannah's Gold, which helps support a Kenyan village through sales of maple syrup!

JANUARY 18, 2010: Julia Alvarez wins the Pura Belpré Author Award for her novel *Return to Sender*, about the children of Mexican migrant workers in Vermont.

AUGUST 27, 2011: A state of emergency is declared as Hurricane Irene hits Vermont; major floods wash away bridges and six people lose their lives.

Vermont

VIRGINIA

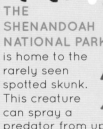

WELCOME TO OLD DOMINION

One of the most historic of all the states, Virginia gained its nickname in the 17th century because King Charles I of England counted it as one of his dominions, calling the Virginians "the best of his distant children." The state is also referred to as the birthplace of America, because the first permanent English colony in the New World was set up on Virginia's shores in 1607. Another of Virginia's nicknames is the "Mother of Presidents" because four out of the first five presidents were Virginians. Indeed, Virginia has always been in the thick of things, playing a lead role in the American Revolution and the Civil War. In fact, more Civil War battles were fought on Virginia's soil than in any other state.

And its beautiful landscape is just as interesting as its history. With its rolling green hills, white sandy beaches, and soaring mountains, visitors to Virginia won't want to leave!

POCAHONTAS
c.1596–1617
This legendary Native American helped the colonists of the Jamestown settlement.

MANASSAS NATIONAL BATTLEFIELD PARK
This park preserves the sites of two major battles of the Civil War.

TURKEY CAPITAL
Rockingham is Virginia's turkey capital. In total, the state produces over 15 million turkeys a year!

WEST VIRGINIA

THE AMERICAN SHAKESPEARE CENTER
in Staunton looks just like the Blackfriars Theatre that "the Bard" and his troupe built in 1600s London.

THE SHENANDOAH NATIONAL PARK
is home to the rarely seen spotted skunk. This creature can spray a predator from up to 20 feet away!

THE NATURAL BRIDGE
Carved by Cedar Creek over thousands of years, this 215-foot-high limestone arch was sacred to the Monocan tribe.

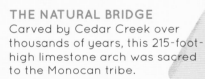

THE BOOKER T. WASHINGTON MONUMENT

celebrates the life of this former slave turned educator, civil rights activist, and presidential adviser.

STONEY POINT RAILROAD
This model town just outside Saltville has a working train, a library, and even a jail, all made from scrap metal!

KENTUCKY

CECE BELL

The award-winning creator of *El Deafo* grew up in Salem and writes about her life with a Phonic Ear hearing aid.

ROANOKE STAR
This enormous neon star stands atop Mill Mountain and can be seen from 60 miles up in the air.

KATIE COURIC
b.1957
Longtime *Today* show anchor, Couric, known as "America's Sweetheart," was born in Arlington.

APPALACHIAN BANJO
Players like Ralph Stanley and the Clinch Mountain Boys keep traditional banjo ballads alive.

MOUNT ROGERS
The highest point in Virginia is 5,729 feet above sea level.

JAMES WEST
b.1931
Some of Professor West's many inventions can be found in cell phones, hearing aids, and microphones.

PHARRELL WILLIAMS
b.1973
This singer, producer, TV star, and composer from Virginia Beach has won 11 Grammys!

CUMBERLAND GAP
This passage through the mountains to the west was an essential shortcut for Native Americans and early pioneers.

TENNESSEE

NORTH CAROLINA

PATSY CLINE
1932–1963
Cline's smooth Country & Western vocals topped the charts with "Crazy."

ARTHUR ASHE
1943–1993
Ashe was the first black man to win the U.S. Open and Wimbledon tennis championships.

THE TOMB OF THE UNKNOWNS
at Arlington National Cemetery is decorated with three Greek figures representing Peace, Victory, and Valor.

WASHINGTON, D.C.

CHESAPEAKE BAY

GEORGE WASHINGTON'S MOUNT VERNON
The first president's home is now a museum. Find out all about him, and even check out his false teeth!

RICHMOND

THOMAS JEFFERSON'S MONTICELLO
The third president was an avid—and experimental—gardener, who enjoyed annual English pea competitions with his neighbors.

COLONIAL WILLIAMSBURG
This living history museum gives visitors a flavor of life in colonial America.

VIRGINIA STATE CAPITOL
The state house in Richmond has statues of George Washington and seven other Virginia-born presidents.

HISTORIC GARDEN WEEK
This tour of 250 beautiful gardens began in April 1927.

BILL "BOJANGLES" ROBINSON
This Richmond tap dancer celebrated his 61st birthday in 1939 by dancing down 61 blocks on Broadway in New York.

MARYLAND

CHINCOTEAGUE WILDLIFE REFUGE
is home to 150 wild ponies, cared for by the local volunteer fire department.

VIRGINIA LIVING MUSEUM
Here you'll find many of the state's animals, including the endangered red wolf.

THE MARINERS' MUSEUM
This museum in Newport News reveals how the Powhatan Indians made canoes by hollowing out trees using fire.

NORFOLK

VIRGINIA BEACH

CHESAPEAKE

ATLANTIC OCEAN

GYM STAR
Born in Virginia Beach, gymnast Gabby Douglas trains six days a week, seven hours a day.

GRACE MURRAY HOPPER
This computer scientist and navy rear admiral designed a programming language that revolutionized the way we use computers. She worked at the Naval Station in Norfolk.

CHILDREN'S MUSEUM OF VIRGINIA
Make enormous human-sized bubbles and discover some 2,000 toys and trains in this Portsmouth museum.

MOMENTS TO REMEMBER

DECEMBER 1607 Near the settlement of Jamestown, Pocahontas (the daughter of Chief Powhatan) is said to have saved the life of English explorer John Smith by throwing herself between him and her father's war club.

NOVEMBER 10, 1921: An unidentified WWI soldier is buried in the Arlington National Cemetery. The Tomb of the Unknowns is guarded 24 hours a day, 365 days a year by Tomb Guard Sentinels.

JULY 1925: The ponies of Assateague Island are rounded up and swim across a channel to Chincoteague for the pony auction, to raise money for the Chincoteague Volunteer Fire Department. This tradition happens every July.

DECEMBER 10, 1953: George Marshall, a resident of Leesburg, receives the Nobel Peace Prize for his work bringing aid to Europe after WWII.

1958: Ella Fitzgerald, born in Newport News, wins the first two of her 13 Grammy Awards. Called "The First Lady of Song," she sold more than 40 million albums.

DECEMBER 19, 1971: The pilot episode of the TV series *The Waltons* is aired. Set in the Blue Ridge Mountains, this family drama continues for nine seasons.

AUGUST 2012: Gymnast Gabrielle Douglas wins two gold medals at the London Olympics.

NOVEMBER 2013: Pharrell Williams releases the first 24-hour music video to his song "Happy," with guest appearances by Magic Johnson, Steve Carell, Jamie Foxx, and many others.

KEY FACTS

CAPITAL
Richmond

LARGEST CITIES
Virginia Beach
Norfolk
Chesapeake

BIRD
Northern cardinal

NAMED FOR
Queen Elizabeth I of England

STATEHOOD DATE
June 25, 1788

STATEHOOD ORDER
10

FLOWER
American dogwood

POSTAL CODE
VA

REGION
South

MAIN TIME ZONE
Eastern

TREE
American dogwood

"THUS ALWAYS TO TYRANTS"

RICHARD BRAUTIGAN
1935–1984
Tacoma-born writer with a quirky style, best known for his novel *Trout Fishing in America*.

HILARY SWANK
b.1974
This two-time Oscar-winning actress spent her childhood in Spokane and Bellingham.

THE DAFFODIL FESTIVAL
is held every spring in Pierce County. It involves four parades in four cities in one day!

SAFE!
Safeco Field, home of the Seattle Mariners, has a retractable roof for rainy game days.

KOOL LIBRARY
If it was laid out flat, the glass in Seattle's library (designed by Rem Koolhaas and Joshua Ramus) would cover more than five football fields!

DO WHALES DRINK COFFEE?
The coffee chain Starbucks was named after the first mate in the novel *Moby Dick*.

PIKE PLACE MARKET
has delicious food . . . and a giant gum wall!

LOVELY LONGHOUSE
The art of the Duwamish tribe can be seen at the cultural center in West Seattle.

SPACE NEEDLE
There have been six parachute jumps from this 605-foot-tall icon!

SAN JUAN ISLANDS

PACIFIC OCEAN

THE TULALIP RESERVATION
was the birthplace of Janet McCloud, a campaigner for Native American rights.

SNOWSHOE SOFTBALL
is played in outrageous costumes every winter in Winthrop.

PUGET PIONEER
The pioneer George Washington Bush and his wife, Isabella, settled here in 1845.

ELK
These majestic animals have been an important part of the area's heritage for thousands of years.

SMELLS LIKE TEEN SPIRIT
Grunge pioneer Kurt Cobain got his musical start in Aberdeen.

SEATTLE

TACOMA

GRAND POWER
The Grand Coulee Dam is the largest supplier of electric power to the U.S.!

WILLAPA BAY
is home to salmon and oysters galore. Yum!

CITY OF DESTINY
Once the railroad reached Tacoma, a trip from Chicago took four days—instead of six months by wagon!

OLYMPIA

WASHINGTON STATE CAPITOL
The granite and stone in the capitol building weigh nearly as much as 9,000 VW Beetles!

CAPE DISAPPOINTMENT
is one of the foggiest places in the U.S.

TROUT FISHING
Some of the best trout fishing in the country is found along the Yakima River.

PREHISTORIC BONES
In 1996 a 9,000-year-old skeleton was discovered in Kennewick. It is one of the most complete prehistoric skeletons ever found.

MOUNT ST. HELENS
During the 1980 eruption, ash drifted over seven states!

YAKAMA INDIANS
In the past, the Yakama people carried their babies on their backs using a cradleboard.

OREGON

CHIEF SEATTLE (SI'AHL)
1786–1866
Leader of the Suquamish tribe, Seattle was known for his compelling speeches and peacemaking.

MERCE CUNNINGHAM
was a world-famous choreographer who started his career learning tap-dancing in Centralia.

WALLA WALLA
is officially one of the friendliest towns in the country, and is home to the sweet onion!

WASHING

MERIWETHER LEWIS AND WILLIAM CLARK
1774–1809 • 1770–1838
Soldiers and explorers Lewis and Clark were sent by Thomas Jefferson to explore the western part of the U.S.

GEORGE WASHINGTON BUSH
c.1790–1863
This African American pioneer was one of the first settlers on Puget Sound. Others followed, causing Britain to yield the land to America.

JIMI HENDRIX
1942–1970
The Rock and Roll Hall of Fame called this guitar virtuoso from Seattle "arguably the greatest instrumentalist in the history of rock music."

CANADA

WELCOME TO THE EVERGREEN STATE

SPOKANE

The award-winning writer Sherman Alexie grew up on the Spokane Indian Reservation.

The nation's 42nd state is the only one named after a president. That's right, the first president, George Washington. And, like its namesake, Washington is a leader in many fields: the Evergreen State is the largest organic apple producer in the world; it grows more red raspberries and cherries than any other state; it is home to Microsoft and many other tech giants; it has the longest floating bridge in the world, and even the largest building in the world (the aircraft factory in Everett).

Washington's lush landscape boasts snow-topped volcanic mountains, vast forests heavy with the scent of evergreens, and beautiful glacier-fed lakes. Its largest city, Seattle, has a world-famous music scene and was the birthplace of Starbucks, the biggest coffee chain on earth. And we can't leave Washington without mentioning Walla Walla, which—in addition to once being named America's Friendliest Small Town—is a lot of fun to say!

MOMENTS TO REMEMBER

NOVEMBER 15, 1805: After a grueling 18-month trip, Lewis and Clark's expedition across the western part of the U.S. finally reaches the Pacific Ocean.

SPRING 1866: Salmon canneries begin to operate along the Columbia River, employing Chinese, Filipino, and Japanese workers.

SEPTEMBER 8, 1883: Construction of the Northern Pacific Railway, connecting the Great Lakes to the Pacific coastline, is finally finished.

JUNE 19, 1910: The first Father's Day is celebrated by its creator, Spokane citizen Sonora Smart Dodd.

APRIL 21, 1962: The 605-foot-tall Space Needle opens. It took a whopping 467 cement trucks 12 hours to fill the foundation hole!

MARCH 30, 1971: The first Starbucks opens in Seattle. There are now over 11,000 in the U.S.

1972: High school friends Paul Allen and Bill Gates start their first company. They go on to found the hugely successful Microsoft in 1975.

FEBRUARY 12, 1974: The efforts of campaigner Janet McCloud (Yet-Si-Blue) finally pay off when the Boldt Decision is made, reaffirming the right of Native American tribes to fish for salmon.

MAY 18, 1980: Mount St. Helens erupts for the first time since 1932, becoming the deadliest and costliest volcanic eruption in U.S. history.

OCTOBER 30, 1988: Nirvana's lead singer, Kurt Cobain, smashes his first guitar. One year later, the band's first album, *Bleach*, is released.

SACAJAWEA STATE PARK
Visit a re-creation of a traditional Wanapum village at this 284-acre park.

IDAHO

TON

KEY FACTS

CAPITAL
Olympia

LARGEST CITIES
Seattle
Spokane
Tacoma

BIRD
Willow goldfinch

NAMED FOR
George Washington, the first U.S. president

STATEHOOD DATE
November 11, 1889

STATEHOOD ORDER
42

FLOWER
Pacific rhododendron

POSTAL CODE
WA

REGION
Pacific

MAIN TIME ZONE
Pacific

TREE
Western hemlock

"BY AND BY"

CHUCK YEAGER
b.1923
This West Virginian ace pilot was the first person in the world to break the sound barrier.

BRAD PAISLEY
b.1972
This country music star and winner of three Grammy Awards learned to play the guitar as an 8-year-old in Glen Dale.

PENNSYLVANIA

FIESTA COLORS
The rainbow colors of Fiesta dinnerware include paprika, peacock, poppy, and plum! The Fiesta factory is in Newell.

OHIO

MARY LOU RETTON
b.1968
This exuberant Olympic gold medalist fell in love with gymnastics in Fairmont.

CYNTHIA RYLANT
b.1954
The award-winning author of the *Henry and Mudge* books grew up in Beaver.

HARPERS FERRY NATIONAL HISTORICAL PARK
runs workshops on making bread in a beehive oven—just like they did in 1809!

GRAVE CREEK MOUND
Around 250 BC, the ancient Adena people buried arrowheads and animal carvings inside this mound.

MARYLAND

BLACK BEAR
The state animal eats fish, flowers, fruit, nuts, insects, and squirrels, among other things!

SHENANDOAH RIVER
Fishing is popular in this river, which features in John Denver's song "Take Me Home, Country Roads."

SAVING SHILOH
Phyllis Reynolds Naylor's three novels about a rescued beagle take place in the town of Friendly.

MARBLE KING
This marble company in Paden City makes one million marbles a day!

MOTHER'S DAY
was first celebrated in 1908 in Grafton, where there is now a shrine.

SENECA ROCKS
Rock climbers flock to this 900-foot sandstone crag.

MONONGAHELA NATIONAL FOREST
Fierce winds keep branches from growing on the western side of trees on Spruce Knob.

THE LEGEND OF MOTHMAN
Some say that a strange creature reportedly seen in Point Pleasant in 1966 was a mutant born from a chemical dump!

PARKERSBURG

PEPPERONI ROLL
Invented by Italian coal miner Giuseppe Argiro as a snack that didn't need refrigeration, the pepperoni roll is now a state icon.

HELVETIA

HELVETIA
This hamlet celebrates its Swiss and German heritage with events like Fasnacht and the Feast of St. Nicholas.

THE GREEN BANK TELESCOPE
sits within the National Radio Quiet Zone. Cell phones are banned to protect the radio telescope from interference.

WEST VIRGINIA STATE CAPITOL
The gold leaf that covers the 293-foot dome was applied in 3.4-inch squares.

CHARLESTON

WEST VIRGINIA RIVERS

HUNTINGTON

CHUCK YEAGER
Born in Myra, this air force pilot made history in 1947 by flying his aircraft faster than the speed of sound.

RED BRICK ROAD
The U.S.'s first brick street was laid in Charleston in 1870.

EXHIBITION COAL MINE
Retired miners lead tours through the passages of an old coal mine in Beckley.

GOLDEN DELICIOUS FESTIVAL
Every year Clay County celebrates the state apple, discovered here in 1905.

GAULEY RIVER
Every September the water in the Summersville Dam is released, creating a thrilling whitewater rafting run.

NEW RIVER GORGE BRIDGE
During the annual Official Bridge Day festival in October, hundreds of base jumpers leap 876 feet into the river below.

SANDSTONE FALLS
These waterfalls on the New River are considered one of the state's seven natural wonders.

THE HATFIELDS & MCCOYS
were rival 19th-century families who lived along the Big Sandy River and had a decades long feud . . . involving the theft of a pig!

THE BLUESTONE RIVER
is home to northern water snakes. Unlike many other snakes, they incubate their eggs inside their bodies, then give birth to live young.

THE GREENBRIER RESORT
in White Sulphur Springs was the secret location of a nuclear bomb shelter, built in the late 1950s. These days it's not so secret, and visitors can take a tour.

KENTUCKY

VIRGINIA

WELCOME TO THE MOUNTAIN STATE

The rugged geography of West Virginia gives one of the country's smallest states its nickname. The beauty of its mountainous scenery, dense with spruce trees, is rightfully a source of pride for West Virginians. Locals refer to their state as "Almost Heaven," taking a line from John Denver's well-loved song "Take Me Home, Country Roads."

This state has captured the attention of other musicians, artists, and writers, too, making an appearance in the songs of Johnny Cash and Loretta Lynn, as well as books like Betsy Byars's *The Summer of the Swans*, Suzanne Collins's *The Hunger Games*, and Phyllis Reynolds Naylor's *Shiloh*. The movie *Super 8* was also filmed here!

Lovers of the great outdoors will adore the Allegheny Highlands, where you can go climbing, caving, hiking, rafting, biking, and skiing. You'll find wild leeks—called ramps by the locals—growing across the state, and some towns even host ramp-eating contests. Just mind that onion breath!

WEST VIRGINIA

MOMENTS TO REMEMBER

250 BC: The Adena people begin building Grave Creek Mound in what is now Marshall County; it is the largest conical burial mound in the U.S.

OCTOBER 16, 1859: The abolitionist John Brown leads an antislavery raid to seize weapons from the U.S. armory in Harpers Ferry.

OCTOBER 1, 1896: Postmaster General William Wilson introduces free rural mail delivery in Charles Town; it then spreads throughout the U.S.

1943: During WWII, the government seizes an important ingredient from West Virginia's Fiesta dinnerware company. It is uranium, used by Fiesta to make its red glaze. The government needs it to build the atomic bomb!

1962–1992: The government operates a secret bomb shelter in West Virginia's Greenbrier Resort, stocked with supplies for members of Congress.

DECEMBER 30, 1970: John Denver first sings "Take Me Home, Country Roads" in Washington, D.C., and is rewarded by a five-minute ovation. It is now West Virginia's official state song.

AUGUST 3, 1984: Gymnast Mary Lou Retton, born in Fairmont, becomes the first U.S. woman to win an Olympic gold for the All-Around event.

JANUARY 24, 1993: Cynthia Rylant, who grew up in Coalridge, wins the Newbery Medal for *Missing May*.

MARCH 3, 2010: Harvard professor Henry Louis Gates, Jr., born in Keyser, becomes the first African American to have his genome fully sequenced.

JOHN FORBES NASH, JR.
1928–2015
This genius mathematician from Bluefield won the Nobel Prize in Economics for his game theory.

HENRY LOUIS GATES, JR.
b.1950
Born in Keyser, this award-winning writer and filmmaker is Professor of African American Studies at Harvard.

KEY FACTS

CAPITAL
Charleston

LARGEST CITIES
Charleston
Huntington
Parkersburg

BIRD
Northern cardinal

NAMED FOR
Queen Elizabeth I of England, "The Virgin Queen"

STATEHOOD DATE
June 20, 1863

STATEHOOD ORDER
35

FLOWER
Rhododendron

POSTAL CODE
WV

REGION
South

MAIN TIME ZONE
Eastern

TREE
Sugar maple

"MOUNTAINEERS ARE ALWAYS FREE"

WISC

LAURA INGALLS WILDER
1867–1957
This well-loved author who was born in Pepin wrote the autobiographical *Little House on the Prairie* books.

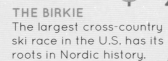

APOSTLE ISLANDS
Kayakers admire and paddle under the ancient red sandstone arches of the sea caves here.

MINNESOTA

THE BIRKIE
The largest cross-country ski race in the U.S. has its roots in Nordic history.

CHEQUAMEGON-NICOLET NATIONAL FOREST
The balsam fir trees found here provide food and shelter for red squirrels and white-tailed deer.

HOME OF THE HAMBURGER
Locals say that 15-year-old Charlie Nagreen sold the world's first hamburgers at Seymour Fair in 1885.

GREEN BAY PACKERS
"Packers" refers to meat packing, because a local meat-packing company sponsored the team's first uniforms in 1919.

AMERICAN GINSENG
is used in herbal medicine. About 95% of the country's crop is grown in Marathon County.

AMERICAN BADGER
The striped state animal has been known to partner up with coyotes to hunt ground squirrels.

THE DEKE SLAYTON SPACE MUSEUM
in Sparta has a scale that shows your weight on Earth, Venus, Mars, and the moon!

THE CHAIR THAT GREW
John Krubsack, a banker from Embarrass, "grew" a chair by shaping box elders in his yard.

GREEN BAY

LES PAUL
1915–2009
This musician from Waukesha developed the solid-body electric guitar, making rock music possible.

DAIRYLAND
There are 134 cheese, 13 butter, and 12 yogurt plants in Wisconsin. Thanks, cows!

CRANE FOUNDATION
If you see a crane strut stiffly with its neck crooked, that's a threat walk! Find out more at this reserve near Baraboo.

PAPER DISCOVERY CENTER
Make your own paper at this museum and workshop in Appleton.

J.M.K. ARTS CENTER
This museum displays the work of artists such as the "Rhinestone Cowboy," who covered his hat, glasses, and dentures with gems!

KEVIN HENKES
b.1960
The award-winning author of *Lily's Purple Plastic Purse* was born in Racine.

"THE BICYCLING CAPITAL OF AMERICA"
is a title proudly claimed by Sparta. The Elroy-Sparta Bike Trail has 32 miles of paths.

THE CIRCUS WORLD MUSEUM
in Baraboo hosts daily live shows in the big top through summer.

WISCONSIN STATE CAPITOL
Every winter holiday the capitol has a 40-foot tree with 2,400 lights!

THE FIRST KINDERGARTEN
was opened by Margarethe Schurz, based on the ideas of German educator Froebel.

MADISON

MILWAUKEE

WILLEM DAFOE
b.1955
This Appleton actor featured in the *Spider-Man* movies, *Fantastic Mr. Fox*, and more.

DANICA PATRICK
b.1982
Go-kart racing in Brodhead kick-started this Daytona 500, Indycar, and NASCAR racer's career.

HOUSE ON THE ROCK
The Infinity Room in this fascinating house near Dodgeville stretches 218 feet over a valley and contains 3,264 windows!

THE MARS CHEESE CASTLE
in Kenosha is a store offering chudge (chocolate cheese fudge) and other cheese oddities— er, delights!

YERKES OBSERVATORY
discovered Uranus's fifth moon and Neptune's second moon.

ILLINOIS

IOWA

ONSIN

LAKE MICHIGAN

HARRY HOUDINI
1874-1926
The magician famous for his daring escape acts grew up in Appleton.

TWO RIVERS
is one of the first homes of the ice cream sundae.

THE OSHKOSH AIRSHOW
Some 10,000 aircraft fly into Wittman Regional Airport for the annual airshow!

WELCOME TO THE BADGER STATE

One thing should spring to mind as soon as someone mentions Wisconsin: cheese! Each year, the state's cheese manufacturers make 2.8 billion pounds of Cheddar, provolone, Gouda, and other varieties—more than any other state.

To work up an appetite, head to one of the state's 15,000 lakes for some outdoor fun. At the Apostle Islands National Lakeshore you can explore by kayak, discovering the islands and sea caves of this special part of Lake Superior. In the winter, adventurers can join some 10,000 skiers in the largest—and one of the longest—cross-country ski races in the country: the American Birkebeiner, or "Birkie," to the locals.

Wisconsinites have an appetite for progressive policies, too, and are pioneers of social legislation: Wisconsin was one of the first states to provide pensions for the blind and old age assistance, and the first to open a kindergarten, in 1856.

MICHIGAN

THE FIRST TYPEWRITER
to be a commercial success was invented here in 1868. It had no keys for the numbers 0 or 1—typists used the letters O and I instead!

FRANK LLOYD WRIGHT
designed 55 buildings in Wisconsin, including Milwaukee's Annunciation Greek Orthodox Church.

THE MILWAUKEE ART MUSEUM
is shaped like a bird taking flight over Lake Michigan.

THE HARLEY-DAVIDSON MUSEUM
in downtown Milwaukee celebrates the 100-year history of these iconic motorcycles.

MOMENTS TO REMEMBER

AD 700: Native American societies begin to build more than 15,000 effigy mounds in Wisconsin.
1856: Margarethe Meyer Schurz opens the country's first private kindergarten, with just five students, in Watertown.
1901: The Northern Paper Mill in Green Bay creates the first bathroom tissue, earning the city the nickname "Toilet Paper Capital of the World!"
APRIL 10, 1911: Architect Frank Lloyd Wright buys a plot near Spring Green on which to build his home, Taliesin. He is later named the "greatest American architect of all time."
AUGUST 11, 1919: Former high school football star Curly Lambeau and sports editor George Calhoun form a new football team: the Green Bay Packers.
MAY 1967: The Elroy-Sparta Bike Trail opens. It is America's first "rails to trails" project, where an old train railbed is transformed into a bike path.
JULY 1968: Mayor Henry W. Maier holds the first annual Summerfest, aka "The World's Largest Music Festival."
JANUARY 10, 1977: The Wisconsin-born artist Georgia O'Keeffe, best known for her paintings of enlarged flowers, is presented with a Presidential Medal of Freedom by Gerald Ford.
JANUARY 2005: Kevin Henkes wins the Caldecott Medal for *Kitten's First Full Moon*. He previously won the Newbery Honor for *Olive's Ocean*.
FEBRUARY 2015: Five friends from Lake Mills carve and stack ice pillars weighing 300 pounds each to create "Icehenge" on the frozen Rock Lake.

KEY FACTS

CAPITAL
Madison

LARGEST CITIES
Milwaukee
Madison
Green Bay

BIRD
Robin

FLOWER
Wood violet

NAMED FOR
Possibly an Algonquian Indian word meaning "long river"

STATEHOOD DATE
May 29, 1848

STATEHOOD ORDER
30

POSTAL CODE
WI

REGION
Great Lakes

MAIN TIME ZONE
Central

TREE
Sugar maple

"FORWARD"

Wondrous Wyoming is home to some amazing landscapes: here you can enjoy both the piping hot springs of Yellowstone National Park and the chilly, snowcapped Rocky Mountains. While the western side of the state impresses with its huge mountain peaks, the scenery in the east, with its rolling prairies, is gentler.

As well as its thrilling landscapes, Wyoming is well known for its incredible history of exploration and adventure. For it is here that daredevils like Buffalo Bill and outlaws like the Sundance Kid, as well as many fearless bucking-bronco riders, honed their skills.

But for all its history of Wild West escapades, the Equality State has long lived up to its "Equal Rights" motto: in 1869 it became the first state where women could vote, and in 1924, it elected the first female state governor in the country.

MARTHA JANE CANNARY
"CALAMITY JANE"
1852–1903
Cannary was an army scout, frontierswoman, and Wild West show star.

WILLIAM CODY
"BUFFALO BILL"
1846–1917
Gold miner, Pony Express rider, and army scout, Cody took the "Wild West" to Europe with his cowboy show.

NELLIE TAYLOE ROSS
1876–1977
Ross won her husband's position as governor after he died. She also became the first female director of the U.S. Mint.

JEDEDIAH SMITH
1799–1831
The explorer Smith rediscovered the South Pass route through the Rockies: a crucial shortcut on the Oregon Trail.

CHIEF WASHAKIE
c.1798–1900
This Shoshone leader negotiated with white military and settlers to ensure that his tribe could stay on their land.

JACKSON POLLOCK
1912–1956
Pollock's abstract style of art, using spatters of paint, caused a revolution in the art world.

OLD FAITHFUL
This world-famous geyser erupts some 17 times a day, firing a jet of boiling water as high as 184 feet.

THOMAS MORAN
In 1871 this artist produced many paintings of Yellowstone, which inspired the government to make it a national park.

YELLOWSTONE
Yellowstone, the world's first national park, is home to bison, grizzly bears, wolves, and elk.

IDAHO

DRIP, DRIP, SPLAT
Jackson Pollock, the great abstract expressionist painter known for his drip paintings, was born in Cody.

GRAND TETON MOUNTAINS
With several peaks over 10,000 feet, the Tetons are some of the youngest mountains in North America.

THE ORIGINAL WYOMINGITES
The Shoshone Indians were one of the first tribes in the region to own and ride horses.

SWEETWATER SETTLERS
Covered wagons traveling west in the 1840s visited the Sweetwater River for water and food.

CONTINENTAL DIVIDE
All water east of this mountain ridge flows toward the Atlantic via the Gulf of Mexico, and all water west of the ridge flows to the Pacific.

TO THE GULF!

MAIL

PONY EXPRESS
Riders such as Buffalo Bill galloped in relay shifts across 2,000 miles of territory 150 years ago to deliver mail.

MINING DISASTERS
In 1923, 99 miners lost their lives when there was an explosion in the Frontier Mine near Kemmerer.

R.I.P.

ROCK SPRINGS DIVERSITY
Prosperous coal mines attracted so many immigrants in the 19th century that Rock Springs became known as the "Home of 56 Nationalities."

CHUGWATER CHILI FESTIVAL
The chefs in Chugwater need to wear rubber gloves to protect themselves from these spicy peppers!

UTAH

WYOMI

MONTANA

BIKELESS BIGHORN
No cars or even bikes are allowed in the most protected parts of the Bighorn Mountains.

MEDICINE WHEEL
Made from 28 spokes of rock, this giant structure in the Bighorn National Forest is used in Native American healing ceremonies.

WYOMING DINOSAUR CENTER
Staff at the dino center in Thermopolis lead budding dinosaur experts on digging tours to a sauropod feeding ground.

CASPER

JEDEDIAH SMITH
survived a savage grizzly bear attack while forging a new trail through the Rocky Mountains.

WANTED
★★★★★★★

BUTCH CASSIDY	THE SUNDANCE KID
$5,000	$5,000

REWARD
DEAD OR ALIVE

THE WILD BUNCH
Butch Cassidy and his robber gang had hideouts all over Wyoming.

WIND POWER
A single wind turbine at Foote Creek Rim can power 150 homes!

LARAMIE

BUFORD
POP 1
ELEV 8000

CHEYENNE

ITTY BITTY BUFORD
This 10-acre town is home to one lonely resident . . . and is owned by a coffee company!

COLORADO

SOUTH DAKOTA

DEVILS TOWER
Sacred to several tribes of Plains Indians, Devils Tower is a huge rock rising over 1,200 feet. The cracks in the surface make for excellent rock-climbing.

ELK EVERYWHERE
Wyoming is home to huge numbers of elk—one of the largest species of deer in the world.

JACKALOPE
Douglas is home to a statue of the mythical jackalope: half jackrabbit, half antelope.

RODEO RIDERS
Fans from around the world come to cheer on bronc riders at Cheyenne Frontier Days, the "Daddy of All Rodeos."

BIG BOY
See one of the world's largest steam locomotives in Cheyenne.

FANCY FRIED LOBSTER
Eat this at the world-famous Little Bear Inn.

WYOMING STATE CAPITOL
The capitol building is topped with a gold-leafed cupola, which is Latin for "small cup."

NEBRASKA

MOMENTS TO REMEMBER

65 MILLION YEARS AGO: *Tyrannosaurus rex, Triceratops, Ankylosaurus,* and other dinosaurs roam prehistoric Wyoming.

1807: Mountain man John Colter (once a member of the Lewis and Clark Expedition) explores parts of Wyoming, including the hot springs near Cody, now called Colter's Hell.

APRIL 1860–OCTOBER 1861: The legendary Pony Express delivers mail from the Atlantic to the Pacific coast in about ten days.

NOVEMBER 18, 1867: The Union Pacific Railroad reached the town of Cheyenne.

DECEMBER 10, 1869: The territory of Wyoming grants women the right to vote.

MARCH 1, 1872: President Ulysses S. Grant declares Yellowstone's two million acres a national park—the first of its kind.

1896: "Buffalo Bill" Cody and others found the town of Cody, named after its larger-than-life investor.

1897: Bighorn National Forest is established.

AUGUST 14, 1923: The heroic efforts of Mike Pavlisin and Clifford Phillips save the lives of fellow miners in the Frontier Mine Disaster.

JANUARY 5, 1925: Nellie Tayloe Ross is sworn in as the first female governor in U.S. history.

JUNE 29, 1986: Patricia MacLachlan was presented with the Newbery Medal for *Sarah, Plain and Tall.*

2010: "Cowboy Ethics" are adopted statewide, promoting living each day with courage and taking pride in your work.

KEY FACTS

CAPITAL
Cheyenne

LARGEST CITIES
Cheyenne
Casper
Laramie

BIRD
Western meadowlark

NAMED FOR
The Delaware Indian word meaning "on the large plains"

STATEHOOD DATE
July 10, 1890

STATEHOOD ORDER
44

FLOWER
Indian paintbrush

POSTAL CODE
WY

REGION
Rocky Mountain

MAIN TIME ZONE
Mountain

TREE
Plains cottonwood

"EQUAL RIGHTS"

KWAME ALEXANDER
b.1968
The Newbery Medal–winning author of *The Crossover* lives in the D.C. area.

FORT RENO PARK
The highest point in the city hosts free summer concerts run by volunteers.

ROCK CREEK PARK
Biking, tennis, and golf are some of the activities offered at this 1,754-acre park.

BEN'S CHILI BOWL
Barack Obama is just one of the celebrities who has enjoyed a chili half-smoke here on U Street.

BUSBOYS AND POETS
This bookstore and arts venue takes its name from poet Langston Hughes, who once worked as a busboy!

LITTLE ETHIOPIA
Restaurants on this block offer dishes like Doro Wat chicken, served up in a tagine pot.

BILL WATTERSON
b.1958
The creator of the *Calvin and Hobbes* comic strip was born in D.C.

WOODLEY PARK
This Metro station has the longest escalator in D.C. proper, with 204 feet of moving staircase!

Woodley Park-Zoo / Adams Morgan Station

ADAMS MORGAN

THE WHITE HOUSE
Before the president's home got its first stove in the 1850s, the food was cooked over an open fire.

THE NATIONAL ZOO
is home to 1,800 animals of 300 different species, some of which you can watch from home on a webcam!

KENILWORTH PARK AND AQUATIC GARDENS
This is the only national park devoted to water plants, such as the water lily.

TAXATION WITHOUT REPRESENTATION
Even though D.C. residents pay taxes, they don't have a representative in Congress, as the states do.

DISCHORD RECORDS
is a punk music record label founded in 1980 by two teenagers with $600.

GEORGETOWN

THE INTERNATIONAL SPY MUSEUM
has oodles of gadgets with secret compartments, including a tube of lipstick, an umbrella, and a pair of shoes.

THE KENNEDY CENTER
This performing arts facility is the busiest in the nation, hosting about 2,000 performances a year!

THEODORE ROOSEVELT ISLAND
The swampy wetlands here shelter the ruby-throated hummingbird, one of the only birds able to fly backward!

NATIONAL MALL

The Capitol has its own private subway connecting it to the House and Senate office buildings.

THE UNITED STATES CAPITOL

CAPITOL HILL

WASHINGTON MONUMENT
This 555-foot-tall monument honors the nation's first president.

DANCE DC
is an education program run by the Washington Ballet. Some 700 students a year take part in classes combining dance with science and math!

THE EASTERN MARKET
was built in 1873 and offers fresh food, flowers, and flea-market finds.

THE VIETNAM VETERANS MEMORIAL WALL
in the National Mall park lists the names of the 58,300 U.S. men and women who lost their lives during the Vietnam War.

LAWRENCE A DODD • DUNN • RICHARD ARLICK • WILLIE G • STANLEY R LEW AN LEE NELLY • W THOMPSON • THO PADARO • RICHAR ETRIE • ROGER L

LINCOLN MEMORIAL
The 36 columns surrounding the statue of President Lincoln represent the states in the Union at the time of his death in 1865.

THE NATIONAL CHERRY BLOSSOM FESTIVAL
is celebrated every year as a sign of the U.S.'s friendship with Japan, and Tokyo's gift in 1912 of 3,000 cherry trees.

THE PENTAGON
Across the river in Virginia, the Defense Department's headquarters is a five-sided, five-story building.

THE NATIONAL AIR AND SPACE MUSEUM
displays key items from the history of flight, including a glider designed by Otto Lilienthal, who inspired the Wright brothers.

FREDERICK DOUGLASS HOUSE
The district of Anacostia is home to the historic house of this abolitionist leader.

ANACOSTIA

VERY CHERRY
The official fruit of the capital has links to George Washington, who is said to have chopped down a cherry tree as a boy.

VIRGINIA

THE NATIONAL MUSEUM OF THE AMERICAN INDIAN
showcases contemporary art, like this pair of beaded sneakers by Kiowa artist Teri Greeves.

RACING PRESIDENTS
Five mascots dressed as U.S. presidents take part in a sprint race during every home game of the Washington Nationals baseball team.

MARYLAND

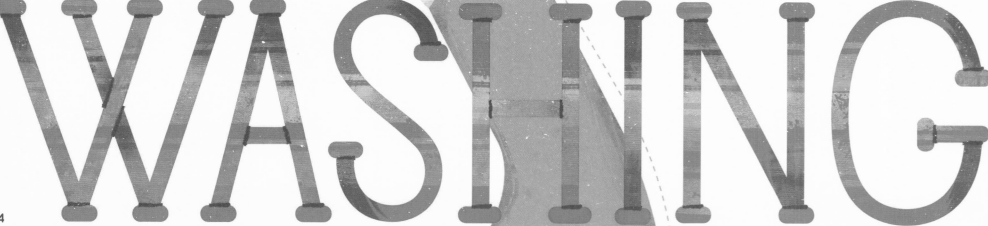

WASHING

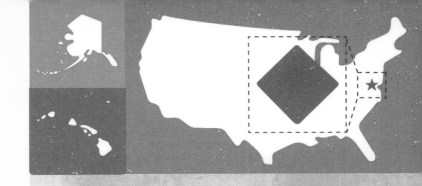

KEY FACTS

ESTABLISHED
June 11, 1800

POSTAL CODE
DC

BIRD
Wood thrush

NAMED FOR
George Washington, the first U.S. president

FLOWER
American Beauty rose

REGION
Mid-Atlantic

MAIN TIME ZONE
Eastern

TREE
Scarlet oak

"JUSTICE FOR ALL"

BILL NYE
b. 1955
This 18-time Emmy Award–winning "Science Guy" graduated from D.C.'s Sidwell Friends School.

DUKE ELLINGTON
1899–1974
This master pianist, bandleader, and composer was born in Shaw.

HELEN CHURCHILL CANDEE
1858–1949
This *Titanic* survivor, writer, and feminist became one of the country's first professional interior designers in D.C.!

WELCOME TO THE DISTRICT

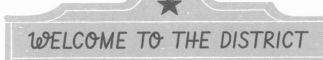

There are capital cities, and then there's THE capital. Washington, D.C., belongs to no state and is not even a city: it's actually a federal district. That could change one day: voters in D.C. have been requesting statehood since the district's early days. The name of the nation's potential 51st state? New Columbia.

Within the capital's 68 square miles you'll find some of the most important buildings in the country. There's the U.S. Capitol (the seat of Congress); the Supreme Court Building; and, of course, the White House itself—the official home of the president.

D.C. brims with iconic monuments, such as the Martin Luther King, Jr. Memorial, commemorating this hero of the civil rights movement. You'll also find incredible museums, like the world-famous Smithsonian, with free entry for all. This is one capital you won't want to miss!

NOVEMBER 1, 1800: President John Adams becomes the first resident of the White House.

FEBRUARY 1926: D.C. resident and historian Carter G. Woodson develops what will become Black History Month, choosing February to honor the birthdays of abolitionist Frederick Douglass and President Abraham Lincoln.

AUGUST 28, 1963: Dr. Martin Luther King, Jr., leads the March on Washington and gives his "I Have a Dream" speech at the Lincoln Memorial.

NOVEMBER 3, 1964: D.C. residents are able to vote in a presidential election for the first time.

MARCH 27, 1976: The Washington Metro opens with 4.2 miles of track and five stations. Today it has 91 stations and 117 miles of track.

SEPTEMBER 9, 1983: Residents petition Congress for statehood, asking to be admitted to the Union as the 51st state with the name New Columbia.

JANUARY 28, 2001: D.C.'s first "Capitalsaurus Day" celebrates the district's official dinosaur, the Capitalsaurus, whose fossil was discovered at the corner of First and F streets in 1898.

MARCH 20, 2009: First Lady Michelle Obama plants a vegetable garden—the largest in White House history—on the South Lawn.

JANUARY 28, 2013: Andrea Davis Pinkney, born in D.C., wins the Coretta Scott King Award for her book *Hand in Hand: Ten Black Men Who Changed America*.

MAY 2013: The Smithsonian museum receives its first gray whale skeleton after the bones are collected by volunteers in Puget Sound, Washington State.

TON, D.C.

CONNIE CHUNG
b.1946
This award-winning television journalist from D.C. was the first Asian news anchor of a major network.

PRESIDENTS

OF THE UNITED STATES OF AMERICA

1. GEORGE WASHINGTON

1732–1799
Term: 1789–1797
b. Popes Creek, VA
First Lady:
Martha Dandridge Custis
Washington

2. JOHN ADAMS

1735–1826
Term: 1797–1801
b. Braintree, MA
First Lady:
Abigail Smith Adams

3. THOMAS JEFFERSON

1743–1826
Term: 1801–1809
b. Shadwell, VA
Wife:
Martha Wayles Skelton
Jefferson (d.1782)

4. JAMES MADISON

1751–1836
Term: 1809–1817
b. Port Conway, VA
First Lady:
Dolley Todd Madison

5. JAMES MONROE

1758–1831
Term: 1817–1825
b. Monroe Hall, VA
First Lady:
Elizabeth Kortright Monroe

6. JOHN QUINCY ADAMS

1767–1848
Term: 1825–1829
b. Braintree, MA
First Lady:
Louisa Johnson Adams

7. ANDREW JACKSON

1767–1845
Term: 1829–1837
b. Waxhaws Settlement, SC
Wife: Rachel Donelson
Jackson (d.1828)
White House Hostess:
Emily Donelson (niece)

8. MARTIN VAN BUREN

1782–1862
Term: 1837–1841
b. Kinderhook, NY
Wife: Hannah Hoes Van Buren (d.1819)
White House Hostess:
Angelica Singleton Van Buren
(daughter-in-law)

9. WILLIAM HENRY HARRISON

1773–1841
Term: 1841
b. Berkeley, VA
First Lady:
Anna Symmes Harrison

10. JOHN TYLER

1790–1862
Term: 1841–1845
b. Greenway, VA
First Lady:
Letitia Christian Tyler
(d.1842)
& Julia Gardiner Tyler

11. JAMES K. POLK

1795–1849
Term: 1845–1849
b. Mecklenburg County, NC
First Lady:
Sarah Childress Polk

12. ZACHARY TAYLOR

1784–1850
Term: 1849–1850
b. Barboursville, VA
First Lady:
Margaret Mackall
Smith Taylor

13. MILLARD FILLMORE

1800–1874
Term: 1850–1853
b. Locke Township, NY
First Lady:
Abigail Powers Fillmore

14. FRANKLIN PIERCE

1804–1869
Term: 1853–1857
b. Hillsborough, NH
First Lady:
Jane Means Appleton Pierce

15. JAMES BUCHANAN

1791–1868
Term: 1857–1861
b. Cove Gap, PA
White House Hostess:
Harriet Lane
(niece)

16. ABRAHAM LINCOLN

1809–1865
Term: 1861–1865
b. Hodgenville, KY
First Lady:
Mary Todd Lincoln

17. ANDREW JOHNSON

1808–1875
Term: 1865–1869
b. Raleigh, NC
First Lady:
Eliza McCardle Johnson

18. ULYSSES S. GRANT

1822–1885
Term: 1869–1877
b. Point Pleasant, OH
First Lady:
Julia Dent Grant

19. RUTHERFORD B. HAYES

1822–1893
Term: 1877–1881
b. Delaware, OH
First Lady:
Lucy Webb Hayes

20. JAMES A. GARFIELD

1831–1881
Term: 1881
b. Orange Township, OH
First Lady:
Lucretia Rudolph Garfield

1829–1886
Term: 1881–1885
b. Fairfield, VT
Wife: Ellen Lewis Herndon
Arthur (d.1880)
White House Hostess: Mary
Arthur McElroy (sister)

22. GROVER CLEVELAND

1837–1908
Term: 1885–1889
b. Caldwell, NJ
First Lady:
Frances Folsom Cleveland

23. BENJAMIN HARRISON

1833–1901
Term: 1889–1893
b. North Bend, Ohio
First Lady:
Caroline Scott Harrison

24. GROVER CLEVELAND

1837–1908
Term: 1893–1897
b. Caldwell, NJ
First Lady:
Frances Folsom Cleveland

25. WILLIAM McKINLEY

1843–1901
Term: 1897–1901
b. Niles, OH
First Lady:
Ida Saxton McKinley

26. THEODORE ROOSEVELT

1858–1919
Term: 1901–1909
b. New York, NY
First Lady:
Edith Kermit Carow Roosevelt

27. WILLIAM HOWARD TAFT

1857–1930
Term: 1909–1913
b. Cincinnati, OH
First Lady:
Helen Herron Taft

28. WOODROW WILSON

1856–1924
Term: 1913–1921
b. Staunton, VA
First Lady:
Ellen Axson Wilson (d.1914)
& Edith Bolling Galt Wilson

29. WARREN G. HARDING

1865–1923
Term: 1921–1923
b. Corsica, OH
First Lady:
Florence Kling Harding

30. CALVIN COOLIDGE

1872–1933
Term: 1923–1929
b. Plymouth Notch, VT
First Lady:
Grace Goodhue Coolidge

31. HERBERT HOOVER

1874–1964
Term: 1929–1933
b. West Branch, IA
First Lady:
Lou Henry Hoover

32. FRANKLIN D. ROOSEVELT

1882–1945
Term: 1933–1945
b. Hyde Park, NY
First Lady:
Anna Eleanor Roosevelt

33. HARRY S. TRUMAN

1884–1972
Term: 1945–1953
b. Lamar, MO
First Lady:
Elizabeth ("Bess") Wallace
Truman

34. DWIGHT D. EISENHOWER

1890–1969
Term: 1953–1961
b. Denison, TX
First Lady:
Mamie Geneva Doud Eisenhower

35. JOHN F. KENNEDY

1917–1963
Term: 1961–1963
b. Brookline, MA
First Lady:
Jacqueline Lee Bouvier
Kennedy

36. LYNDON B. JOHNSON

1908–1973
Term: 1963–1969
b. Stonewall, TX
First Lady:
Claudia Taylor ("Lady Bird")
Johnson

37. RICHARD NIXON

1913–1994
Term: 1969–1974
b. Yorba Linda, CA
First Lady:
Patricia Ryan Nixon

38. GERALD FORD

1913–2006
Term: 1974–1977
b. Omaha, NE
First Lady:
Elizabeth Bloomer Ford

39. JIMMY CARTER

b.1924
Term: 1977–1981
b. Plains, GA
First Lady:
Rosalynn Smith Carter

40. RONALD REAGAN

1911–2004
Term: 1981–1989
b. Tampico, IL
First Lady:
Nancy Davis Reagan

41. GEORGE H. W. BUSH

b.1924
Term: 1989–1993
b. Milton, MA
First Lady:
Barbara Pierce Bush

42. BILL CLINTON

b.1946
Term: 1993–2001
b. Hope, AR
First Lady:
Hillary Rodham Clinton

43. GEORGE W. BUSH

b.1946
Term: 2001–2009
b. New Haven, CT
First Lady:
Laura Welch Bush

44. BARACK OBAMA

b.1961
Term: 2009–2017
b. Honolulu, HI
First Lady:
Michelle Robinson Obama

45. DONALD TRUMP

b.1946
Term: 2017–
b. New York City, NY
First Lady:
Melania Trump

INDEX

To the educators at Broad Ripple High School, and everywhere else. — GSB
To Jogu, Uli, Elo and Poncho. — SL

Author Acknowledgements
Kudos first to the attention of the inspired publisher that is Rachel Williams and the artistry of the talented Sol Linero.
What happy luck to have stumbled upon you both! Also, praise to Camille Baptista, Mollie Galchus and Amy Jean, for their
relentless and cheery research support. And finally, to my very proficient and very favorite family, friends, and innocent
bystanders, who endured and answered my endless questions about all things state.

Illustrator Acknowledgements
Rachel, Gabe, and Nic, our key star team players who made this book possible. Jogu, my lovely husband, for all the support by making
parenting a joint project. Juli, my dear friend and work partner, for always giving me the right answers. Albert, for the hard work (you are the best
in every possible way!) Ari and Ignacio, you rock! Laura, for the advice. My Mom and Dad, for giving me the tools to become the person I am.

The Publisher would also like to thank the many librarians and fact-checkers in every state who freely gave their time and energy
to make this book the best it could be. Thanks also Laura Dellinger for efforts in checking the Native American facts, and to Erik Niemi
for his encyclopedic knowledge and amazing collection of vintage maps. It's time for a road trip!

Wide Eyed Editions
www.wideeyededitions.com

The 50 States copyright © Quarto Publishing plc
Illustrations copyright © Sol Linero 2015
Text copyright © Gabrielle Balkan 2015

First published in 2015 by
Wide Eyed Editions, an imprint of The Quarto Group, The Old Brewery, 6 Bludell Street, London, N7 9BH
www.QuartoKnows.com

A catalogue record for this book is available from the British Library.

ISBN 978-1-84780-711-3

The illustrations were created digitally
Set in Quicksand and Cursive Script

Conceived and commissioned by Rachel Williams
Design assistance and project management by Nicola Price
Editorial by Emily Hawkins, Jody Revenson, Jacqueline Hornberger and Jenny Broom

Manufactured in Guangdong, China CC112020

18

KEY REFERENCES

NELSON, KADIR, *Heart and Soul:
The Story of African Americans.*
Balzer + Bray, 2011.

HERRERA, JUAN FELIPE, *Portraits
of Hispanic American Heroes,*
Dial Books, 2014.

VARIOUS AUTHORS, *America the
Beautiful series,* Children's Press, 2009.

THE LIBRARY OF CONGRESS:
AMERICA'S STORY
www.americaslibrary.gov

NATIONAL PARK SERVICE
www.nps.gov

FURTHER READING

SIS, PETER, *The Train of States,*
Greenwillow Books, 2007.

VARIOUS AUTHORS, Discover America
State by State series, Sleeping Bear
Press, 2010–2011.

AMERICA COMES ALIVE
www.americacomesalive.com

STATE FLAGS

OF THE UNITED STATES OF AMERICA

ALABAMA

ALASKA

ARIZONA

ARKANSAS

CALIFORNIA

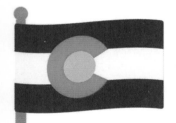
COLORADO

CONNECTICUT

DELAWARE

FLORIDA

GEORGIA

HAWAII

IDAHO

ILLINOIS

INDIANA

IOWA

KANSAS

KENTUCKY

LOUISIANA

MAINE

MARYLAND